Merry Christmas;
Best to you in
2016!
"LBR"

Nebrasketball

Nebrasketball

Coach Tim Miles and a Big Ten Team on the Rise

SCOTT WINTER
Foreword by TOM IZZO

University of Nebraska Press | Lincoln & London

Publication of this volume was assisted by a grant from
the Friends of the University of Nebraska Press

Library of Congress Cataloging-in-Publication Data

Winter, Scott.
Nebrasketball: coach Tim Miles and a Big Ten team on the rise /
Scott Winter; foreword by Tom Izzo.
pages cm
ISBN 978-0-8032-9892-7 (cloth: alk. paper)
ISBN 978-0-8032-9930-6 (epub)
ISBN 978-0-8032-9931-3 (mobi)
ISBN 978-0-8032-9932-0 (pdf)
1. Miles, Tim, 1966– 2. Basketball coaches—Nebraska—Biography. 3. University of Nebraska–
Lincoln—Basketball. I. Nebraska Cornhuskers (Basketball team). II. Title.
GV884.M544W56 2015
796.323092—dc23
[B]
2015014446

Set in Scala OT by M. Scheer.

For Dave and Dusty Kromarek and all the other kids who loved basketball with everything they had, but were never given a fair shot to play.

CONTENTS

PHOTOGRAPHS

Following page 162

FOREWORD

I met Tim Miles on the road a few summers back and felt like I got to know him when I jumped on an airplane with him. Then I really got to know Tim Miles when he kicked our ass in East Lansing in February 2014. And I hated him. I'll be mad at him forever for beating us at home like that.

I don't know why the hell I'm doing this foreword for a book about him. I don't know why I recorded a video for his team banquet at the end of the 2013–14 season, when I told him, and his whole program, how ticked I was because I didn't get any flowers or candy when Tim Miles won the league's Coach of the Year Award after we were so instrumental in that. We never really recovered from that game. It may have cost us a shot at winning the Big Ten. I mean, I really don't like you, Tim Miles.

But seriously, Tim is one of those guys you meet for just five minutes and you feel like you've known him for a lifetime. He has an appreciation for the game and the league, and I have an appreciation for how he runs his program and how he's turned around programs throughout his career.

When he got to Nebraska, he understood where the program was and where it needed to go.

I've been a head coach in the Big Ten for twenty years, and when I was the young buck here, veteran coaches really took care of me and showed me what it took to win in this league—legendary coaches such as Purdue's Gene Keady, Illinois's Lou

Henson, Minnesota's Clem Haskins, and Indiana's Bobby Knight. They respected me because I wasn't a cheat or a jerk or this or that, and they thought I was doing it the right way. They looked out for me, and I want to do the same thing for young coaches like Tim, who have done things the right way. I'm so sick of the cheating that goes on in college sports, including basketball. Tim gets that, too.

He's turned around programs pretty humbly. Tim always gives other people credit. He's refreshing. He's got a fun personality, but he strikes a commanding presence. But one of the things I like most about him is he can laugh at himself. It's one of the great things you can have as a human being. I can laugh at myself. I make a fool of myself at things like Midnight Madness. I see that in Tim, too. And he's pretty transparent and brutally honest, which also serves him well in this league.

People ask me all the time: "What is your gift as a coach? Is it rebounding? Is it defense? Is it toughness?" Well sure, players play, but tough players win. All those things are important in the Big Ten, for getting wins in the National Collegiate Athletic Association (NCAA) Tournament, and for winning a national championship, which we did here in 2000. Well, Tim Miles posed that question to me on that airplane a few summers back. I told him that many of these players are looking for a male influence they can trust. So, you have to spend time with them, learn about who they are and what it takes to get them to Big Ten titles or the Final Four or the National Basketball Association (NBA). Earn their trust. My best thing isn't defense and rebounding; it's spending time with my guys. They know what I want, and I know what they want. That was my advice to Tim.

He's one of the up-and-coming quality coaches in the country, and he treats people the right way. I never hear anybody bad-mouthing him. Win or lose, people will get mad at you, but I can read a person, and what I read is he's ready for a long, great career.

It's been fun watching him grow the program at Nebraska and other programs over the years. The one good thing, for us, is now he's going to be expected to win. Now he'll know what the pressure is like for the rest of us who have been here.

Good luck, Coach.

Tom Izzo
Michigan State University

ACKNOWLEDGMENTS

First of all, thanks to my kids, Jasmine and Jake, for giving me the time and support to crank out this book. Jasmine hates basketball and Jake loves the Minnesota Gophers, so I couldn't assume their help on transcribing notes. I still owe them some cash for all those hours.

Thanks also to my mother and my father, Abe, the Red Smith of North Dakota, for embracing nepotism to get me into journalism.

Thanks to Tim Miles and Marc Boehm, for believing in the project and trusting me with full access to the program. They took a chance on me and stuck with me because the team seemed to be winning only when I was in the locker room (15-0 at one point).

Thanks to all the assistant coaches, staff, student managers, and players for tolerating my audio recorder, my wardrobe choices, and my existence. I asked them all to pretend I wasn't there, and they, for the most part, refused to oblige.

Thanks to the Miles family—particularly Tip and Alyce and Karin—for never saying no to a request. I even appreciate the coach's siblings who chose to ignore my calls and texts rather than be overtly rude.

Thanks to all the professional folks at the University of Nebraska Press, particularly Rob Taylor, who took a chance on the idea.

Thanks to many friends and colleagues who offered ideas

and editing, especially Peter Salter, Dirk Chatelain, Joe Starita, and Michelle Hassler.

Mostly, thanks to my wife, Deena, who is my best friend and editor and probably rewrote this sentence. She pulled me through some dark months on this project and in life.

Nebrasketball

PROLOGUE

Tim Miles would meet only at a Lincoln coffee shop that was a corporate sponsor of the Huskers. He'd survived his first season at the University of Nebraska–Lincoln (UNL), a losing season at 15-18, and he was in full recruitment, golf, and guest-speaker mode in the summer of 2013.

He'd just finished talking to a group of boosters and potential boosters. He knew what I wanted before the question could be asked: to write the Tim Miles Story. What he didn't know was that I wanted to write his *Season on the Brink*, an homage to John Feinstein's 1986 book about Bobby Knight and the Indiana University (IU) Hoosiers. Knight cussed, joked, and exploded through a turbulent year, and Feinstein had unprecedented access to the team. Anyone who loved 1980s college basketball, such as Tim Miles, loved Feinstein's book.

Miles had a pivotal season coming up with the Huskers: a plush, new $186 million arena paid for by the city; new transfer players who had hammered the Husker starters all last season as redshirts in practice; high expectations locally and low expectations nationally. He was going up against a history of losing basketball at the University of Nebraska. The team had never won an NCAA Tournament game and hadn't made the tournament in sixteen years.

"No way," he told me. "We can't do a book this year."

He didn't want a book because this team was unpredictable.

He wasn't sure they'd be any good, much less a story worthy
of a book. And he'd had mixed results during the second years
of his stops at Mayville (ND) State, Southwest Minnesota State
(SMSU), North Dakota State (NDSU), and Colorado State (CSU).
And worse, they weren't going to win.

Do it next year or the following one, in year three or four, but
not now in year two, he argued.

"We're gonna win," he said, and he meant it. "But we're not
going to win this year." He meant that, too.

He also didn't really want a book at all, he said. Well, he wanted
one. He has an ego, and a book would feed it, but he didn't want
an insider's look at his program.

"It's my mom," he said.

The forty-seven-year-old coach didn't want Alyce Miles, who
raised him in Doland, South Dakota, to know how consistently
he uses what she would call "vulgarities." When Tim Miles is
happy, angry, energized, distraught, dismayed, shocked, hyped,
winning, or losing, he's often swearing.

His assistant coaches joke about the mileage their boss can get
out of four or five cuss words in any basketball scenario, whether
imploring his 280-pound center to keep the ball up high or teas-
ing his farm-boy student manager about his date last night.

Early in Miles's six-year tenure at North Dakota State, athletic
director (AD) Gene Taylor had to be direct with his basketball
coach. At the Bison Sports Arena, the basketball team practiced
in a multisport venue, surrounded by an indoor track, adjacent
to the wrestling room and softball batting cages. Another coach
had said something to the AD about Miles.

"Coach," Taylor said from behind his desk, "we've gotten complaints you're using the *F* word too much."

"Gene," Miles said, "you can't take that word away from me.
It gets their attention."

Eventually, Taylor relented.

"Just keep it down, okay?" he said.

When Miles's Bison played in Orlando for a holiday tournament, some South Dakota snowbird friends of Alyce and Tip Miles sat behind the bench to support the family's baby boy and couldn't believe the words they heard in a time-out. Afterward, they called Alyce in Sioux Falls to rat him out.

"I came home to find Mom crying on the couch," oldest daughter Karin said.

After three days of tears, Karin called her brother Kevin and told him to call Tim. They couldn't have Mom crying for the rest of her life.

Tim tried to explain to his mother that he sometimes resorts to the only language his players understand.

"I don't give a hoot," she said.

Another time, when Miles was in the middle of his five-year run at Colorado State, Lutheran friends from Colorado called Alyce the day after a game to ask whether her son learned such language at his Catholic college.

Alyce called Tim right away in horror.

"Mom," he explained, "[Duke coach] Mike Krzyzewski swears all the time, and he's won national titles and the Olympics."

"I don't care about him," she said. "I don't hear about him. I hear about you. Little kids can even hear you."

Alyce still monitors her boy's weekly radio show down in Nebraska on the computer, and when she hears an occasional "Oh, my God," she'll text him to watch his language.

"What's a mother to do?" Alyce says.

A few weeks later, Miles relented and agreed to the book. With help from above from Husker Athletic Department administrators and even more assistance from below from coaches and team staff, Miles gave full access to him and his program—in team meetings, in practices, in game-day locker rooms, and on the road. Or at least as much as he could handle.

By season's end Miles was wrong about how good his team would be in 2013–14, but he was right about pretty much everything else. And his recipe for transforming losing programs into winning cultures revealed itself on a daily basis, through mis-spelled words on marker boards that became team battle cries, through expeditious decisions that cured locker-room chemis-try problems, and through joking his way through pressure sit-uations. He pulled every solution to every problem from lessons learned in his first four program transformations. By March he liked the idea of a book so much, from a public relations stand-point, that he started offering up book titles, such as "Tougher-ness" and "The 50 Days That Changed Nebraska Basketball." He also offered up clues about why he is the way he is—an attention-deficit-disorder marketer, an obsessive-compulsive recruiter, a religious-superstition believer, a relentless jokester who needs to win not just every game but every room.

As for the swearing, just like the deal Tim Miles made with Gene Taylor ten years earlier, we agreed to just try to keep it down.

One

Money at the Bank

1

Tim Miles cracks out his Doland stories when he speaks to new audiences. Tonight, he's in Fremont, Nebraska, which is eighteen miles closer to Creighton University (CU) in Omaha than it is to the University of Nebraska in Lincoln. The banquet hall fills with bankers and their clients, who have all been to the cash bar at least once before Miles even showed up. They cluster around the buffet of meatballs, vegetable trays, and loose-meat sandwiches.

The point tonight, just days before the 2013–14 basketball season opens, is to win over Fremont.

"I'm from a small town in South Dakota called Doland," Miles starts.

"I graduated seventh in my class. There were 13 of us. Actually, there used to be 14 of us. But one guy dropped out in the spring of my senior year, leaving us with 13. So now, I'm below average in everything I do."

He pauses for his first laughs.

"I'm not saying I'm bitter, but I'm kind of pissed off. So, I'm Doland. I'm average."

Miles, the second-year Husker basketball coach, wants the crowd of 100 or so to know he's a regular guy. That he's like them. So he can win them over, which he will. Hey, they're already laughing.

"Doland's a fascinating town," he continues. "When you come into town from the east, the sign says 'Doland: Pop. 306.' And when you come in from the west, it says 'Doland: Pop. 297.' So, there's 9 missing people, which is why I always ask if someone is from Doland, so I can find them."

Already today, late in October, Miles ran a practice to prepare his team for opening night of the new Pinnacle Bank Arena

(PBA) next week against Florida Gulf Coast University (FGCU), a team that became a national story during the first weekend of March Madness the previous season when the Eagles made the Sweet Sixteen. Miles's Huskers haven't even made the tournament since the millennium. He's memorized FGCU's playbook, but wants to memorize the strengths and weaknesses of each player. He's also shot a thirty-second commercial for the Athletic Department in one take—"I'm one-take Timmy." And he's called four recruits from the passenger seat of his black Cadillac Escalade during the sixty-minute trip northeast on Highway 77. He's being paid $500 for this speaking engagement, but he's not here for the money. He makes $1.5 million in the second year of a seven-year contract.

"Tonight," he said in the SUV, "we have to win Fremont. We sold out that arena, but we need to always be selling. Always. Be. Selling."

His seventy-minute talk includes how he turned around perennially losing programs at his coaching stops at Mayville State, Southwest Minnesota State, North Dakota State, and Colorado State. He was asked to speak for only twenty or thirty minutes, but he tells stories and drinks Coors Lights—a corporate sponsor in his last job at Colorado State University—until midnight, when he grabs his jacket, forgets his $500 check on a table, and watches film clips of Florida Gulf Coast the whole way home, his eyes lit up by the screen of his MacBook Pro.

"I think we won Fremont. Now, how are we going to beat Dunk City?"

Dr. Tom Osborne is a decision maker. In the eleventh year of his twenty-five-year career as Nebraska's football coach, he chose to go for two points against Miami at the end of regulation in the 1984 Orange Bowl. He went for the win, and he lost the game and the national championship. But Nebraska football diehards swear that decision cemented his legacy and led to three national titles that came a decade later. An upcoming ESPN *30 for 30* documentary film is dedicated to the bold move.

One of Osborne's last decisions at the Husker Athletic Department wasn't seen publicly as overly bold. As athletic director he fired his friend Doc Sadler in the spring of 2012. Sadler had gone 4-14 in Nebraska's first year in the Big Ten and 12-18 overall.

"Doc Sadler was a popular guy," Osborne said, "an engaging, outgoing, friendly person. There were some people who didn't want to remove Doc. But with Doc's situation, he had a few years where he wasn't successful, and it was affecting recruiting, with opposing coaches telling kids, 'Look, you can't win there,' and it was becoming a self-fulfilling prophecy."

Osborne and executive associate athletic director Marc Boehm had to find a new coach. Together, they had procured the $18.7 million for a training and practice facility for the men's and women's basketball teams that many considered the best in the nation. They also cemented the basketball programs as the main tenants of the new $186 million arena owned by the city of Lincoln, set to open in eighteen months. In all, the West Haymarket project, which included the arena as its anchor, cost taxpayers $378 million. Picking a coach to lead Nebrasketball into the new arena era was a big decision.

"We had to get it right," Boehm said.

They combed through coaching portfolios from coaches across the country. In interviews coaches would walk Osborne and Boehm through those slick, shiny portfolios. All but one.

All Tim Miles had was a blank notebook.

In the offices of a downtown Atlanta law firm, Boehm started off the interview by showing Miles a DVD on his laptop that featured the Hendricks Training Complex and detailed plans for the arena. A few minutes into the video, Miles pushed Boehm's laptop aside and pulled out a white legal notepad.

"I know about all that," Miles said. "Let me show you what we're going to do here."

Osborne, who had been quiet in his chair, perked up. As
Boehm remembers the moment, Miles scribbled his offensive
philosophy on the first sheet. Then he flipped to a second sheet
and scribbled out a defensive philosophy. Then came a communication philosophy. Recruiting philosophy. Player evalua-
tions. Coaching responsibilities. Philosophy after philosophy.
Page after page.

"I looked over at Coach Osborne, and I could tell that he got it,"
Boehm remembers. "There was an edge to Tim that showed he
wasn't just some coach Nebraska fans hadn't ever heard about."

Externally, Miles was winning the conference room at that
high-rise law firm. Internally, he was reeling. When he recalls
the moment two years later, he doesn't even mention the interview itself. What he remembers is everything before the meeting. His Colorado State Rams had just been blown out 58–41 in
a first-round NCAA Tournament game by Murray State, which
would lose its next game to Marquette, which would lose its next
game to Florida, which would lose to Louisville, which meant
his team hadn't been all that close to making a run. But he knew
he'd have a shot the next year with most of his rotation returning
the next season and two redshirts playing significant minutes.

He flew to Atlanta the night before the 8:00 a.m. meeting and
woke up at 6:30 a.m., which was 4:30 on his Mountain Time
internal clock. He hit the snooze twice and then worked out on
the hotel's treadmill. He downed some coffee and went downstairs to meet an employee from the law firm.

"I'm feeling good," he said. "I'm not nervous about the interview, but I'm a little nervous about Tom Osborne. He's a quiet
guy, and I'm not sure how I'm going to read him."

The law-firm employee makes Miles sign a confidentiality
agreement to keep the meeting secret.

"It says something like, 'If you tell anyone you're here, we'll
take your son. He won't be able to procreate,' or something like
that," Miles remembers. "And I like Gabe, but I sign the deal."

Truth is, he's fine with confidentiality because he doesn't

want the interview leaked in the media, either. He's got a great job at Colorado State and has worked to win fans away from the University of Colorado, pro teams, and mountain slopes. The problem is that he's still sweating, ever since the workout. A hot shower didn't help. Sitting down to sign away his child in the lobby didn't stop the sweats. The law-firm guy notices and finds Miles a towel. Nothing helps. Now, he's walking the sidewalks of downtown Hotlanta with his book bag and suitcase. It's not even 8:00 a.m., and it's in the seventies with full humidity.

"I'm pouring sweat. My collar is damp. We go up to the fifteenth floor in this building, and the guy asks me three times if I'm okay."

Miles says he's great. He stops in the bathroom and uses paper towels to try to pat down the sweat. Nothing works. Now, he's worried.

"A lot of times when you meet a famous person, you get all worked up," Miles says now. "But when you meet Tom Osborne, it all dries up."

Osborne was impressed. He saw an energetic coach who had a clear plan that went beyond the Xs and Os, though those were important to the retired coach, too, as much as anything. But many coaches could do that. Not many of them could articulate their plans like this guy from Doland, South Dakota. Still, Osborne did his homework. He checked with old coaching friends; his former football assistant coach Craig Bohl, who coached with Miles at North Dakota State; former Husker volleyball coach Terry Pettit, who had consulted with Miles's teams at Colorado State. Osborne had even reached out to University of Colorado coach Tad Boyle, a longtime friend, to get him to apply for the job, but Boyle suggested he chase Miles.

"I thought he was trying to get rid of his competition or something," Osborne remembers.

Osborne and Boehm searched for a reason not to hire Miles. Boehm knew experience might be a problem, considering the quality and experience of coaches in the Big Ten—Tom Izzo,

Thad Matta, Tom Crean—but Miles hadn't shied away from those big names in the interview at all. He wanted the Big Ten. He had a reverence for it that started in his youth, when he traveled east to games at The Barn in Minnesota. He wanted to coach against—and beat—those guys in the Breslin Center at Michigan State (MSU) and Assembly Hall in Indiana.

"Overall, I was able to get a pretty good read on him from people I knew and trusted," Osborne said. "He had a good understanding of what he wanted to do and how he wanted to go about it. He was very positive, not a lot of hang-ups. We needed someone who could engage the fans. And Tim does that as well as anyone."

After a long day of interviewing, Boehm and Osborne were about to call an experienced candidate for one last interview. Boehm met Osborne in the lobby outside their offices before they made the call. Instead, Osborne went for two. He looked at Boehm and said, "I think we already have our guy."

2

Ryan Hanigan and Patrick Nee sat right behind the Husker bench in December 1994, when Jud Heathcote brought his fifth-ranked Michigan State Spartans to Lincoln's Bob Devaney Center for a nonconference game. The teens were juniors at Pius X High School. Hanigan's father, John, a stoic accountant and prominent Catholic, was a season-ticket holder for Nebraska basketball. Nee's father, Danny, a former high school teammate of Lew Alcindor in New York and a Vietnam veteran, was the Husker coach, on his way to the most wins in program history.

Nee's Huskers were coming off four straight NCAA appearances and a surprise Big 8 Tournament title, despite finishing with a .500 conference record. Michigan State was fifteen years removed from Magic Johnson's title run, but ranked in the top five nationally. The Spartans would go on to lose only five games that year, and this would be one of them.

The boys had to catch the Pius team bus about ninety minutes after tip-off for their own road game. But Hanigan crisply remembers backup Husker guard Tom Wald getting fouled at the end of regulation on a three-pointer with the Huskers down three. Wald hit all three free throws, and there was no way Ryan and Patrick would ditch the overtime. Nebraska won 96–91, and the boys jumped in Patrick's Oldsmobile Delta 88 and drove one hundred miles per hour to their game at a private school an hour east on I-80 in Omaha.

They showed up late, and the coach held them out of the first quarter as punishment. Pius trailed by the time they entered the game. Ryan's father showed up and watched Pius win.

"My dad was pissed and said I was irresponsible," Ryan remembers. "But then he added, 'At least you saw a hell of a game worth being suspended for a quarter.'"

Ryan loved those Husker teams. His older sister was a college buddy of Husker center Rich King, who showed up at one of Ryan's seventh-grade Small Fry games. King, a senior that year, spread his seven-foot-two frame across all three rows of bleachers in the Salvation Army Rec Center gym on North Twenty-Seventh Street. Six months later he was the lone Husker ever taken in the first round of the NBA draft, when the Seattle Supersonics picked him fourteenth. He lasted four years in the league, starting just two games. With King cheering, Ryan was the team hero that day.

In Ryan's eighth grade year, he played a pickup game at the Lincoln Racquet Club that included Husker Beau Reid. The six-foot-eight, 220-pound forward got loose on a breakaway, and Ryan tackled him to stop a dunk.

"He got up and wanted to fight me," Ryan said.

Once he saw that a 130-pound kid had taken him down, Reid was embarrassed.

During those years Danny Nee's teams were relevant on the

national scene, Ryan Hanigan's favorite memories of spending time with his father all played out three rows up in Section C9 at the Bob Devaney Center with his father, who would rarely speak, except to mumble about the referees or a bad play.

Nee's teams from 1986 to 2000 would make five NCAA Tournaments and lose all five first-round games. He brought in future NBA players such as Erick Strickland, Eric Piatkowski, and Tyronn Lue. The 1997–98 team was the last to make March Madness, with Lue losing to Nolan Richardson's "40 minutes of hell" Arkansas team by nine points.

Sixteen years later Ryan Hanigan was a graduate of Creighton University, the only nationally relevant program in Nebraska since the millennium. Married with three kids, he lived in Omaha, where he worked as a physical therapist. He was what Husker fans seemed to hate more than even the University of Texas. He was a Jaysker fan: a Husker football fan in fall who switches his Big Red gear for Bluejays gear in wintertime to cheer Coach Greg McDermott's perennial NCAA Tournament team. He was pretty cranked about cheering for the Bluejay coach's son Doug, projected to be the national player of the year, and the team had moved to the Big East Conference to prove itself against historic programs, such as Georgetown and Villanova. Hanigan's father, John, now semiretired, was excited about Doug McDermott, too, because the coach's son played a disciplined and fundamentally pure offensive game worthy of respect. But Dad still held on to his Husker season tickets and wanted to see what this Tim Miles character could do in this first season at the new arena, even though news just broke in his *Lincoln Journal Star* newspaper that Nebraska was picked to finish last in the Big Ten.

Neither father nor son had any idea how this Husker season would change both of their lives.

At tonight's late-September open scrimmage at Pinnacle Bank Arena, Tim Miles will take the microphone to get seventy-five hundred fans riled up. For many of them, this will be their first experience at the Pinnacle Bank Arena, part of the biggest public works project in Lincoln's history. Their tax dollars will pay for the $378 million project. They need a good time. That means Miles will have to show his big grin. He'll have to lead chants. He'll have to call some play-by-play over the public address system. He'll have to talk up his team, his product.

He can play that role. He's made fans care about perennial loser programs at Mayville State in North Dakota and Southwest Minnesota State in Marshall. He's handed out free tickets to students in dorms at North Dakota State. He's hosted his own reality TV show for Mountain West Conference fans while at Colorado State. He can play Miles the Marketer.

But those players are going to pay dearly for tonight's praise in advance with this last practice, three hours before the doors open to the new arena. The currency will be defense. Miles the Marketer can also play Miles the Tyrant. Miles often says being around his team is like being in an episode of *Seinfeld*, but many practices, including this one, are more *Breaking Bad* than situation comedy.

Assistant coaches stand at center court in their futuristic Adidas sweat suits, arms folded and eyes darting from player to player stretching methodically to strength coach Tim Wilson's set routine. Wilson used to work in the NBA, so players follow his routine without question. Hip-hop music breaks in the new arena sound system to keep things loose, and Wilson lines up the team to start warm-up drills from baseline to baseline.

When the head coach finally appears, with his handwritten and photocopied practice outline from the coaches' locker room, the music devolves into rapid-fire *F* bombs. Miles makes a beeline for the scorer's table and tells student manager Skylar Sullivan to cut the sound.

"If you're not going to give me a better playlist, we're not going to play music," Miles says to the team. "I don't give a shit."

If swearing is going to be done in the arena this afternoon, he'll do it. Players, especially first-year guys, don't know if this anger is genuine or for effect. Sometimes the assistant coaches don't know, either, though they have their suspicions. If Miles wants to direct their excitement about tonight's public scrimmage—and halftime dunk contest—into an efficient and strenuous practice, the lyrics were a convenient excuse to get their attention. And the punishment starts right away.

Miles calls for the Iba drill, named after legendary coach Henry Iba from Oklahoma State. He's the coach who most American basketball historians say had the 1972 Olympic gold medal stolen from him, his team, and the country by referees in Munich, Germany. He's also the father of Moe Iba, the first Nebraska coach to take the perennially losing Husker program to the NCAA Tournament, where the Huskers lost to Western Kentucky, 67–59, in the first round in 1986. Moe Iba was also Don Haskins's assistant and main recruiter at Texas Western when the unknown school shocked Adolph Rupp's Kentucky team in the NCAA title game in 1966. That game was college basketball's Jackie Robinson–esque civil rights moment. Unless these Husker players can connect the dots from watching the movie version of the story in *Glory Road*, they have a limited knowledge of such history. And their freshman starting point guard, Tai Webster from New Zealand, can't even name three-quarters of the teams in the Big Ten. But they all know Nebraska has never won an NCAA Tournament game, which Miles promised to Husker fans when he took the job.

All that starts with the GATA drills. GATA is a Miles acronym for Get After Their Asses. And among those drills is the Iba drill, which goes something like this: A player takes a charge, then a ball is rolled out to midcourt, where a player must dive for it and hurl it back the way it came to an assistant coach, all in one motion. Then he must get up quickly to sprint back, take a return a pass from the coach, and try to score a fast-break layup. Waiting at the rim is Skylar Sullivan, the six-foot-four, 200-pound lead student manager. Coaches and players call him

Woody because he's a doppelgänger for Disney's *Toy Story* cowboy, facial expressions and all. Some players don't even know his real name. Woody holds a Husker red blocking pad that looks like it belongs on the football practice field, and he uses it to both protect himself from the force of incoming scorers and deliver blows once they're midair.

"This is the Big Ten, boys," Miles often calls out. "You gotta take the contact. Hit him, Woody."

Woody is the hardest part in the Iba drill. He scored thirteen points per game as a high school senior in Grand Island, about a hundred miles west on I-80. Now, he submits to any abuse Miles might send his way in his dream of becoming a college coach himself.

Some players can't score on Woody and his padded weapon. They must track down their misses and try again and again, hide their pain from the body blows, more tired with each attempt. Freshman Nick Fuller, a three-point shooter from Wisconsin, takes nine shots to score, slowing down each time he rebounds his own miss to prepare to drive hard to the hole again. After the eighth miss Miles, in the sweetest voice he can devise, asks, "Do you want to pass the ball back out to Coach Harriman?" The question actually means this: "Do you want to show your teammates who you really are and quit? Maybe go home to Sun Prairie in the land of cheese and admit you can't make it on this level?" Passing the ball to coach without scoring is an admission of defeat.

Instead, Fuller blasts through Woody's swinging pad to score with his off hand.

Point guard Benny Parker, nearly a foot shorter than Woody, takes four shots to score. Forward David Rivers struggles with his first two blasts, but knocks Woody backward on the third try and scores. Division I redshirt sophomore transfers Terran Petteway and Walt Pitchford score easily on their first tries. They're full of nervous energy because of tonight's open scrimmage, where they'll finally get to play in front of Husker fans after more than a year of waiting.

Near the end of the drill, forward and captain Shavon Shields, the son of Husker All-American offensive lineman Will Shields, an NFL Hall of Famer, gathers and plants his shoulder into Woody and his football pad, knocking the student manager onto his tailbone and out of bounds beneath the hoop. This spot on the new arena floor will be the setting for the team's defining moment of tonight's scrimmage. For now, this moment belongs to Woody, who is dazed on his back under his blocking pad with Shields standing over him, offering him a hand up.

"You got to be tough, Woody," Miles yells, before realizing his manager might actually be hurt. His question isn't as syrupy as the one he asked Fuller a few minutes ago: "You okay?"

Woody shakes his head as if to fight off an oncoming concussion, and Miles moves forward to grab the pad from him to take the next shots himself, which gets freshman Nate Hawkins excited. He's last up in the Iba drill and would like a shot at the coach. But Woody shakes his head again at the coach and gathers himself in front of the hoop, waiting for Hawkins, his eyes glassy. Miles slaps the student manager on the butt.

"Let's hear it for Woody," he yells, and the team starts screaming Woody's name and clapping. Assistant coaches grin and yell even louder. Assistant coach Chris Harriman, in particular, is a physicality junkie, eyes lighting up and teeth showing, like Jack Nicholson's as he peeks through the ax-broken door in *The Shining.* Then everyone starts yelling for Hawkins as he dives for his ball past midcourt and throws it back to Harriman while sliding backward. Hawkins picks himself up and sprints to get the return pass. He plants two feet in the lane to gather himself for Woody's hit. He misses and has to retrieve the ball and try again, and again, before he gets it in. Cheers for both of them.

Miles loves the punishment of the Iba drill so much he made his 1999 Southwest Minnesota State team perform it in warm-ups in front of the crowd before games, "just because I was so pissed at them." On the road the effect was hushed awe from opposing fans. At home the gym exploded with fan noise.

For these Huskers there's no rest after the Iba drill. No water. And the next drill hurts even more.

Players get in three lines to drive right into the body of a defender, who must take three straight charges. The defender, standing a few feet in front of the rim, gets run over by a driver coming down the right side of the lane. Then the left side. Then down the middle. Defenders must fall and get up as fast as they can for the next hit.

Terran Petteway, the new cocaptain, wants to go first. Petteway transferred from Texas Tech and sat out last season. He's most famous in college basketball circles for taking a swing at a Kansas Jayhawk as a Texas Tech freshman in the Big 12 Conference. Miles calls his dreadlocked transfer guard-forward the hardest worker on the team, but he also calls him an emotional perfectionist.

"Do I fall back on my hands?"

"No," Miles shouts. "You might hurt your wrists. Fall on your butt."

When walk-on freshman Tim Wagner is last to take his turn, guard Deverell Biggs, a new transfer from Omaha, cuts in front of some teammates to get the first shot at him. Biggs delivers a forearm shiver follow-through to send Wagner sprawling beneath the rim. Biggs grins at teammates. He doesn't help Wagner up. Others do, led by Shavon Shields. The team claps, and Miles moves to fundamentals. He gets the team lined up in their defensive stances. Butts down, fingertips to the ceiling. A grade-school drill. Something he has his summer camp coaches drill into third-graders. He walks around, pointing out weak stances.

"Lower, David. Butt."

He can spot his best defensive players from how low they get into their stances and how hard they work in such a tedious drill. They react to assistants moving the ball right or left or miming shots. Move right, left, hands up.

"Lower, lower, Tai."

"That's some weak sauce, Terran."

Players must stay down in the stance until Miles blows the whistle to stop them.

"Sergej, if you don't get down, I'm not gonna blow the whistle."

"Sit in it, baby, sit in it," Harriman shouts. "Make it feel good, Terran."

"I'm hurtin'. I'm hurtin'," Shields says through gritted teeth. He will be hurting later tonight in the scrimmage, but not from playing defense.

"That's what good stance feels like: it hurts," Miles says, without looking away from Sergej Vucetic, who can't seem to lower his butt without leaning forward and dropping his head. "Most of your guys' stances are straight legs, head out in front, all like that."

The team starts smiling and clapping while still in stance. And Miles notices some boosters, including two women, have shown up in the stands to tour the arena, and he blushes and smiles.

"That's only for certain ears," he says, after a joke about the perils of bending over too much.

"Last one if it's good. Ready?" He blows the whistle.

Harriman nestles up chest to chest with the team's best defensive player, Parker, who is fighting for minutes with two new point guards. Parker was recruited by previous coach Doc Sadler and started for half of Miles's first year. But nobody's talking about Benny Parker now in the media or on message boards. Fans are buzzing about Webster, the point guard Harriman brought in from across the globe off the New Zealand national team. And they're talking about Biggs, the Omaha Central three-time state champion, the first Nebraska scholarship recruit in the past decade. And Miles's first recruit as Husker coach. Parker needs a good practice, a bunch of them, to earn back his job. Harriman starts trying to push him over and out of his stance and takes the ball and tries to get by him. He can't.

"Benny, you can take that shit all day from him," Miles says before blasting the whistle.

Next, players jump into a team defense drill. The offense

passes the ball around the three-point line, and the defense must shift into the right positions, being able to see both their man and the ball. When the offense cuts to the rim, the defense must make things difficult.

"If they come into the lane, they're coming on our terms, not their terms," Miles shouts.

Miles is known in coaching circles as an offensive savant, but he knows this team needs to win with team defense, which many of them have never really had to play in lower-level basketball.

When Miles finally likes the defensive reaction to the ball, he allows the offense to attack the basket, and play is live. Players perk up, and Petteway takes over. He drives down the middle of the lane and over three players for a layup. He hits a three-pointer after dribbling between his legs. He dunks. But on his first play on defense, he gambles for a steal and turns his back on his guy, and walk-on point guard Trevor Menke beats him for a layup and draws a foul.

"Terran, give me five push-ups," Miles says. "You let a guy from Beatrice, Nebraska, cut in front of you. Wait 'til a guy from Columbus gets through there, too."

Eventually, new center Leslee Smith takes a charge, which shows he was paying attention in the previous drill, and half his teammates run to him to help him up, including some players on offense. The teams break into post players at one basket with assistants Chris Harriman and Kenya Hunter working on lane defense and perimeter players on the other end trying to close out on shooters with assistant Craig Smith.

Miles wanders to both ends of the court four times during the ten minutes.

With his right hand on his chin, he watches Walt Pitchford struggle to close out on shooters and return to rebound the ball. He's six feet, ten inches tall and can shoot three-pointers, but Miles wants him to control the lane and rebound. As Walt struggles and Hunter makes him repeat the drill a third and fourth time, Miles calls players down from the other end to watch.

Walt's on display now. Coaches and managers and teammates shout his name.

"Let's go, Walt."

"This is yours."

"You never quit," Hunter yells. "You never quit until you get that rebound."

Walt finally gathers the board.

"Get a drink," Miles says to all of them. "I think Walt [needs a break]."

Miles works Walt over more during some post defense drills in the lane. As Walt gets scored on repeatedly, Miles walks over to the scorer's table to Teddy Owens, the newest member of the coaching staff.

Miles looks down his practice outline to find one of his favorite drills, and the one the Huskers will repeat most in practice all year: a GATA drill called "Getback," which focuses on up-and-down transition defense. Essentially, he wants his team to always sprint back on defense to stop the ball and avoid giving up transition points after made or missed shots. He wants muscle memory. Score? Get back. Miss? Get back. Turn the ball over? Get back. That's Getback. Biggs and Webster, battling for Parker's starting point-guard position, go after each other physically for their respective red and white teams. After four or five solid defensive possessions, Biggs throws the ball away.

"What happened on that pass, Dev?" Miles says.

Magnanimous, Walt raises his hand and says, "That's my fault. My bad."

He does five push-ups without being asked to do them. Miles shakes his head.

Biggs misses a shot and gets beat back on defense. Miles rides him, and Biggs argues under his breath. Later, he beats everyone back and stops the ball, then just takes it from Webster.

"That's good, Deverell," Miles says to the entire team. "Listen, I'll tell you when you're good and tell you when you're bad. You were good, there. That was good."

The Getback devolves, like the prepractice hip-hop, into playground basketball.

"You're tired," Miles says. "When you get tired, you get sloppy. Next basket wins."

Petteway scores on a sweeping drive from the right side. Miles starts slow clapping, and the team runs toward him, clapping with him and quickening the tempo until they're all making a racket at the free-throw line.

The open scrimmage starts in an hour.

"You guys get your lipstick on," Miles says. "Get your makeup on. And let's be ready to go. Good job, guys."

A team meal awaits them on silver platters in a meeting room.

An hour later Miles lets his team introduce themselves to the seventy-five hundred fans who are seeing the new arena for the first time. Then he takes the microphone.

"This is just an awesome night," he says. "You can see the energy level is through the roof. It's just a different time for Nebraska basketball. Let's hear it for Husker basketball."

He throws the ball out, and the team scrimmages while Miles walks the sideline with his microphone to make fun of his team.

"Deverell, did you have a nickname growing up? It's not Dee-Nasty? Shavon said it was Dee-Nasty, but I wasn't sure."

"Hey, Sergej, have you ever seen *Rocky IV*? Can you give me an 'I must break you'?"

He hands the microphone to his seven-foot Serbian backup center while Sergej's loping down the court.

Sergej Vucetic's impression of actor Dolph Lundgren as Ivan Drago is unintentionally perfect, except it sounds like a question, not a threat: "I must break you?"

The crowd laughs, watching Miles as much as the basketball.

Then he picks on Mike Peltz, one of his two seniors, who was a big scorer in high school in the Nebraska panhandle before walking on for the Huskers. He has long hair and the biggest bench press on the team. But he's most known for scrapping with Creighton's Grant Gibbs a year ago at the Devaney Center when the Bluejays, the Huskers' biggest nonconference rival, smoked Miles's first Husker team, 64–42. The game was an embarrassment for Miles, mainly because he had somehow sold out the Devaney Center for the first time since 2006 for a non-conference game, and the highlight was Peltz scrambling for a loose ball against Gibbs and Avery Dingman for the Bluejays. Gibbs wound up with a three-inch scar on his face. Peltz got a standing ovation.

"That's a nice headband, Mike. My daughter has the same one."

Players jack up three-pointers on both ends, playing at about three-quarters speed, but fans react wildly.

"Reminds me of my high school team. Shoot the three, play no D."

The game then picks up offensively, with four consecutive dunk attempts—one missed—and on the last one captain and crowd favorite Shavon Shields flies in on a breakaway from the right side. Walt Pitchford chases him down from the left and undercuts him, sending Shields sprawling to the floor in the same spot where he had hammered Woody in the afternoon practice a few hours earlier.

Miles sets down the microphone and goes to Shields. The crowd is silent for a full minute until Shields gets up to stifled applause, and the momentum is lost for the night. Miles sits with his assistants and doesn't smile.

"I didn't say a word [to Walt]," Miles would say later. "He came over to Shavon and said, 'I'm sorry. I lost my mind for a second and didn't know what I was doing.' That was enough for me. Though it took all the energy out of the gym."

Miles had told the team not to be too physical in the scrimmage, to allow free layups, to not undercut each other. But Walt had gotten caught up in the dunks, and in the moment, and that kind of emotion would haunt him, and his team, all year.

In the next month Miles would survive having to suspend last year's No. 1 three-point shooter in the Big Ten two games for violating team rules, he'd have a reserve forward leave the team to officially "focus on his education," he'd give a speech to bank clients in Fremont, and he'd steal the show at the Big Ten Media Day in Chicago.

Through it all he had a team picked to finish last in the Big Ten and the official Pinnacle Bank Arena opening night coming up against Florida Gulf Coast, the team known as Dunk City during its run to the Sweet Sixteen in last year's NCAA Tournament, upsetting Georgetown and San Diego State as a No. 15 seed.

Again, the Husker program hadn't even appeared in March Madness since 1998, sixteen seasons ago. And it had never won a game in the tournament, going 0-6 in first-round losses, losing by an average of nine points. But those embarrassments didn't belong to Miles, he's always quick to mention. He'd turned around programs on five levels of collegiate basketball in his last four stops. For some teams the transformation took a year. Others took up to four. For now he's focused on figuring out who is smart enough and tough enough to play for this team, which almost lost its most significant returning player on a teammate's undercut in a public scrimmage. Through anger, comedy, and calculated confrontation, he'd have to get this team ready for Dunk City and a sellout crowd.

"All I want to do is win," he said. "That's all I think about."

3

Before flying to Big Ten Media Day in Chicago, Tim Miles knew that everyone, including the Big Ten media, picked Nebraska to finish last in the conference. That's twelfth in a conference called the Big Ten. That hurt him emotionally and psychologically. Or, at least, it didn't make much sense to him. In his first year the Huskers had won five Big Ten games, including upsets at home over Iowa and Minnesota, which would go on to win an NCAA Tournament game over the University of California at Los Angeles (UCLA). They also upset Purdue in the first round of the conference tournament. Yeah, they had a losing record—15-18 overall, 5-13 in conference—but they finished ahead of Penn State (psu) and Northwestern.

"I felt like we had good momentum," he said in his office after returning home. "And I think our players and fans had to believe that we think we're going to get this done. You can pick us last all you want. They may have that reality, but I'm not going to accept it. Losing doesn't make you a loser."

So a simple plan worked its way into Miles's brain before he reached the microphone at the O'Hare Airport Marriott meeting room to be the first coach to talk to the media.

"To me, the plan was partly standing up for our program and saying that in a very nonconfrontational way," Miles said later. "And they don't care that much, but it's an idea, too, that I understand where we stand, but I don't accept it."

So here's the short version of what he did when the moderator introduced him:

"I'm pleased to be back here at Big Ten Media Day. I see we're picked twelfth out of twelve again. And it's not just by you guys. I see it's by everybody.

"Like anybody, you take that to heart a little bit. . . . I came home to talk to my wife, and she says: 'Why aren't you out recruiting?'"

Big laughs.

"I understand why we are. Facts in life are really interesting. I've always tried to ignore them. I take the Mayville State job, all these places you guys have never heard of. They've been 2-22, 2-22. And we win. Southwest Minnesota State had one winning season in thirteen, and we find out how to win. . . ."

He talks about transforming North Dakota State from a Division II run-of-the-mill program playing to minuscule crowds to a Division I independent winner, filling the gym. Getting Colorado State from a winless conference team to a March Madness team.

"And in Nebraska we're not viewed as much, obviously, and I just, I don't believe it. I'm a dreamer. I really do believe in

Nebraska. I really do believe in what we are doing and how we can do it."

He sounds as if he's trying to convince himself of his beliefs, as much as he's trying to convince the sportswriters and broadcasters. But he knows they aren't really here to talk to him. They're waiting for the big shots. So he's really talking to his fan base.

"I believe in our guys," he says. "So, I don't think we're going to end up twelfth, and I think it's going to be a good thing. . . . I know we have a way. I know it works. It's worked every little place you've never heard of and some others you might have heard a little bit about, and it's going to work in Nebraska.

"Now, this team's interesting. You know, we're young. We're impulsive. I don't know if you ever were young or impulsive. But these guys—somebody said, 'Oh, they're going to be like a roller coaster.' I said, 'No, we're going to be like an EKG.'"

Laughs.

"I don't think you're probably going to have many questions after that. So, let's keep this to a minimum. I'm putting in a new directive that if you're picked first, you have to take the most questions, and as you get down to be picked at the end, you get to take the least questions. So I'm taking one."

The laughter is more reserved this time. Miles's mouth smiles at the group, but his eyes don't as they look impatiently over the crowd of video cameras, voice recorders, iPhones, and notebooks, locking eyes with reporters.

"And there's one guy that didn't vote us last, so he can ask it," he said.

A reporter asks about the new arena's ability to help him recruit and drum up local support. Miles brags about selling out season tickets six months in advance of the season. He brags about the seventy-five hundred fans at the open scrimmage. He brags about the beauty of the arena and the state-of-the-art practice facility. But he cautions them that none of that matters—not to players, not to recruits or fans, and certainly not to him—unless they win.

He jokes about both his team and the Husker women's team, coached by Connie Yori, being ranked the same.

"Connie and I are both picked twelfth. She's twelfth in the country; I'm twelfth in the league."

More laughs.

Miles likes winning over the media. He thinks most everyone who has ever interviewed him or reported on his teams has been fair. He doesn't like that reporters may use anonymous message-board material in their work, but that's his only complaint. He ends this press conference by repeating that he loves Nebraska and its rich athletic history and that it's time for his program to do its part. Then he says this before leaving the microphone:

"I asked one buddy of mine, 'What do I say? We were picked twelfth again.' He said, 'You've got them right where you want them.'"

At practice that night in Lincoln, the team stands in what would be an almost perfect alignment for a team photo as it awaits Miles to finish discussing the day's practice plan with assistants. Miles walks over to them and rattles off five things he'd like to do in a quick practice, but his mind is still stuck on the press conference. He stops talking and looks over two of his few veterans from last year, Benny Parker and David Rivers, who are both worried about making this year's rotation. Miles looks down at Parker, the shortest guy on the team, then up to Rivers and his headband full of dreadlocks.

"D-Riv? How many days until we play in the Sweet Sixteen?" Miles asks deadpan.

Rivers's eyes get big, like someone has just handed him a hundred-dollar bill he's not sure he deserves, and everyone smiles. Miles smacks him on the shoulder.

Thirty minutes later the team struggles through a full-court drill against pressure. The red and white teams are divided evenly, and neither side can avoid turnovers. On the red team Terran Petteway makes a big play or a turnover every time he touches the ball. All or nothing.

"If we're not going to do this right and we're going to be pissy and whiny after a day off," Miles yells, "then we're just going to run."

"Come on," Petteway shouts. "Let's go, red. Let's go."

Mike Peltz fumbles the ball away for the red team, and Miles stops everything to clarify life for his walk-on guard.

"Peltz. You can help us, but you have to do two things: You have to take care of the ball great. Well, three things. And you have to know what the hell's going on defensively, and know what we're trying to do here against pressure."

Peltz immediately steals the ball from Parker and feeds Terran Petteway on the fly for a no-dribble dunk. Within a few months he'd learn that such defensive plays in practice would earn him a second-semester scholarship.

By the end of the drill, though, Peltz's comeback isn't enough to satisfy Miles that his team is ready for Dunk City—or any opponent. Maybe they will finish last in the Big Ten. The losing team in this drill was supposed to run, but that wasn't enough incentive to play well.

"Both teams on the baseline. Twenty burpees. Count them out."

Up, down, out, in. One. Up, down, out, in. Two. Up, down . . .

Nebraska director of basketball operations Jayden Olson is a North Dakota guy who joined Miles's staff at Colorado State and followed him to Lincoln. Miles calls early-season practices "Etch-a-Sketch days," Olson says.

"You teach them something, and they go do it," Olson says from the bench at an October practice at the Pinnacle Bank Arena. "They have the talent now to do it well."

He's referring to the talent level of the entire team, but mostly indicating the new redshirt sophomores, Terran Petteway and Walt Pitchford, who transferred in from Texas Tech and Florida.

"But they come back the next day, and they've shaken that Etch-a-Sketch that is their heads and it's gone."

So the team is back in the Getback GATA drill. Trying not to screw up. Miles learned the GATA acronym in high school football back in Doland, South Dakota. His coach Chris Lund had stolen the idea from a Georgia Southern football coach, as far as Miles could tell. Their first four drills would always be GATA stuff, relentless-pursuit-of-the-ball kinds of drills, "and you'd be bleeding fifteen minutes into practice."

When Miles got his first coaching job in 1995 at tiny Mayville State in North Dakota, GATA came back into his coaching lexicon after a strange confrontation with the women's coach, Chuck Gremmels, who hadn't been around all summer. "The guy just didn't exist," Miles said.

Miles had been scrambling to put a roster together, calling a buddy in Wisconsin to come through with some junior college (juco) transfers. The day before classes started, Miles was still worrying about not having a full team and having to teach multiple classes—bowling class, racquetball class, coaching class—for his twenty-seven-thousand-dollar salary. The town was tucked a few miles off Interstate 29 between Fargo and Grand Forks along North Dakota's Red River Valley. Population: 2,156. The Comets generally couldn't outdraw the local high school teams, especially not after going 2-22 each of the past two years.

So Gremmels bangs on the office door frame and starts right in on Miles.

"You're the new basketball coach now, right?"

"Yeah. Hi, I'm Tim Miles."

"What makes you so special?" Gremmels said. "What's your edge? How are you going to beat Mary and Minot? Those guys have players. They get all the best players. You're at Mayville. Jamestown is even loaded right now."

Then Gremmels digs deeper.

"Is the aura of Tim Miles going to beat those guys? What's your edge? The last three guys who sat in that chair got fired."

All Miles could think about after that inquisition was GATA. He thought his team's edge would be some kind of essence that his team would not stop. Ever. That his players would be relentless and energetic. He knew everybody gets smacked in the face, and Mayville had lost forty of its last forty-four games. But this team would learn to recover from getting smacked and Get After Their Asses. That would be his team's identity. He'd seen St. Cloud State's team motto of "Run and Fun" and had seen Clem Haskins's University of Minnesota teams wear shirts that read "Play Hard."

"I knew at the time it had to be GATA," Miles remembers. "Regardless of what happens, we are going to stay after it, and we can do it. That's what it really comes down to is we can do it."

In his career he'd have shirts made with GATA on them, even on practice shorts. His Husker staff received long-sleeve gray practice Ts with "GATA" along the bottom of the back as soon as he arrived at Nebraska.

Miles remembers everything about that moment with Gremmels nineteen years ago. "It just really resonated with me. We coaches still always say, 'What's our edge?'"

He admits, though, that as the Florida Gulf Coast game approaches, the team views GATA simply as playing hard, not surviving turmoil and coming together to win. That gnaws at the coach.

"Maturity takes time," he says in his office while sketching out a practice plan. "Discipline takes time. My challenge is, how brutal do I make practices?"

Pretty brutal. If the Huskers were to avoid last place in the Big Ten in the 2013–14 season, they'd have to embrace GATA as their edge. And embrace the Getback, which works like this: Coaches break players up into even red and white teams. The team on offense must score in a half-court set, and then guards must sprint back and the three "bigs"—forwards and center—must get back within two and a half seconds, and the whole team must get a defensive stop. If they do that twice, they get two points. If not, they go back to zero. Then the other team gets a shot.

Midway through October at the two-year-old Hendricks Center, the Getback isn't going well. The white team wins when freshman guard Tai Webster and junior forward David Rivers repeatedly score on the red team, which is loaded with Walt Pitchford and captains Shavon Shields and Terran Petteway. Red now has to run baseline to baseline and back three times in fewer than thirty-three seconds as punishment. In nearly two decades as a coach, Miles has figured out that eleven seconds is a reasonable time for players to run the length of the court and back and not like it, which is what he wants. And if he wants to make them dig a little deeper, he'll make them run twice in twenty-two seconds. But he's angry now, so he's going full throttle with three sprints in thirty-three. The reds all make the baseline before the horn blows, except for Pitchford.

"Do it again," Miles says.

Some players, including Shields, complain that the clock was too fast.

"I'm just going on the information I got," Miles says to Shields. The reds run again.

Pitchford barely makes the buzzer this time.

Miles grimaces but doesn't make them run a third thirty-three.

"Let's give red one more shot."

Pitchford hits a three-pointer and hustles back, and red gets a stop. Then he hits another three.

The team is tired. For every mistake players are subbed out to run on a treadmill beside the court. They must run at ten miles per hour for thirty seconds under the supervision of strength coach Tim Wilson.

After a water break red gets a point when Mike Peltz steals the ball from Tai Webster, who automatically drops to do ten push-ups before the coach can tell him to run on the treadmill.

Miles looks over at Craig Smith, his top assistant. "Should I let him do that ten or run him for thirty?"

"Run him."

"Go run, Webster. Treadmill."

Webster smiles.

"I ran ten miles an hour for twenty minutes on that thing this morning, Tai. Don't cheat me."

Webster smiles bigger, and Wilson cranks up the treadmill. Miles's attention switches back and forth between the court and Webster running in the corner.

Teddy Owens's father, Ted Owens, coached the Kansas Jayhawks from 1964 to 1983. He's sitting in on practice and likes Miles's attention to detail.

"He doesn't miss anything," Owens says to his son at the scorer's table. "He sees mistakes and addresses them right away. And makes them run. And watches that, too, to make sure it's done right. Doesn't miss a thing."

Later in practice, Webster starts pounding the ball in a half-court offense drill that limits the players to one dribble each. Miles blows the whistle and shakes his head. Webster starts for the treadmill.

"No. You can play. You can play. I'm not going to make you run for playing stupid."

Ten minutes later Miles tries to put in a new play. The team keeps messing it up. Webster tries to sneak a pass through three defenders on a pick-and-roll, and backup center Sergej Vucetic fumbles it out of bounds.

"Tai, you're running."

Treadmill. Fifteen seconds later Deverell Biggs turns the ball over. Then Ray Gallegos. Soon, all the guards are waiting in line for the treadmill. Finally, Wilson fights the barrage by making some of them do push-ups rather than the treadmill.

"Gallegos, get back in here and play D," Miles says. "And stop throwing it off the walls."

For the last fifteen minutes, Miles loads up the red team with his top eight players on his white board in his upstairs conference room. Assistant Chris Harriman takes the white team and psychs players up to mess up the offense. Which they do. After several turnovers Harriman is screaming support for his team and clapping in Miles's face. The head coach smiles and starts a slow clap to bring the team together to end practice.

"Today, I think we got better," he says, as if to convince himself. "We moved the ball better. Turnovers were down. People were in better shape. We got better."

But they didn't get much better.

4

After a week of similarly frustrating practices, Miles decides to blast the team in a prepractice film session in the team classroom beside the practice court. Afterward, he invites the Big Ten Network's (BTN) Stephen Bardo to give the prepractice speech. Bardo played for Illinois in the late 1980s for Lou Henson and made the NCAA Tournament all four years, the Final Four as a junior. He was also the Big Ten Defensive Player of the Year.

"Do you mind saying a word?" Miles asks him as the team circles the two of them. "I want him to talk to you guys because nobody's been through more of what you're going to go through than him."

"Trust the process," Bardo says. "Let him kick your ass every day. Trust the process. Trust your coaches. . . . The toughest thing for coaches across the country is to get you guys to go hard every day. It seems silly. But you think you're going hard, but you can go harder."

The speech feels like a setup. But Miles swears he didn't coach Bardo on what to say.

"We need a good practice today," Teddy Owens says from his spot at the scorer's table, where he's working with PhotoShop on his laptop.

The NCAA allows only three assistant coaches for each team. The rest of the staff have other titles, such as Owens's "administrative coordinator" title or Olson's "director of operations" title. Basically, that means Owens can do anything to help the team except directly coach players. So he offers advice to assistants. Lines up recruiting trips. Works with boosters. Puts on youth events. Anything but directly coaching the team. At practices he takes notes on anything from players' body language to tracking points in drills. Today, he's working on his design skills to build a sign for the locker room tomorrow and maybe for a late-night text to players tonight. On the file he's pasted a Florida Gulf Coast University logo, and over that he's typed, in bright Husker red, "8 PRACTICES UNTIL FGCU BEATS YOUR ASS!"

Miles has used a line item in his budget to hire three officials from Omaha for today's practice. The NCAA has tightened up the rules on hand checks, arm bars, and defensive players setting their feet before collisions in the lane, and Miles is worried his team's lazy defense in practice will translate into a mess of foul calls. He wants his team to adjust now and not have to figure it out during a game. He wants them to stop fouling.

The team is crisp in warm-up weave drills. The ball rarely ever hits the floor, and nobody misses layups or dunks. Miles works the team up from one-on-one defensive drills to two-on-two, and the refs rarely blow whistles. A half hour into practice Miles is pleased enough to offer an early water break.

The red team plays defense against Florida Gulf Coast plays run by assistant coach Chris Harriman and his white scout team of mostly walk-on players. Miles is loose and rides Harriman for overcoaching his scouts.

"Let's go, Belichick," he yells across the court to Harriman's huddle, referring to New England's three-time Super Bowl–winning coach.

An hour into practice things seem to be going too well, so Miles calls for the Getback drill. He comes to the sideline to explain it to Bardo, who takes notes for future telecasts on the Big Ten Network.

Right away Miles's red team messes up. Biggs gives up a free layup to Benny Parker and gets sent to the treadmill for thirty seconds at ten miles per hour. He walks. And Miles notices, but doesn't say anything.

A referee whistles Shavon Shields for a hand-check foul. Treadmill. He sprints to the corner of the gym.

Ray Gallegos turns the ball over. Sprints to the treadmill.

Peltz, on the white team, steals the ball from Biggs and goes in for an uncontested layup, which he butchers off the back of the rim. He falls to the floor in frustration.

"Red team on the line," Miles yells. "White off [the court]. Good job, Peltz. Woody, put twenty-two seconds up there."

Red takes off for two baseline sprints, but Miles is still talking.

"When you're running, you're running as hard as you can, and when you get back, somebody show some leadership."

The white team claps for the red team from the sideline while drinking water from green Gatorade bottles. Scout players all know the practice can go one way or the other from this point.

"Peltz!" Miles turns on his senior guard. "Next time you miss a layup, I don't want you laying on the ground. Go run."

Peltz smiles and runs for the treadmill, and Miles turns to watch the red team on its second trip down court and covers his mouth to hide his own smile. And without looking toward the treadmill he yells, "And cut your hair. You make three great defensive plays and have nothing to show for it. Now, let's go."

Back in the Getback, red fouls again.

"Peltz! Get a red jersey."

Miles pulls Ray Gallegos, his other senior, aside and launches into a tirade about leadership and defense and every mistake he made on the court in the drill and throughout the fall practices and throughout his junior season.

"Let's go, Ray," Terran Petteway shouts.

"Hey, Ray, you got to make a play," assistant Kenya Hunter calls out. "Whether it's offense or defense, you got to make a play."

Leslee Smith turns the ball over. Treadmill.

Peltz misses another layup, but puts in the offensive rebound.

Biggs fouls. Treadmill.

"Consistency, discipline, boys," Miles yells. "She's either pregnant or she's not. We either have discipline or we don't. We don't right now."

Petteway starts taking over on offense, hitting drives and threes. Then he misses a putback and fouls Peltz, who is back on the white team and beat him for the rebound. Petteway hacks at Peltz in frustration, ninety-four feet from the basket where he's supposed to be sprinting to in the Getback, the whole point of the drill.

The gym is silent as Petteway is sent to the treadmill.

"Attaboy, Peltz!" Harriman screams. He loves messy practices. He loves his scout team battling the guys who might start against Florida Gulf Coast. If he makes things tough for them here, they might handle the pressure of opening night at the Pinnacle Bank Arena in front of a sellout crowd. Someone has said a surprise guest is supposed to be at the pregame ceremony and everything.

Eight practices left until Dunk City beats Nebraska's ass.

Leslee Smith is built like a commercial furnace. At six-foot-eight and 255 pounds, the junior forward looks like a Big Ten post player. Tim Miles likes to refer to him as his island prince because Smith was born in the British Virgin Islands and because Smith walks around with his chin high, a princely dignity. Today, Miles will blast away at that dignity.

The truth is that Miles's team will struggle to defend or rebound in the bulky and physical Big Ten, picked again to be the top conference in basketball this 2013–14 season. He doesn't have many guys who can take up space in the lane or force their will against players like Michigan State's Adreian Payne or Michigan's Mitch McGary. Smith has never been much of a scorer or rebounder in his brief career at Southern Methodist or even Seward County Community College in Kansas, where guard Deverell Biggs also played. But strength coach Tim Wil-

son praised Smith's NBA-like power in summer drills, including his ability to push heavy sleds across the gym floor. Smith's
strength rivals that of any player Wilson coached while working with the NBA's Milwaukee Bucks. But Miles has yet to see
that power in practice this fall.

Miles has scheduled an early practice for the last day of fall
break. He's doubling down on GATA drills. He's been worried
he's spent too much time in practice on the new guys, all transfers who redshirted or played at a lower level a year ago: Terran
Petteway, Walt Pitchford, Tai Webster, Biggs, and Smith.

He'd like to spend more time on guys who suited up for the
Huskers in last season's 15-18 season. The leader from that team,
Brandon Ubel, graduated and is playing pro ball in Belgium.
Miles salivates at the thought of having Ubel's leadership and
inside presence on this team. He'd tried to talk the six-foot-ten
center into redshirting last season, when Miles knew he'd lose
more games than he'd win. But Ubel was too smart. He could
have graduated a semester early and wasn't going to wait three
full semesters to walk across the stage. Four other guys who
played significant minutes on that team—Ray Gallegos, Benny
Parker, David Rivers, Mike Peltz—are fighting to make the rotation. Only Gallegos—and his Big Ten–leading three-point percentage—seems to be a lock for significant game minutes. But
he's not going to be able to focus on any of them today.

Today is Leslee Smith Day at the Hendricks Training Complex.
In the first GATA drill, a four-on-four battle, Smith has already
been sent to the white team for allowing a walk-on to get to the
rim. After another mistake he's sent to the treadmill. He makes
a grimace and walks toward the corner of the court. He makes
three long, dignified strides before Miles explodes.

"Leslee, get over there," Miles yells while play ensues. "I'm
not watching you dog it on my time and then walk over there."

Miles turns back to the court to see Petteway dive out of bounds
for a loose ball. The entire red team sprints to the sidelines to help
him up, a physical symbol for what Miles calls "togetherness."

"All right, Leslee, get out here and do it right."

Smith lumbers back into the Getback fray. Immediately, his entire white team must do ten push-ups for not being in position defensively. Leslee's tired.

Freshman Tai Webster turns the ball over and gets ten push-ups.

Gallegos and freshman Nate Hawkins turn the ball over. More treadmills.

"We'll be playing three-on-three Getback if we keep running out of players," Miles says.

Freshman Nick Fuller starts hitting threes and a few layups for the white team. He's not ready to play in the Big Ten, not quite quick enough to guard anyone or get his shot off, but he's tearing up Miles's red team. And the coach isn't having it. He sends little Benny Parker to the treadmill for a turnover. Parker jogs to the corner.

"Benny? Why are you walking? Add thirty seconds, Coach. Let's go. You should be eager to get to that treadmill."

His point is that Parker, who started as a freshman point guard, should be outworking everyone to beat out Webster and Biggs. He's on the white team and should be ticked off about it and do something about it.

Webster runs again. Gallegos gets sent for a third time. When he gets back in, he runs a play incorrectly.

"Red on the baseline. Eleven seconds on the clock," Miles says to everyone, but never stops glaring at Gallegos. "You either don't know how to run the play or you don't care. Go."

Biggs gets sent to the treadmill for a turnover. Then Petteway turns the ball over. Treadmill. He sprints to the machine and starts running before Wilson can even get there to time him.

Leslee Smith powers to the rim to score on the red team, and Miles is satisfied enough to give the team a break with a free-throw shooting drill and water. But not until red runs a thirty-three—three times down and back.

That's the last thing Leslee will do right for the next hour.

Miles puts the teams in a shot-selection game in which they get extra points for making shots within the offense or off assists, and they lose points for turnovers. He allows Petteway and Gallegos to draft their teams to make them even. Petteway takes his fellow captain, Shavon Shields; Benny Parker; David Rivers; and some walk-ons. Gallegos takes Deverell Biggs, Leslee Smith, Tai Webster, Nate Hawkins, and walk-ons. Miles visibly cringes a little. He hates having cliques on the team, and clearly Gallegos's white team has all the new guys, except Petteway.

The white jerseys run a terrible offensive set before Webster bails them out with a tough floater in the lane.

"We've got four guys standing around on offense," Miles says, stopping the action. "That will work sometimes. But we can't be 'sometimes.' We can't play smart sometimes and beat Indiana. We can't play smart sometimes and beat Michigan and Michigan State. We can't play sometimes and beat Florida Gulf Coast at home. We have to play smart all the time."

The next play: Smith fumbles a perfect pass at the rim from Webster. The ball goes out of bounds. Miles starts in on him from a foot away. Leslee has to look down at his coach, but he looks all the way to the floor. Apparently, that's a bigger mistake than the turnover.

"Leslee, look at me," Miles screams. "Do you want to play juco basketball? . . . Time to man up and say, 'I messed that up.'"

"Come on, Les," Petteway says, even though he's leading the other team.

Miles subs Smith out and keeps talking to him on the baseline.

"Embarrassing to watch," Miles says, and keeps glaring at him. "You had a great practice earlier this week. Then this."

Nate Hawkins slaps Smith on the butt.

Another assistant, Chris Harriman, came to Nebraska from St. Louis University, where he earned what he calls his "coaching PhD" from Rick Majerus. Harriman learned to never allow what Majerus called "slippage." Deal with even the smallest of mistakes right away. Confront. Confront. Confront. So Harriman loves these public call-outs. He shows a kind of smiling snarl in these moments.

The team's new assistant coach, Kenya Hunter, was taken a little off-guard by these tirades in early-season practices. He's a fifteen-year veteran from East Coast programs. He's coached in the Atlantic 10 and Atlantic Coast Conference and most recently the Big East, with Georgetown. He's been working hard with Leslee Smith on his post moves, and his style is to be positive. His most common phrase in practices and locker rooms is "Let's go, fellas," delivered in a heavy bass followed by a couple of claps. So it's hard for Hunter to watch Smith being torn down after he's worked so hard to build him up. But Hunter understands why Miles confronts players in front of the team because it's a form of complete transparency.

"For some coaches, it's a fine line where they would go in yelling at players," he says. "Most do more individual talking instead of out in front of the team. But I'm on Miles's side because we address things out in the open. The alternative is you tell one guy something in private, and they think they're his favorites or they're getting picked on. This way, everyone knows. And it doesn't matter if you're Terran Petteway or a walk-on. Not too many coaches are able to do that and still bring out the best in them."

Miles's thought process has a philosophical foundation. He likes to read both sports and nonsports books about psychology and philosophy. More so, he picks up stories here and there on the Internet. He read recently that most adults don't leave adolescence until age twenty-eight.

"So what am I dealing with, like, prepuberty here on this team?" he says.

He also read companies are hiring something called "reassurance managers" because people need constant encouragement and immediate feedback. In Miles's pragmatic translation of those facts, that means parents constantly praise kids. Students immediately receive their test scores. They frantically need to know how they're doing. So in practice Miles offers constant critiques, but not sugarcoated ones. And the drama of confrontation is born out of this generation's inability to confront each other on anything, Miles says. They just don't want to do it.

"I say, 'Man up, let's go, eyes up,'" he says. "I feel like you have to confront issues, especially in front of the team, so everybody knows this is what I expect out of this guy. And when it's not going well, he's not meeting expectations. Now, is that calling a guy out? Okay. But if I don't, it's going to get contemptuous. Which is killer."

Miles defines *contempt* as a form of passive aggressiveness that tears teams apart. If Miles blasts a player privately to an assistant, he's not confronting the problem. He's gone down a path of contempt. If some players overhear the contempt, they go to the locker room to complain about the coach "screwing me and messing with my game." But if Miles says everything in the open, nobody can complain in the locker room or the showers or on the Internet or anywhere because the teammate who hears the complaint knows what the coach wants. He was there when it all went down.

Miles smiles. "I always say, 'If you think I'm messing with your game, then you ain't got no game.'" Then he admits he stole the line from former Minnesota Gophers coach Clem Haskins, who had a more earthy version.

The point is that Miles wants no slippage, and he wants no contempt in the locker room. To ensure that he'll meet the next day with a player he blasts in practice, or text him later that night, or pull him into a corner of the gym after practice to explain his intentions, to field questions, and to be sure he's sucked any contempt out of the player or his relationship with that player. And, of course, they need the reassurance. They're not horrible players. They're not being picked on.

"Look, I'm not getting off here on making your life miserable," Miles says. "I'm about winning. This program's got to win."

...

Twenty more minutes into the shot-selection game, the turnovers haven't slowed down at all. Body language isn't good. Miles confronts the entire team, but this time he's using his elementary education bachelor's degree voice rather than his Bobby Knight.

"Things are getting a little bitchy," Miles says. "A little whiny. A little fatigued. Nothing's going your way. How are you going to play like a winner? Earlier, Tai Webster has his hands on his knees. He looks like he's thinking, 'We'll lose, and I'll run, then the game will be over.' I'm looking for nonverbal cues on all you guys. I jumped on Leslee. I'm looking to see how he'll react. Guys are reacting to everything that's happening. This is the way a game goes sometimes. It tests you. Now, find a way to win."

Two minutes later, without looking at his island prince, Miles softly says, "Leslee, get Serge."

Miles's anger is spent, or his strategic anger spent—nobody knows for sure except him. The tone of his verbal critiques has changed. In a formula Miles uses repeatedly, he will call out players publicly and turn up the heat, but he'll follow that up not only with individual postpractice or next-day meetings with the player he besmirched, but by bringing his comedy routine out to repair everyone's psyche.

As he puts the red team in a zone defense that Hunter brought with him from Georgetown, Miles moves Petteway from the left block to the right.

"You see, we want our best rebounder on the left side in this D," he says deadpan. "This guy [Petteway] had something like 101 career rebounds at Texas Tech, and he hasn't gotten a defensive board yet here. I don't know where we're going to hide him."

Petteway smiles.

Miles adds specific game situations into the drill. Shields forgets about the shot clock and doesn't get a shot off.

"Shavon, I told you there were ten seconds left on the shot clock. You want me to change your diapers, too? I'll bring the wet ones, Shavon."

Shavon smiles. So does Petteway.

Shavon tries to make up for the mistake with a hard drive down the middle, but Leslee Smith takes a charge and the walk-ons on the white team help him up.

"You go at it, Leslee," Miles says. "Way to respond. Good job."

He claps twice. When Biggs misses horribly on a wide-open three, he falls backward on his butt, trying to get a foul call.

"You can't flop after missing a wide-open three, Dev. You can join Shavon in the diaper club."

Shields dives for a loose ball, and Petteway runs up to him and screams in his face. Red team wins.

Miles senses he needs to stop practice on that moment, that image.

White has to run two in twenty-two seconds, then Miles slow claps the team together. This is what he wants them to understand today: "It seems like an easy game, doesn't it? But it's not easy," he says. "I saw guys getting real negative, and I jumped on you. But you guys have to step in, too. That's one way to be a team. Ultimately, what matters is how we find a way to win."

Six days later Miles's island prince would grade out as the team's most efficient player in an exhibition blowout over Nebraska-Kearney in front of fifteen thousand fans at the new arena.

5

Tim Miles has a philosophy about scheduling opponents that is complicated, but he can articulate his ideas in a bullet-point fashion. The goal every game is to win. Those are the battles. But the war is to make the NCAA Tournament. Or to get the selection committee to choose you and your résumé. To do that, you must beat legitimate teams with strong RPIs (ratings percentage indexes) so that your team finishes with a strong sos (strength of schedule). So you can't schedule 10 University of Nebraska–Kearneys or any teams in the bottom 100 among the 349 Division I teams.

"The trick is, who do you get that is 75–150?" he says. "Now, your strength of schedule is top 30 or 40 [in the country]. So if you have any type of season, you're an NCAA team. You can be 18-13 and still be in. If you have enough top-100 wins, you're going to get in. But if you don't play well, you're 13-18.

"Essentially, I always build the schedule so that even if we're 18-13, our numbers are so solid that they are taking us."

That's how he got Colorado State into the tournament in 2012. The team won twenty games, lost eleven, and beat enough good teams, or lost to enough very good teams, to get itself into March Madness. He was so strategic with then-AD Paul Kowalczyk in schedule making that *Sports Illustrated*'s Luke Winn, the next fall, used CSU's schedule as a case study for a term he coined as *the exploitable gap*, in which teams use a flawed RPI system to schedule their way into the tournament. Winn's essential assertion: "They had managed to play a non-conference schedule that, in actuality, was middle-of-the-road, but it was so well-tuned to exploit the RPI's flaws that, in the eyes of the selection committee, it looked elite." In other words, Miles had tricked the selection committee. Pretty smart for a below-average kid from Doland, South Dakota.

ESPN basketball writer and author John Gasaway was so jealous of Winn's piece he referenced it, and Miles, in his book *Basketball Prospectus* as part of a chapter that was essentially a rant against the NCAA's use of RPI. Miles, at Nebraska by this time, sent a direct email to Gasaway, defending and justifying his methods and his team, and won the writer over. Gasaway, to this day, seeks to destroy the NCAA's use of the RPI, but is somewhat of a Miles devotee.

This 2013–14 season, with the Big Ten loaded, Miles figured the Huskers should have one of the top schedules in the country, like they did last season in 2012–13, his first at Nebraska. That team had the tenth-toughest schedule in the country by season's end, mostly because so many teams in the Big Ten had strong RPIs. So, despite going 15-18, his team finished ninety-eighth overall in the RPI. If the Huskers could somehow win half its conference games, play some strong teams in the non-conference schedule, and win them, they could conceivably finish in the thirties or forties nationally and make the tournament a few years before schedule.

To do that he and his administrators built a nonconference schedule that included an assortment of teams that were picked to win or at least do well in their smaller conferences—Massachusetts (U-Mass), Alabama-Birmingham (UAB), Western Illinois. He also had some pushovers in Northern Illinois, the Citadel, and South Carolina State, but those could help with team confidence. He also had reluctantly agreed to play Cincinnati, a perennially loaded team, as part of a football-basketball scheduling package at the behest of his new athletic director, Shawn Eichorst. Last, he had the annual in-state rivalry game with Creighton. But he didn't want to think about Creighton yet. With a schedule intact, all he had to do now was win. That's all.

He thought the team would have to go 10-2 in the nonconference schedule to have a chance.

The first team on the schedule was Florida Gulf Coast.

"I don't know, I just thought Dunk City would be a fun team to play in the opener at the arena," Miles said three days before the game.

The next day he suspended his most experienced player.

Practice was supposed to start at 3:00 p.m. on the first Wednesday of November at the Hendricks Training Complex. The structure opened in October 2011, before Doc Sadler's last year. The eighty-four-thousand-square-foot palace houses the basketball and wrestling teams and is basically an addition to the Bob Devaney Sports Center, where the Huskers played basketball until this season.

Coaches have offices up in the rafters, essentially, with windows that look down onto the court, and a balcony to allow visitors to watch, too. Players have the best offices, though. As they walk a hallway to the locker room or gym, hip-level glass basketballs along both walls light up Husker red.

"That's for recruits," Miles says.

In the locker-room lounge sits a pool table with Husker pool balls, a nutritionist-stocked kitchen, seven-foot-deep couches that face a wall of TVs that always seem to be on the Big Ten Network or some ESPN channel. Players have iPads embedded into their lockers that they can program to play their own music directly to their preferred shower stall forty feet away, past the whirlpools. The bathrooms have adjustable TVs. Want to look up at them? Down at them? Up to you. Take your time in there. Sinks, urinals, toilets, and showers are all stainless steel.

The Hendricks is a symbol of a decade of unprecedented growth in college sports revenue, as much as the Nebraska Athletic Department is a symbol in itself. In the past ten years the Huskers have renovated the Devaney Center for $20 million and Haymarket Park for $4.75 million and expanded the Memorial Stadium twice for $50 and $63.5 million, among other projects.

As drivers enter Nebraska's capital city from the north on I-180, they now not only see the promised land of Memorial Stadium on the left, but also see the plush Hawks Field at Haymarket Park for Husker baseball on the right, followed by the Jiffy Pop/spaceship–looking Pinnacle Bank Arena. Many of the millions came from Athletic Department donors, but the baseball park was paid for in a partnership with the city, and the new arena, well, that was all city money, and both projects were built on complicated tax-increment financing agreements. But the millions haven't received much criticism in the public or the local media. Aside from a small group opposed to the $378 million price tag of the entire arena project, the biggest public works project in Lincoln's history, voters approved construction by a twelve-point margin in 2010.

In the *Lincoln Journal Star*, Mayor Chris Beutler, who spearheaded the project, said he was surprised by the margin of victory for the arena. But the margin shouldn't have been a shock. The newspaper had done many stories over the years about the cause-and-effect relationship between Husker success and the health of the economy. Stories had been done on the amount of domestic-abuse rates in relationship to Husker failures and successes. In the *Daily Nebraskan*, the student newspaper, Tom Osborne once lamented the football team's—and essentially the entire athletic program's—relationship to the mental health of the state's citizens: "I just know the realities of the situation. If the football team goes south on us and is really bad—it does affect the psyche of the state. Not everybody, but it affects a lot of people in terms of how they feel about themselves, in terms of just the general mood of the state. You lose a big game, and they tend to go in the tank a little bit."

And the basketball program had tanked for sixteen years.

On the first Monday of November, the Huskers hammered Nebraska-Kearney 91–60 in an exhibition that was essentially the second soft opening of the new arena. Thirteen players got into the game, five of them scored in double figures, and nobody got hurt. Terran Petteway had foul trouble and took himself out of plays defensively by gambling, but nothing in the game really surprised Miles. The arena, though, was little more than half full, with 7,804 fans.

Now, the hard opening was coming in two days, the first game of a season of presold sellouts. The momentum of the arena, the entertainment district surrounding it, and the Husker program needed to crescendo, or at least continue.

In the Hendricks gym players talked and took shots casually, with assistants joking around with them. They were waiting for Miles, who was more than his usual ten minutes late. When he showed up he pulled them into their film room, filled with three tiers of black and red leather seats. Rotation guys in the front row. Walk-ons and bench players in row two.

Coaches in back. And he told the team shooting guard Ray Gallegos would be suspended for two games for breaking team
rules. Gallegos led the Big Ten in minutes at 37.5 per game
and three-point shooting last year. Usually, breaking "team
rules" means partying too much. He had already released the
suspension news to the media. On top of that junior walk-on
Jordan Tyrance had left the team to focus on other priorities.
Already, the team would be without new guard Deverell Biggs,
who would serve a three-game suspension for a DUI the previous winter.

To the media Miles had said this: "It's disappointing. At the
same time, I'm not so sure Ray's not going to come back better
from this. Give him a couple of weeks to collect his thoughts."

Miles brought the team out to the court to warm up and sat
on the bench to watch.

"This is what I've been dealing with the last two days," he said,
leaning forward to watch his team stretch and run. "Ridiculous."

As he waited for players to get ready for drills, he looked at
Teddy Owens's defensive statistics from the Nebraska-Kearney
exhibition game. His analysis was that Petteway and Smith
hadn't played as well as they thought they'd played. He'd have
to address that, too. Meanwhile, Gallegos and Biggs would
move to the scout team to help the team prepare for Florida
Gulf Coast.

He worried about whether this team could actually learn how
to win. Now, he's got distractions that exacerbate the problem.
So he got philosophical.

"Maturity takes time. Discipline takes time," he said. "Lessons
are oftentimes learned the hard way. Right now, we're preaching
to a group of guys that doesn't understand the consequences of
their actions. The consequences will be losing. We're going to
lose some games."

He had plenty of reasons to justify anger, but he had decided
that wouldn't be productive today. Instead, he spent the short
practice teaching and encouraging his players. As assistant

coach Craig Smith ran FGCU plays in half-court sets, Miles spoke individually to players on the sidelines or interrupted play to fix screen-and-roll and post defense. Players were getting it.

Biggs, playing with the scout team, blew by freshman Tai Webster for a layup. Miles pulled Webster aside. Biggs then air-balled a ten-footer with Webster contesting.

"We got a 7–2 lead, red. Let's screw it up. Leslee, you're in for Walt."

Then Gallegos started heating up for the scout team. He hit a couple of threes, and in the second game white led 8–0.

"Let's go, red. Figure it out."

Petteway then took over to close the game to 16–13 and later 22–21. Red couldn't stop Gallegos and Biggs, but Walt Pitchford hit a three to tie and Webster, frustrated by getting beaten consistently by Biggs, drove down the lane for a tough score to put red up, 26–24. Miles immediately ended the game on that spurt of positivity.

Assistant coach Craig Smith had assigned himself the first big scout of the season. He spent much of the week leading up to Pinnacle Bank Arena's opening night breaking down FGCU's plays and personnel. During a game-day forty-minute film session and walk-through, he repeatedly said the opponent is athletic and dangerous, but the truth was Dunk City had lost half its players. Its coach, Andy Enfield, had parlayed the team's tournament run into a new job at the University of Southern California for more than $1 million a year. Because of that half of Smith's film clips are of the Kansas Jayhawks. Coach Bill Self's longtime assistant Joe Dooley replaced Enfield. The more Miles watched film in the darkness of the back row at the Hendricks Center classroom, the more fired up he seemed to get.

"We are going to defend these [guys]," Miles said. "I would be disappointed if they come in here and we let them dunk all over us."

. . .

Ethan Rowley once owned his own portable disc jockey business. He's got degrees in both advertising and physical education. Sometimes he has lamb-chop sideburns that could have gotten him elected president in the 1800s or cast as a lone-wolf detective on a '70s crime drama.

He brings a combination of seriousness and goofball to his job as director of fan experience. He's the guy who can get fearsome football coach Bo Pelini to carry a kitten into Memorial Stadium at a spring game. He's also the guy who can pull off a football-game jet flyover by coordinating the Reserve Officers' Training Corps, the band, and the Lincoln airport, all during a government sequester. In his head he must keep it straight that the Husker basketball team plays in the Pinnacle Bank Arena on the First National Bank court, while Tim Miles appears on the *Bank of the West Nebraska Basketball Show.*

For a guy like Ethan Rowley, Tim Miles is a bottomless bank account of possibility. And the new arena is a marketing Fort Knox. He smiles through the pressure of getting everything coordinated.

NCAA Division I basketball is a sport. And it's a billion-dollar business. An entertainment business. Tim Miles's job is to put a product on the floor that's entertaining; Ethan Rowley's job is to squeeze the most out of that product.

For the official first game in the PBA, Rowley's team has been brainstorming and executing plans for months. A sports marketer's job is 90 percent work for a 10 percent payoff, he says. And just as Miles's team can't screw up the energy of this first game, Rowley can't screw up the opportunity of this moment. Really, if everything works right, this night could be historic.

So his people put together a marketing recipe of traditional home-cooking staples of scarlet-and-cream dancers, cheerleaders, pep band, and hip-hop music. They rely heavily on their HuskerVision video team to produce highlight videos and team-introduction slow-motion shots. But before all that they add some spicy appetizers. They bring out the football marching band to blast a record 15,119 fans while Mötley Crüe drummer Tommy Lee deejays a synthesized explosion from the north concourse. Lee had been the star of *Tommy Lee Goes to College,* an NBC reality TV show shot on the Nebraska campus nine years earlier. He was also famous for his sex tape with wife Pamela Anderson.

Rowley's fan-experience team has taken some chances: lights, music, rock star, basketball.

The HuskerVision production on the 16.5-by-20-foot high-definition scoreboard screen crescendos to slow-motion video of Walt Pitchford screaming and flexing as chalk flies. The fans, particularly the students surrounding the south and east sides of the court, lose it for every player introduction. But they cheer more loudly as Tim Miles's name is announced.

Pop group Karmin, a duo that includes Nebraskan Amy Heidemann, sings the national anthem. Miles talks to the musicians after they're done.

Right off Pitchford's tip Terran Petteway hits a three-pointer within the flow of the offense. Then Pitchford launches and nails two threes the next two times he touches the basketball. Shavon Shields puts back a rebound and gets fouled. Three minutes into the game Shields squares up the free throw, and the arena is silent for the first time since the gates opened. As it arcs toward the rim a student behind the Husker bench screams: "We love you, Tim Miles!" The Huskers are up 12–5. The lead would reach twelve by halftime.

From the tunnel Miles delivers his trademark halftime tweet by putting his arm around sports information director Shamus McKnight and yelling it in his ear over crowd noise: "The first five minutes are important. We stalled at the end of the half and have to regain the momentum."

In the second half FGCU makes a run, but Benny Parker comes off the bench with a steal and a couple of layups to spark a 10–0 run, and Dunk City never recovers. The Huskers would double their halftime lead for a 79–55 win.

The captains scored forty-five points, twenty-eight by Shields, who consistently bullied his way into the lane and finished twelve for twelve on free throws.

In the locker room Miles points to his two suspended guards—Ray Gallegos and Deverell Biggs. "You boys in blue jeans, that's the way it's done," he says. "Great job. I'm impressed. Everybody contributed well. We got a little sloppy at the end. [But] we did a really good job. I'm not one to hand out game balls. Shavon had a huge night. But this is a team ball. We're going to mark this up and place it somewhere so you remember how this feels. Because this was a great ass-kicking night."

"Dunk City, my ass," Petteway yells.

Miles then chooses to rein them in, a little. "Now, here comes the tough part," he says. "Western Illinois is going to make it a root canal. Western Illinois isn't going to let you have any fun. We are going to have a strong mental capacity. The way we play, we can beat anybody, but anybody can beat us. So we need to be ready to go.

"Energy's high, but lay low. Go to Mom and Dad. . . . Stay away from the girls. Great job. Let's take a knee."

They kneel on the carpeted floor of their classroom behind their locker room at Pinnacle Bank Arena and pray for seven seconds before Miles can't contain himself any longer, breaking the silence by screaming a high-pitched and elongated, "Woo hoo!"

Petteway follows with his customary postpractice "Team on three," but Miles cuts him off before the team can chant.

"No," he says. "Money at the Bank."

They chant: "One, two, three, money at the Bank."

TWO

Making Do

6

Alyce Miles looks down and shakes her head. She hates to admit it, but there's no two ways about it. She spoiled her son.

She had her reasons, and she still regrets them. Tim Miles was the youngest of her five kids, and as they grew up she had more time to spend on him. Plus, he was the only grandchild among thirty who had those smiling brown eyes. But the real reason was bigger.

In 1968, when Tim was a year old, Alyce had trouble conceiving a sixth child. She'd had three girls and then two boys within eleven years. She and husband Tip wanted another boy. A doctor told her she had stage-V cancer in her uterus and ovaries. Today, ovarian cancer gets graded only to stage IV, but in the late 1960s doctors and university researchers were still experimenting with chemotherapy and radiation treatments. She didn't know anything about all that in rural South Dakota. Instead, Tip drove her fifty miles east on Highway 212 to Watertown for a hysterectomy.

She made a full recovery, but the health emergency changed how she treated her littlest boy.

The grandparents were taken with him, too, and apparently everyone in Doland, South Dakota, which had one hundred more people back then. Everyone except his oldest sister, Karin, who claims she raised him and had to deal with him twenty-four hours a day while Mom ran the weekly newspaper they owned and Dad worked in Redfield at a state school for the developmentally disabled.

Norbert "Tip" Miles served in World War II, but showed up to the Pacific theater too late to ever see any real action. He enlisted November 6, 1944, and the army deployed him to the Philippines just as Harry Truman sent a B29 bomber to Hiroshima.

Weeks later, his company hopped on a navy tank-landing ship in a typhoon of forty- and fifty-foot waves on the way to Japan. Down on the tank deck, the navy sailors asked each other, in front of the nauseous and panic-stricken infantrymen, "Do you think this ship will survive another storm like this?"

When her boys joined World War II, Tip's mother started saying rosaries for them, and eventually she would say them for her one brown-eyed grandson, who would call her to pray for wins before rivalry games.

Here's the kind of letter Tim Miles occasionally gets. This one's from a banker from Omaha. Miles opens it. It's written professionally in what Miles's Doland High School typing teacher would call the block-style business letter:

Dear Coach:

I would first like to congratulate you on the completion of the new basketball arena. This leads me to my next topic. It will make me so happy when Creighton comes to Lincoln next year and blows your squad out of the water. In the meantime, good luck preparing for Creighton on December 8, 2013, because you will need a miracle to win. All in all, please remember that there is, and will only be, one basketball powerhouse in NE. Go Jays!!

Sincerely,

The letter's last line serves as a belated counterpunch. More than a year earlier the Nebraska football team was blowing out an overmatched Idaho State on the Big Ten Network when sideline reporter Damon Benning, a former Husker, interviewed Miles to try to keep the broadcast interesting. As Miles remembers the moment, Benning asked him how he liked his new job. Miles started raving about how Nebraska didn't have to compete with Colorado's mountains or professional sports teams for fans and finished that argument with this line: we're "the only game in the state."

Creighton coach Greg McDermott must have been watching or getting lit up with text and Twitter messages because Miles remembers that McDermott tweeted out something like this: "That's an interesting perspective."

"Then Creighton fans poured it on," Miles said.

The next day *Omaha World-Herald* columnist Tom Shatel put together a column that started with Miles and went on to degrade the program's relevance:

> I know of at least one Creighton alum who couldn't have liked that one: NU women's coach Connie Yori, whose hoops program actually wins and plays for conference championships and in the NCAA tournament.
>
> Around gyms in eastern Nebraska, Eric Behrens' Omaha Central program gets more buzz than Husker Hoops.
>
> Creightonians should relax. Laugh. You're above getting riled up by Nebraska basketball. The Jays are a top 20 program now, with an All-America kid and their sights set on the Sweet 16.
>
> CU coaches and players are focused on trying to beat North Carolina [UNC] in the NCAA tourney. They aren't thinking about Nebraska. They also know that the only time Husker Hoops is the show is when it's playing Creighton.

Message boards exploded, quoting the column and hammering the new Husker coach.

Miles was steamed, mostly because Shatel didn't call him for clarification on his comments. Instead, Shatel had made fun of the Huskers, putting them behind not just Creighton but the Husker women's team and Omaha Central High School as far as hoops relevance. His team had been dismissed.

The truth is Miles and McDermott are buddies who play golf together, or at least against each other. McDermott preceded

Miles for one season at North Dakota State in 2000–2001, and Miles has always respected the way McDermott's teams played. And McDermott had earned that respect. McDermott's Wayne State teams beat Miles's Southwest Minnesota State teams six times in three years in the Northern Sun Intercollegiate Conference in the late '90s. Then McDermott's Iowa State teams beat Miles's North Dakota State teams twice a decade later. Add in last season's 64–42 blowout at the Devaney Center, and McDermott was 9-0 against Miles, who didn't want to drop to 10-0.

"Mac's a friend," Miles says, "but that doesn't mean we can't have a friendly rivalry."

Odds were against the Huskers. They would be for the next month.

One of the great things about high schools across America is that for every one that gets built, another one emerges for that school to hate. Maybe that has something to do with capitalism, or Darwinism. For Doland athletes that school was Clark High School, fifteen minutes east on Highway 212 toward Watertown.

In 1982 Miles sat on the Doland Wheelers' bench as a freshman when the gym went dark just before the end of the District 4B title game, which would have sent Doland to regionals for the first time in decades. Miles's brother Kevin was a senior starter on that team, and Tim had been coaching Kevin on his free throws from the bench.

"He went, like, two for six in the game anyway," Miles said.

With eleven seconds left the fluorescent lights went out on the Clark side of the court. Down one point, the Doland Wheelers brought the ball to half court before the referees blew their whistles. Once the problem got fixed, the officials made the Wheelers inbound the ball on the other end of the court again. Crunched for time, Doland missed a game-winning shot, but put back the rebound for the win. One official waved off the basket—too late—and pandemonium took over, both teams cutting down the nets in victory. Clark was given the win, and Miles had three more years of needing to "beat those pricks." As John Papendick of the *Aberdeen American-News* reported in a nostalgia column twenty-one years later, Miles told him, "It was not a good night for the Wheelers. We're still in recovery stage."

Again, as with any opponent, Miles didn't necessarily hate the town of Clark, the team, or the Comet players, but hating a rival helped him find an edge, and an edge is everything, no matter how you find it.

"You know, they played in an A conference, and we played in a B conference," Miles says of South Dakota's two-class system. "Then they would drop to B for the postseason, so we really wanted to beat them. Plus, I dated their girls."

In college in North Dakota, Miles's University of Mary team had Minot State as a rival. In his first job at Mayville State, the Comets wanted to pound Valley City State, merely because it was good and Miles respected longtime coach Al Olson. A few years later at Southwest Minnesota State, Miles's teams weren't traditionally good enough to have earned a rival, "So I just told them it was Northern State," where he'd been an assistant coach for six years and where most of his family went to college.

In 2001, when he arrived at North Dakota State in Fargo, the Bison had a century-old multisport rivalry with the University of North Dakota, seventy-three miles up I-29 in Grand Forks. Miles remembers a fight nearly breaking out in January 2003 when his Bison beat the then–Fighting Sioux 64–57 at UND's Ralph Engelstad Arena, or the Ralph, which most hockey aficionados call the greatest hockey venue on earth.

"We just outscrapped them in an ugly, physical game," Miles says.

Soon after, the Bison jumped to Division I, and then-UND coach Rich Glas was so furious about the move he yelled at Miles in a sports bar while they were both recruiting at a Mr. Basketball camp in Kearney, Nebraska, and took the Bison off his schedule.

"There's no comparison to a rivalry like that," Miles says. "You know, U N D would release its enrollment numbers in a morning press release at 12,025 students. Then N D S U releases its numbers the same day at noon, and of course it's 12,127. Same thing when we were at Colorado State. Boulder [University of Colorado] sends out that its average A C T [American College Test] score for its incoming freshmen is a 25, so later that day Colorado State says its freshmen are coming in at 25.25 or something like that."

Colorado State's rivalry with Colorado was similar to the Nebraska-Creighton rivalry in that the teams played once per year and were in separate conferences. So that annual game was about bragging rights for all of Nebraska, including sending a message to the state's recruits about the directions of both programs.

For Nebraska's upcoming December 8 game with Creighton, all that was at stake.

7

Tip Miles is the kind of guy who will spend twenty minutes telling you his wife does all the talking. Growing up with talkers like Tip and Alyce helps a child own any interview, press conference, or speaking engagement and win over E S P N writers and play-by-play announcers from across the country.

Tim Miles's parents say their youngest son was a talker from the start. And yes, spoiled, too. He sucked a pacifier until just before he entered school, and Mom didn't have the heart to take it away. In fact, as he played on the sidewalk outside the family newspaper that he'd later dominate with 144-point headlines, Alyce kept extra pacifiers ready in the mailbox slots in the newsroom for when he dropped his in the gutter.

One summer day, though, an older woman visiting the Miles home on the unmarked Main Street told Tim he couldn't bring that pacifier to start school that fall. The kids would make fun of him. Tim kept sucking and spinning around the living room.

"He was definitely A D H D [attention deficit/hyperactivity disorder], criminy," Alyce says. "No doubt." Then the old woman cut the boy a deal, and Tim Miles liked deals.

"I tell you what," she said. "I'll give you a brand-new dollar bill for that pacifier."

Tim stopped playing and sat with perfect posture in a living room chair, staring at her. When she got up to leave she pulled out the crisp dollar, and Tim handed over the pacifier. That night oldest sister Karin was watching Tim, and Mom told her where the extra pacifiers were if Tim was struggling. But he went to bed without complaint. The woman gave Tim a dollar every year on his birthday after that and eighteen dollars when he graduated, which still makes Alyce shake her head and cluck her tongue when she thinks about it.

Money mattered to Tim—Tip and Alyce figure—because they didn't have any.

"You know," Alyce says, "you didn't have credit cards back then. What you had was what you had, and if you didn't have it, you couldn't spend it. You had to make do."

The family newspaper, a weekly, had a circulation of about a thousand and struggled to get by, maybe netting the family $20,000 in a good year. Tip still remembers being broke before Christmas in 1968, when Tim was still just one year old. He and Alyce bundled up one day and circulated through the small towns in the county, trying to sell some advertisements, mainly going to businesses that had bought ads in the past and hadn't paid up. Essentially, he was trying to collect on some outstanding debts because he had no money to buy Christmas presents. Tip would do the talking, and Alyce would handle the ledger on her lap in the car. As dusk set in at about six o'clock, Tip pulled in to a hardware store that hadn't paid for the smallest of ads. Before walking in the storefront, Tip told Alyce he'd just try to sell a Christmas ad. The owner looked at Tip and cut him off before he could launch into his pitch.

"Tip," he said, "I think I owe you some money."

"You do?" Tip said in shock. "How much?"

"I don't know."

Alyce had the number on her lap. The hardware store owner wrote a check.

"I went to the bank around the corner and told Alyce we're going to Aberdeen to do some shopping," Tip said.

That story reminded Alyce of something else. When Tim was in high school he had to have Nike Air Jordans, the dominant gym-rat shoe of the '80s. He bugged his mother for days because she was his best shot. She couldn't say no to him, or anything like no, since he'd been born. She drove him to Redfield and saw the price tag: $100. She had never worn shoes worth half that, or even a fourth of that. But she bought them.

Years later, when Miles started making a six-figure salary in coaching, he bought his mother a plaque that essentially said he'd been proud to walk in her shoes. She thought that was nice, but didn't understand why he had given it to her. Then, once he got married, he seemed to always ask his mother, or especially his father, if they needed shoes. Visit after visit, year after year.

"Finally," Alyce says, "I said to him, 'Tim, you're just obsessed with shoes.'"

Tim smiled at his mom and said, "Mom, I know that you couldn't afford those Nikes, and you got them for me anyway."

Alyce smiles and looks over at Tip to her left on the couch on the second floor of the new St. Joseph's Catholic Housing apartments, right on the property of the diocese in Sioux Falls, South Dakota, where they can walk to Mass every morning. Close enough for oldest daughter Karin to drive them to Lincoln for big games.

"Tim is like that," Alyce says to her husband. "He remembers."

Winning at Creighton was urgent for more than rivalry and recruiting reasons. Miles needed the team to go 10-2 in the non-conference schedule to have even a shot at the postseason, with those two losses most likely coming at home against Florida Gulf Coast or Miami, or at Creighton or Cincinnati. The Huskers had rolled FGCU and were 3-0 after easy wins over Western Illinois and South Carolina State.

Next up was the Charleston Classic in South Carolina. Miles had said in his first radio show of the season that tournaments were important because coaches were able to fast-forward the building of their team's identity. Progress was crucial for this team, which was playing only three guys who had seen significant Big Ten minutes. Some of his newest players were still struggling with simple Tim Miles vocabulary, such as *hedge* and *raid*, or offensive sets such as UCLA or *Princeton*. His freshman point guard, Tai Webster from New Zealand, couldn't name many teams in the Big Ten, and in practice days earlier he asked the coaches this question:

"What's Princeton?"

Miles told the story to the crowd of about thirty-five fans pounding *chile con queso* at Carlos O'Kelly's in North Lincoln. Miles had arrived a half hour late for his first radio show of the year because he went to the wrong location and had to call in for the show's first segment while traveling five miles up Twenty-Seventh Street in Monday-night traffic.

"So Tai says, 'What's Princeton?'" Miles said into his microphone. "He's so innocent, you know? And we're, like, 'Don't worry about it. You're on a need-to-know basis.' We're just acclimating him to everything."

Acclimating him to college basketball. Acclimating three starters to Big Ten basketball. Acclimating new assistant Kenya Hunter to the Midwest from the East Coast.

"I asked Kenya, 'Why did you leave Georgetown? Were you tired of winning?'" Miles told his listeners before introducing Hunter for a segment the following week on the show.

So, yeah, the tournament in Charleston would be important. And what was the goal? "To win. Of course." They were 3-0 going into the tournament, and Miles wanted to be at least

5-1 on the flight home, which could happen. Maybe 6-0 could happen.

"I've had teams I thought would be good that stunk in tournaments like this," he said. "I've had teams that weren't very good but found ways to win tournaments like this. So, we'll be curious to see how it comes out. We'll give it our best shot, but you don't really know how it's going to come out until you get smacked in the mouth pretty good."

They got smacked in the first two games, a 96–90 loss to the University of Massachusetts in a game the Huskers led late and an 87–74 loss to Alabama-Birmingham. Miles's worries about his team fouling too much had been a premonition, not a fear. The Huskers fouled thirty-four times to give U-Mass forty-three free-throw attempts, which decided the game. Then they fouled twenty-four times against UAB to get outscored twenty-four to twelve at the line, which sank them again, before salvaging the third game with a win over Georgia. Until that game, Miles's guards had been overmatched, which led to constant drives to the rim, fouls, and huge scores that his offense couldn't match.

Back home his team had two weeks of practice and games with Northern Illinois and Miami before heading east on I-80 to Omaha to Creighton and the McDermotts. Those two weeks would start with a film session. Miles ordered video coordinator Greg Eaton to cut video clips of all eighty-one fouls from the tournament. They would watch each one.

"There's three things we're among the worst in the country at right now. Give them to me," Miles says in the film room at the Hendricks Training Complex. The front row of players names them, in order. "Yeah, defensive rebounding, assists, and fouls. Yes, the foul rate is terrible. So let's get together and figure out why."

All the players sink deep into their leather-cushioned seats, except for cocaptain Shavon Shields and scout teamer Trevor Menke, who lean forward into the onslaught.

Miles calls out guys on nearly every play. He repeats plays if he doesn't think they understand their "defensive errors," a stat operations guy Teddy Owens charts every game. Play after play, Massachusetts guard Chaz Williams flew by Tai Webster, Terran Petteway, and Deverell Biggs. Petteway and Biggs gambled for steals, sometimes successfully, but mostly Williams got by them, forcing a teammate to pick up a foul at the rim or messing up the entire defensive rotation to give up layups.

Sometimes, Miles gets creative to explain his points in terms he thinks his guys will understand. "Here's what I mean," Miles says from the middle of the front row, with Biggs on his left, Webster on his right, and his remote-laser pointer in hand. Their faces are all illuminated in the dark room by the light of Williams's white jersey driving through the defense again. "Right there, Dev. Shoot your hands in and out. If you and I were gonna go, all right? And you were gonna punch me and I stood like this."

Miles stands up on his heels with his hands down in front of Biggs.

"Would it go well for me? No. It would not go well for me. And that's what I look at. He's got the ball. He's doing the punching. He's punching it to the rim, and if you stand there and take it with your hands down, you got no chance. You got to get your hands up and protect yourself."

The next foul is another Petteway gamble.

"Terran. Now, I'm telling you, you're our hardest worker, but you're making way too many defensive errors. When seeing defensive errors as coaches—we met yesterday—guys are going to have to come out of the game. There's only one way to learn, sometimes, and that's being over here as an assistant coach, all right? And you better willingly and eagerly accept that if you're going to make errors, there's some accountability on that. Nobody's got a free pass 24-7."

He shows Petteway's man getting by him, getting an offensive rebound, and Shields picking up a foul on the play.

He stands over Petteway now, and he turns to the screen and

rewinds the play. The foul clip shows the reaction of the team after the whistle, with Petteway jawing at Ray Gallegos.

"What did you say to Ray?" Miles asks.

"I told him that's my fault," Petteway says, barely audible.

"Oh. Good. Because if you're blaming Ray, I'm like, 'What the hell?' Right?"

Next, the Alabama-Birmingham loss comes on the big screen, foul after foul, and Miles cringes, but he is in teacher mode now. He's called nearly everyone out on the team, but now he turns more philosophical, and Eaton had clipped another play long, so the team reaction to the whistle is on-screen.

"Terran, this is one of the things," he says without getting out of his chair or looking at his top scorer. "The refs came over to Kenya and said, 'Hey, [No.] 5 is doing too much talking.' So, Terran, what happens is you don't hardly touch the guy. So, [the ref] is just looking for you. The shot's up, and he's not looking at anyone but you. So, if there's any kind of bullshit, he's not going to let things escalate. So, you have to understand that if you're out there running your mouth or talking, you're just a target. And you're hurting yourself and you're hurting the team."

Petteway sucks air in through his teeth and, stretching out to his left in his seat, takes a deep sigh and nods.

Miles points out that he started Benny Parker at the point in the third game because he could guard the ball. The message to Tai Webster is clear, but Webster had responded off the bench and played nearly the entire second half, putting the game away with layups and free throws for the win over Georgia.

Near the end of the game, Nebraska had shown the Bulldogs some of the zone Kenya Hunter brought with him from Georgetown University. At certain points players seemed to be unsure of where they should be in the scheme. On one play backup center Leslee Smith seemed lost, unsure whether to protect the basket or attack the ball as a player hit a jumper from the free-throw line. With Smith at 255 pounds of muscle, Hunter needs him to control the lane in the zone without being indecisive.

Miles to Leslee: "You got to guard him. You've got to come guard him. Can't give him a free pass."

Hunter: "Well, Coach, in Leslee's defense, if he sees someone behind him, he has to give up that shot because we'd rather give up a twelve-footer than a dunk at the rim."

"Kenya," Miles says, "what's Leslee doing? Playing the guy behind him?"

Hunter: "Yeah. I hope that was what you were thinking, Leslee."

Miles: "Well, he is now. Good talking on defense, Les, but as soon as you start talking, what do you do?"

Leslee smiles and covers his face and says nothing.

Hunter speaks for him: "Stands up."

Miles: "You stand up like a coach. You just stand straight up. You can coach with me all day, but we need your ass down right now, right away. We need you ready to play."

Miles turns off the projector and stands up to face his team. Eaton turns on the lights.

"What did we see there?"

Nothing.

"Hello?"

Still nothing. He doesn't wait for any responses. He never does.

"Look, men lie. Women lie. Numbers don't lie."

Miles hands out a packet of statistics that he's marked up in blue and black pen. Later in the season, he'll go to multiple-colored highlighting. The numbers are mainly the work of Teddy Owens. Miles, an elementary education major, wants to teach some simple math to justify his themes of team defense, rebounding, and sharing the ball. Using his numbers, he jumps particularly hard on Benny Parker for his inability to score (6 for 17 from the floor), Mike Peltz for not making a shot all season (0 for 3), and David Rivers for numbers that point to a lack of effort (1.8 rebounds per game and less than 1 defensive rebound per game).

"It really comes down to the same thing, Dave," he says. "I don't know what I can do to get you to rebound. Anything that I've told you, you just ignored. And that doesn't go well usually between a coach and a player. So, if it's time for someone else to play, if it's time for whatever it is, time to give Sergej a chance, to give Peltz a chance, whatever. I mean, there's only so long a guy can tolerate. And this is not a trend. It's the same issue. And it doesn't matter enough for you to change it. I don't believe you can only get me 2 rebounds a game, playing as many minutes as you're playing."

He hammers main ball handlers Tai Webster, Deverell Biggs, and Terran Petteway for having more turnovers than assists. Shavon Shields hasn't hit a three all year (0 for 7).

What he doesn't mention is that Parker, the third-string point guard, has 9 assists to 1 turnover and Rivers shoots above 50 percent.

The rest of the film session he launches into a thirty-minute analysis of defensive and rebounding errors, bad shooting percentages, and shot choices. By the end his voice reveals little emotion, and the players look like they've been sitting in calculus class for a full Friday afternoon with a bow-tied professor.

"We dropped two games," he finishes. "That was one too many. We're talking about the NCAA Tournament. Where did we need to be at the break? Maybe 9-3 or whatever. We have to get going. Every game matters for the next game. Northern Illinois is playing teams tough, but I'm more worried about us. Getting things done. All right? Are there any questions?"

No pause.

"All right, coacher," he says to strength coach Tim Wilson. "Get them loose and get them going for a good one."

Hunter: "Let's go, fellas."

The players rush out, as if trying to escape a submarine that's been below the surface for months.

Miles holds a stern face until the last player leaves, and then he smiles at his coaches and they joke about a player who hasn't practiced in two weeks. They have a running bet over when he'll finally say he's healthy enough for full drills. Lunch is on the line. An expensive one, too.

The team went on to execute its best practice of the year. Petteway led every drill, every eleven-second trip down court, and he hit every big shot.

The next practice, the last before Thanksgiving, was a disaster. A full-on Etch-a-Sketch day, as the assistants would say, using Miles's metaphor. Then Northern Illinois nearly beat them three days later with about four thousand empty seats in the arena, but the Huskers got four free throws at the end of the game from Deverell Biggs, who scored a season-high eighteen points, which would be a high point of his brief career with Nebraska.

8

Alyce Miles laughs when she thinks about her son majoring in elementary education at the University of Mary in Bismarck because he had no interest in elementary education as a kid.

Her worst days of the year as a mother, without question, were days she walked across the street from her house to Tim's parent-teacher conferences. She knew her boy was trouble and feared how much he caused his teachers. Tim refused to work on numbers or letters as a preschooler until he felt there was something in it for him. One day he sneaked away from his mom at the newspaper. He crossed the street to the Golden Pheasant Café, also called the East Side Café—a double name is common to any small-town business that has endured multiple owners—and walked right up to the waitress.

"Ethel," he said, "I want you to teach me to write my name so I can charge [food] like my dad does."

Like everyone in town, Ethel was tickled by the boy, as Alyce puts it.

Alyce wasn't. Parent-teacher conferences in a town the size of Doland can get pretty personal. When your son is "a pain in the keister," everyone finds out about it. She dreaded walking across the street to the school. Everything is across the street in

Doland, Miles would tell you, but their house was directly across the street from the Doland school.

One year the third grade teacher was particularly honest with Tim Miles's mother. Alyce remembers the conversation like this:

"You know, Mrs. Miles, he just talks all the time," she said. "He disrupts the whole class."

"Well, tell him to shut up."

"Well, he won't."

"Well, where does he sit?"

"He sits over there in the back."

Alyce turned to the back of the room, then back to the teacher. "Well, bring him up front."

"I can't do that."

"Of course you can."

"No, I can't. He stands up all day. He won't sit down. He does all his work standing up, when he does his work."

The problem, really, was that nobody could really stay mad at him. By the time he hit high school, he'd talked his way out of jams with all his teachers. The school didn't allow students to leave for lunch, but Miles, who admits to being the most finicky eater at any table, refused to eat school food. Instead, he slipped across the street to his house for Chef Boyardee ravioli or Tombstone pizza or both while catching up on *Days of Our Lives*. The high school staff would try to catch him coming back, but he'd circle around the back of the school, through the elementary classrooms, where he'd play along the way with the little ones, who loved him for every point he'd score in basketball games and the jokes and stories he told, disrupting each grade on the way.

"The principal sat me down and said, 'Alyce, I know he's sneaking home for lunch, but it's okay. He's just going across the street.'"

Alyce told the principal to not let him get away with it, but nobody would listen. Not even Tim.

Again, she would just have to make do.

In his first season at Nebraska, when he was now making

more than $1 million, the Doland residents filled up a charter bus to Lincoln to watch Nebraska battle eighth-ranked Michigan State to a 73–64 loss at the Devaney Center. The game was nicknamed Doland Day by the Husker Athletic Department, and even a high school math teacher—who barely tolerated Tim Miles in class—wound up taking a spot on that bus. Eventually, Miles had won his teachers over, too.

The tune-up game before heading to Creighton would be at home against the University of Miami, a Sweet Sixteen team the previous year. The Huskers held the Hurricanes to thirteen first-half points, and Miami never came closer than within five points the rest of the game.

At the shootaround before the game, Miles had been joking with ESPN broadcasters who were trying to get to know him and gather anecdotes for the broadcast.

"What was Bismarck like?"

Miles: A smile. No answer. He won't feed off that bait.

"Who's your mentor?"

Miles, who was coming up on 250 career losses, said: "My mentor is losing. That's taught me everything."

"What about the rule changes and tighter officiating?"

Miles: "Something's got to give."

The Huskers fouled just sixteen times. Miles was handing out compliments afterward like they were free Runza sandwich coupons, which fans redeemed if the team scored seventy points, which they didn't after the 60–49 win.

"Honestly, you guys did a hell of a job," he told his players in the locker room after his postgame interview on ESPN. "Here's what happened: you guys guarded the ball, you got out on outside shots, and you rebounded like you can."

He complimented assistant coach Chris Harriman on his scouting work on Miami. The Australian had told them to accept that they'll make mistakes: "Just keep playing. Keep playing."

The team clapped for Harriman, who admitted throughout the season he still gets nervous when he has to run the scout on the upcoming opponent, but assistant Craig Smith had trusted him with this one against a strong team.

Miles went on: "I'm just telling you, this is the advertisement. This is the advertisement. We know where we're heading right? [He points east.] It's in Omaha. We got it. [Creighton] is the biggest rivalry game all season. It's bigger than any Big Ten game to our fans. It is the most important game. For you guys that don't know, this is the one I hear about all the time. They are a great team, a team of a lifetime. I would love nothing better than to go to Omaha, right? Hometown of Deverell? And just beat 'em. We gotta have this, right? Only, it'll be fifteen thousand against us. And they are Jays fans, and that's fine. We'll show 'em our best shot, what we got, and we owe 'em one. Last year we weren't quite complete, and this year we're coming down the line. We're getting better every day and better every game, and we gotta prepare now. . . . We'll go hard prep on Friday and Saturday, then Sunday at 5:00 in Omaha it's on Fox Sports One, so tell your parents. Congratulations. Team on three."

Terran Petteway: "One, two, three, team."

Hunter: "Good job, fellas."

Miles isn't telling Doland stories the next night in front of the Big Red Roundball Club, which listens to Miles sell his team on the first Thursday of each month. He's got a team that's struggling, not really even getting along with each other, much less its head coach. And he's facing some important alumni from the Omaha area. These guys all are (at least) middle-aged and have country club–type money. The tallest is Dave Hoppen, the all-time leading scorer at Nebraska.

This situation would be a tough room for most coaches. These guys have the potential to donate to the program, which Miles cares about, as does his boss, Marc Boehm, who will introduce him to the crowd. More important, though, these guys wear suits in Omaha, where they're surrounded by Creighton fans. They've had to hide, or at least tone down, their enthusiasm for Husker hoops since the Danny Nee era of the '90s. And they're sick of it. They want Nebraska to blow out the Bluejays in a national TV game less than forty-eight hours away. They want to know how Coach Miles plans to get that done. They want insider information. So they've sent a Leisure Limousine SUV to pick him up. The vehicle is almost as nice as Miles's Escalade, but not quite. Having a hired driver allows Miles to give operations guy Teddy Owens a night off from driving him. Miles swears he isn't a prima donna. He just doesn't want to drive so that he can watch Creighton plays on his laptop all the way to Shadow Ridge Country Club in West Omaha. He's prepping for the game, not the speech.

"So," he starts when he gets on the microphone, which he doesn't really need, "we got a ball team this year, and they're a little psychotic, you know? . . . You might want to take out some life insurance if you're in the front six rows."

His players, he explains, come from places all over the country where they were The Guy. If a coach wanted to win a game, he told them to take over. And they were good enough on that level of high school or Amateur Athletic Union (AAU) basketball to do that. And they could gamble on defense to get steals and layups or dunks. Miles's favorite metaphor for this phenomenon is football. He says he's loaded with guys who think they are running backs and wide receivers, touchdown scorers. But he needs blockers, linemen, guys who will do the dirty work inside, quarterbacks who get the ball to the skill players.

"They have an idea of what they're about, but not an idea of how to win," Miles says. "That's my single focus. Get guys here, hope they grow up a little on the way, get their degree, and we win."

This season is his fifth year two in a program, Miles explains. At this point he's pretty happy with his talent. He swears that his team, on a good night, can handle any team on the schedule, including Michigan and Michigan State. And he couldn't say that last year, when the Huskers took beatings by more than twenty points seven times from seven teams.

"I like our team, and we can do some things. But we're also capable of crapping ourselves," Miles admits to big, and some uneasy, laughs. "Going out there and just freaking out, and we've already done that. But the thing with dealing with them is they all want to get better; they just don't know how to do it.

"Some teams don't want to get better. This group isn't like that. I usually watch body language. We're down to one or two guys who it depends on their mood. . . . These guys truly want to figure it out. I like them from that aspect. We just have to teach them."

That's where his elementary education background boosts his coaching, along with his master's degree in physical education from Northern State in Aberdeen, South Dakota.

"There's just a different mentality sometimes between coaching and teaching," Miles says. "And I think what this group needs most is to be taught how to be unselfish and to be taught how to play for one another."

That difference, in Miles's philosophy, is that a teacher can bring a struggling student from performing at 70 percent success up to 80 percent and say, "Hey, I did my job today." A coach, however, wants perfect execution right now. Of every screen, every inbounds play, every post move, every switch, every drill.

"So frustration sets in in a lot of coaches, I think, and if you just stick to teaching, I don't think you get as frustrated and you're able to stay patient with people."

He starts running through those people out loud to his crowd. Leslee Smith handles the ball like it's made of ice, and it flies out of his hands. Shavon Shields needs to play more aggressively on offense. Terran Petteway makes defensive errors because he's too aggressive, which is a symbol for this team so far. He logs more hours of watching film on his iPad than anyone else, but he leads the team in defensive mistakes.

Miles shakes his head, smacks his forehead, and sighs dramatically, and the crowd loves it, the honesty and transparency. They feel like they know things no other fan knows. This stuff isn't in the newspapers or on the Big Ten Network.

What he's really doing here—consciously or not—is tempering expectations for Sunday for these Omahans, who will all be in attendance at the CenturyLink Center, a minority among fourteen thousand Bluejay fans, the only place in conservative Nebraska where blue always outnumbers red.

We're not ready in year two, he's saying. Maybe year four. Then he shifts tone, which usually means returning north to Doland.

"I just want you to know," he says, pausing to lock eyes with as many listeners as possible, including *Omaha World-Herald* basketball beat writer Lee Barfknecht, "my parents owned a newspaper, a function of the community. You know, 'Melva and Mavis hosted Marla and whomever, and a good time was had by all.' And I want you to know this: don't believe everything you read in the paper."

Miles says the *Coloradoan* in Fort Collins published a story in 2007 claiming he walked into a job in which he returned the most talent in the Mountain West and should finish first in the conference. Within four months he lost ten players. One pointed a gun at another, then fired into a couch. Felony identity theft. Drug charges. Domestic charges. DUIs. Miles had to jettison them as fast as he could until he had no talent. Colorado State went 0-16 in the Mountain West. With a seventeen-game losing streak, the Rams had to face Wyoming in a play-in game just to make the conference tournament at the Thomas & Mack Center in Las Vegas, which would win them the right to get hammered by No. 1 seed Brigham Young. Miles's CSU team trailed by five at half, but ground its way back to win 68–63 in a game in which neither team ever led by more than seven points.

"It was the greatest day of my life," Miles said, and in his career he had already logged upset wins over Wisconsin and Marquette, both on the road, with his North Dakota State teams.

His point: fixing a losing culture is a process. If that wasn't clear, he was going to make sure, like a moral at the end of a fable.

"My boss, Marc [Boehm], says it's a process, because we grilled him to say that for four years because, you know, you don't get an extension right away," he said.

In year four Colorado State was a nineteen-game winner. By year five it was in the NCAA Tournament.

Once he gets his message across—turning Nebraska into a winner will take time—he contradicts himself by telling this crowd what he knows it wants to hear. He says the first question everyone asked him when he got to Lincoln was "Who's going to guard Doug McDermott?"—Creighton's All-American forward, *Sports Illustrated* cover boy, and coach Greg McDermott's son.

The second question: "Can you beat the crap out of Creighton for us?"

His answer: "Everywhere I go, all I hear about is the Creighton game, and I don't want to hear about us losing to Creighton. So let's get ready to go."

He refers to last year's 64–42 home loss at the Devaney Center, where the biggest cheer was for Mike Peltz, his Nebraska-panhandle backup to the backup shooting guard, after he got into a tussle with Creighton guard Grant Gibbs. He talks defensive strategy, of going small, of being physical with the All-American McDermott, of playing like George Washington University did when the Colonials upset the Bluejays the other day.

Then he talks about his lead strategist: "My wife had some ideas for Mike Peltz on Doug," Miles says. "Listen, you guys can say what you want, but my wife says, 'You better beat these guys.'"

Kari, his wife, is a physical therapist who came to terms with the hours Miles worked to recruit and develop a winning team, but her point is that if he's going to spend that much time, he'd better win. She ran cross-country in college because her track coach said the miles would help her in sprints. She qualified at cross-country nationals.

"Talk about being competitive," Miles continues. "Nobody wants to beat Creighton more than my wife. If we don't beat them, I'm on the couch until we beat someone like Michigan.

"So, we're going to come up here Sunday and try to punch them in the mouth. See if they like the taste of their own blood. I know they've got All-Americans, they're the team of a lifetime at Creighton and all that, but we can be the villain for a day." The Huskers even prepared to wear black uniforms to play that villain role. "I want to beat them because my wife wants me to beat them. And I want to beat them."

On the way home Miles asks his driver, Paul, about his job, his company, and his life. Then he digs into his seventeen-inch MacBook Pro to figure out how to beat Creighton.

9

On game day Miles finishes off a treadmill workout wearing all-black Adidas, from baseball cap to shoes, while players loft shots they'll try to take in the game. They're loose. Assistant coaches aren't. They're making last-minute suggestions to Craig Smith, who will go over Creighton's offense and personnel one more time in the film room.

As Smith launches into his litany of reminders—screen-and-roll defense has to be perfect, Bluejay forward Ethan Wragge has to be guarded out to NBA three-point range, attack the rim all night, take smart and makeable shots—Miles cuts him off. He's prepared a film intro that should focus his team. He looks over to video coordinator Greg Eaton, who has the idea cued up on the big screen.

"E, hit it," Miles says.

He shows them three sets of clips from last year's blowout loss at home to Creighton:

Doug McDermott dunking in transition and against the press.

Ethan Wragge hitting a thirty-five-foot three-pointer.

Creighton guards dribbling out the last thirty seconds of a mostly vacant Devaney Center.

"The great part about this is you get to pick your own ending every year," he says. "You determine what's going to happen. They earned it last year. If we're gonna win, we're going to have to earn it this year. Nothing is going to be easy. They came in here and whipped our ass. Today, whatever it is with effort, concentration, whatever, you need to be locked in."

Smith takes over. He says all five guys will be guarding McDermott at all times. Wragge gets no room once he crosses half court. Grant Gibbs is the ultimate GATA guy—coaches aren't afraid to use their Get After Their Asses mantra to describe opponents. He's the soul of their team, a tough guy, an agitator, but double off of him to help out on McDermott and Wragge.

"All right, coacher," Smith says to Miles, who nods and releases the players.

Still in the film room, the coaches debate how to guard inbounds plays and then some fine points about guarding in the half court. Harriman and Miles don't agree on a few strategies, and Smith tries to mediate. Miles trusts Smith more than anyone on *X*s and *O*s, especially on defense, sometimes admitting that his assistant coach, who has been with him for most of his coaching years, could probably outcoach him in a game. He may not really believe that to be true, but he likes to compliment his consigliore whenever Smith isn't close enough to hear.

Miles was in his second year at Mayville State when a friend called to say he had to meet Craig Smith, a guy about to graduate from the University of North Dakota. He was twenty-two, a small-town kid from Stephens, Minnesota, and all he wanted to be was a college basketball coach.

So Miles met Smith and Smith's fiancée, Darcy, thirty-five miles north in Grand Forks at the Ground Round, which is like a small-town Applebee's chain. Every kind of food on the menu, but Smith ordered a salad and wanted to know about how many onions and tomatoes were in the mix.

"You're really finicky, huh," Miles asked and stated at the same time. He can recognize finickiness because he's got the same gene. By the end of lunch he told Smith to come down to Mayville sometime Monday.

At nine on Monday morning, Miles was watching the 1996 NCAA Tournament press conferences on ESPN in his underwear in his Mayville apartment when his athletic director called from campus to say Smith was waiting for him.

Miles tried everything he could to talk Smith out of coming to Mayville State because he couldn't really pay him. He had turned a loser program—2-22 for two straight years—into the North Dakota Collegiate Athletic Conference champs in one year, going 9-3 in the NDCAC and 17-11 overall. But he still had no budget for a full-time assistant.

Smith wanted the job, he insisted in Miles's office, claiming he could learn everything he needed to know about coaching from Miles. This interview happened in the spring, as the sitcom *Seinfeld* was just reaching its popularity peak. Miles, who still references the show today, noticed Smith was a Loud Talker—not a Soft Talker or Close Talker like characters from the show, but a Loud Talker, ridiculously excited about everything Miles said, every question he asked.

"He's Mr. Superlative," Miles says. "Everything is always great."

Smith also wore a white shirt that was almost obscenely see-through, "like a Bo Derek thing," and Miles knew Smith was a character, but he still didn't really want to hire him.

He said he'd call him the next Monday and forgot. Tuesday, he tried to talk Smith out of the job. Smith wouldn't let him. "Coach," Smith said, "I already moved to town. My wife already found a job." So, Miles hired him.

That fall Miles held a fund-raiser in which fans could donate a dollar or five bucks for every free throw his players made, and it raised a few thousand dollars, which bought him some cotton shooting shirts and about thirteen hundred dollars for his new assistant. Smith got a paying job supervising study halls at Mayville-Portland High School and Darcy, a nurse, found three jobs in the area, and they moved three doors down from Miles.

Since then Smith has followed Miles at every coaching stop except Southwest Minnesota State. He also replicated Miles's turnaround at Mayville State seven years and two coaching regimes later, taking his team that had been 1-25 and carrying the Comets to the National Association of Intercollegiate Athletes Tournament three straight years, making the final in his third year, when he was NAIA Coach of the Year.

In that first year out of college, Smith made more money as a study-hall babysitter than a college coach. Darcy worked constantly. Then the flood of the century hit the Red River Valley.

Tough time, and Smith loved it. Mr. Superlative.

At Colorado State Miles elevated Smith from an operations guy to an assistant, then brought him to Nebraska as his consigliore, his right- and left-hand man, who runs the defense, in-game substitutions, and coordinates opponent scouts.

"I have no doubt, he's a smarter coach than I am, when it comes to game planning," Miles says now. "But I'll figure it out. Matchups are what he's great at—'This guy should guard that guy; this guy can only guard drivers.'"

As the coaches disagree over what to do under the basket against Creighton, Smith makes the final call.

"We just have to roll with it," Smith says, grinning.

Miles shakes his head at the board, where he's drawn three possibilities for defending inbounds plays.

"They're gonna get something," he says.

Kenya Hunter, the new guy from Georgetown, has been silent, but he finally speaks up. "Pick your poison," he says.

Creighton would be lethal.

The Creighton-Nebraska game, for Miles, was a chance to break out of a lifetime 0-9 record against Greg McDermott teams and, more important, a chance for his team to make a statement in year two. They were ready now.

For backup guard Deverell Biggs, the night was a chance to play in front of friends and family. He'd grown up in Omaha and won three state championships for Omaha Central High School, less than a mile from the arena and just blocks from Creighton's downtown campus. His former high school coaches had shown up to early-season practices to learn more about the new Husker coach and how he ran things. They'd probably be at the game, too.

Biggs started games on the bench, but had often been on the floor in the final minutes, hitting free throws to seal wins. He was the team's second-leading scorer at nearly eleven points per game in just nineteen minutes of playing time. But many of his points came on one-on-one plays, blasting his way into the lane to get fouled, gambling on defense for steals, but getting beaten for layups when he didn't pick opponents clean. He had more turnovers than assists, but he was as talented as anyone on the floor most nights.

Biggs had been Miles's first recruit at Nebraska, and like he wanted to win the towns of Fremont and Omaha, he wanted to win the entire state of Nebraska. Recruiting the best of the slim basketball talent in the state was crucial. He had recruited Omaha, Fremont, and the panhandle well while at Colorado State, and those players were key pieces in the Rams' turnaround. Nobody wanted Biggs to play a big role in a Husker transformation more than Miles, but Biggs was exactly whom Miles was talking about when he said his players are too used to being The Guy or that their play often depended on their mood that day. If Biggs played well against Creighton that Sunday, it was good for everyone at Nebraska, now and in the future.

As much as Nebraska basketball culture had been excited about Miles, the new players, and Lincoln's new arena, Creighton had as much, if not more, to be excited about. In moving from the Missouri Valley Conference to the Big East over the summer, the Bluejays had traded rivalries with Wichita State and Northern Iowa for the likes of Georgetown and Villanova, traditional powers that had won national championships. While Nebraska still had never won an NCAA Tournament game, Creighton had won tournament games in the opening round each of the last two years as favored seeds. Then it had been knocked out in the next rounds by North Carolina and Duke.

Now, Greg McDermott figured his team would be more tested after a Big East schedule and ready to make a run in the tournament. And his son was a senior who had a shot at being a John R. Wooden Award winner as college basketball's best player. He was the only returning All-American in the country and the leading returning scorer. At least eight NBA scouts, including former all-star guard Tim Hardaway, would be in the secondary press box for the game to get a bird's-eye view of McDermott for next summer's draft. On top of that, the Bluejays had lost two out of three games on a California trip during the past week, which had knocked them from the Associated Press Top 25. They were good, hungry, and simply didn't lose at the CenturyLink Center, where they were 51-7 in Coach McDermott's career.

"I'm just worried about stopping them," Miles said while planning before the game. "Just, they're so skilled and so smart offensively—I just don't know if we can stop them."

They couldn't.

10

As had been an early-season trend, six-foot-ten sophomore forward Walt Pitchford started the game with an immediate three-pointer, and missed it badly. Terran Petteway jacked another one early in the next possession.

Creighton's Ethan Wragge hit a deep NBA three.

The Bluejays' first inbounds play produced a wide-open layup, and the assistant coaches all grimaced at each other.

Doug McDermott hit a three-pointer in transition after another bad shot from the Huskers.

Creighton 8, Nebraska 0.

Tai Webster drove through the lane and powered his way to a layup. Creighton scored the next ten points.

Creighton 18, Nebraska 2.

Later in the half Ray Gallegos hit a three-pointer, and Shavon Shields scored a post move. Creighton scored the next ten points again.

Creighton 38, Nebraska 8.

Everything assistant coach Craig Smith had warned them about—taking good shots, finding Wragge and McDermott, the fanaticism about inbounds plays—had been lost in the pressure of the moment, the gravity of the game. Just seventeen minutes into the game, McDermott had seventeen points and had outscored the Husker team himself.

At the half Creighton led 51–27.

At Carlos O'Kelly's the next night, Miles would recall that halftime locker room: "Our win-one-for-the-Gipper halftime speech went like this: I said, 'Raise your hand if you think we can win this game.' Who lied? All their hands are up. Wow. I think they lied. No, I think they believed in it. So, I said, 'Let's get this down to fifteen with ten [minutes] left.'"

Creighton's lead rose as high as thirty-two points, but the Huskers, through frenetic full-court pressure, finally cut the lead to fifteen with 2 minutes remaining. Too late.

With 1:48 left Creighton's GATA guy, Grant Gibbs, and Petteway battled for a loose ball. Petteway dove to grab the ball, and then Gibbs dove on top of him, punching the ball free. In slow-motion replays later, Husker coaches would swear that Gibbs, still on top of Petteway, took a right-hand cross at Petteway's head, but missed. Petteway than performed a textbook wrestling reversal on Gibbs and pushed down on his chest as he got up. The whistle blew and Creighton fans erupted. The referees pulled Petteway away from the play as Gibbs got up and clapped. Then officials checked the replay and talked. They checked it again. Then discussed again. Lead official Tom Eades called the two coaches to center court to discuss the call. The public address announcer said officials had assessed both players flagrant fouls and ejected them from the game. Petteway untied his shorts and left the bench with a stoic face. Gibbs left to hand slaps from teammates and fans and another eruption from the crowd.

Smith had warned his team about Gibbs, too.

Though the Huskers outscored Creighton 42–31 in the second half, with Petteway scoring seventeen before being ejected, not much of that mattered. The game had been over in the first 13 minutes.

"That escalated in a hurry, huh?" Miles said to open his postgame press conference, trying to force a smile as he quoted Ron Burgundy from *Anchorman*. "You're looking up there like, 'Wow.' My son is a nine-year-old, and I've seen some games like that. But that's not supposed to happen in college basketball."

Reporters asked about the Gibbs-Petteway play.

"Terran, the kid's tore up in the locker room," Miles said. "And the first thing he does is apologize to his teammates for his behavior."

The team had Etch-a-Sketched everything it had been told about Creighton.

The next day Coach Greg McDermott tweeted out a photo of Gibbs diving through the air above Petteway with both hands stretched out before him, with the words, "My guy @DoubleG-for3 . . . . . . gotta like his hustle! Thanks again to all our fans for creating a great environment!"

The Husker assistant coaches would talk about that tweet more than once that day. They would meet with players individually to look at film and figure out where their heads were.

At the weekly radio show at Carlos O'Kelly's, Miles would

avoid talking about the game, even if that meant talking about trying not to talk about the game.

"I can't go the whole hour not talking about the Creighton game?" he asked host Greg Sharpe.

Instead, he talks about Irish superstitions and Doland. He talks about Olympic wrestler Dennis Kozlowski teaching him a single takedown move. Anything to avoid the game.

His wife, always very private, texts him to stick with basketball.

Miles reads her texts: "Don't talk about your siblings." "Don't read this on the air."

During the broadcast two sisters and a brother text him to correct his facts in his Doland stories. Alyce will call him later to tell him not to say the Lord's name in vain, especially not on the radio. Criminy.

When he finally talks about the Creighton loss, he keeps his thoughts abstract and philosophical: "Good players make things happen; bad players have things happen to them. They're left wondering what happened. That was us."

Miles turns the show over to Chris Harriman as part of his plan to prepare his assistants for head-coaching jobs and to escape the microphone. Harriman admits to Husker fans that Miles took the loss hard.

Meanwhile, Miles takes selfies with the fifty-odd fans at the restaurant. He signs door prizes. He asks a seven-year-old girl and her mother, who will attend every show together all year, if they'll be at the next game. Then, at a side table in Carlos O'Kelly's, Miles tells media-relations guy Shamus McKnight and others close to the program to say the team had a players-only meeting. Walt Pitchford told him about it.

"I don't care," Miles says. "I told him just to be ready to practice hard tomorrow. I don't care. I have to ride herd for three weeks. . . . I'll have to shake up the lineup, kick somebody out of practice."

He smiles.

"Don't worry. I'll think of something. I have to keep them thinking. That game was a defining moment."

He's also still talking about the Gibbs-Petteway play, defending his guy. But in the end, even before he hit the postgame locker room, Miles thought about his own mistakes. What could he have done differently?

"What I really respect is he looks at himself first," Harriman would say later in the week. "I love that about him, you know? And us being opinionated coaches, as we are, we told him, 'Coach, we could have done this better. We stayed in this offense too long. We showed our immaturity and inexperience. They jumped on it with their veteran leadership.' A perfect storm. We've been humbled."

Omaha World-Herald beat writer Lee Barfknecht has covered the Huskers for the paper since Moe Iba coached the team in the '80s and in the late '70s for the *Daily Nebraskan* while in college. He had seen Husker teams lose every way imaginable, but he couldn't imagine this result.

"The thing that I thought was really startling that day was how Nebraska quit competing early in the game," he would say later. "Thirty-eight to eight. Just didn't think I'd see that from a Tim Miles team. . . . I thought there was a possibility it could really send them in a tailspin."

His colleague at the paper, columnist Dirk Chatelain, grew up loving Husker basketball so much in the Danny Nee years that he used masking tape to build a replica Bob Devaney Center court on the red shag carpet of his parents' basement in Columbus, Nebraska. In his journalism career he'd seen coaches Barry Collier and Doc Sadler bring moments of hope to Nebraska basketball, but not enough wins. He figured Creighton would get all the attention this season, but he hoped Nebraska would be a story, too.

"The consensus from everyone I talked to after that game was that was kind of the first time that Miles really got embarrassed like that," he said. "They were bad last year, but they didn't get embarrassed like that. And if they did, it was in a place it was more acceptable to get embarrassed, like at Michigan. You just don't lose to your in-state rival like that. They looked scared and played scared. That they looked scared and played scared was sort of Collier-esque. And that was a signal to me very early on in the year that they're two years away. These things are supposed to work in a trajectory, and if that's where they were on December 8, that signaled to me the trajectory was slow."

Miles didn't have the team that he needed to play the way he wanted. Like his parents before him, he just had to make do.

When Tim Miles grew up, his family went to the post office every day but Sunday to get the mail because they really had no real address. They lived on what residents called Main, but Doland had no street signs back then.

Later, Main was named Humphrey Avenue because Hubert Humphrey spent much of his childhood there and graduated from Doland High. His dad was the town pharmacist and served as mayor. Humphrey would be a major player in the Democratic Party in Minnesota, where he united the party with the Farmer-Labor Party to create the DFL. On the national level he served as a U.S. senator, as Lyndon Johnson's vice president, and as the Democratic nominee for president in 1968, losing to Richard Nixon. Not bad for Doland. Miles regularly slips it into motivational talks or regular conversation that Doland High School produced four military generals. But his mother thinks the Doland heroes who most influenced her son were the Koslowski brothers.

The Koslowski twins lost their mother to brain cancer at age two, and later in adulthood Dennis Koslowski would admit that his father never really recovered, dealing with the loss by drinking and shipping the kids off to relatives. They went off to a farm, attacked their chores, started wrestling, rammed heads together, and turned themselves into Greco-Roman wrestlers at the 1988 Seoul Olympics, where Dennis medaled and Duane finished eighth. Dennis then returned, at thirty-two years old, to compete in the 1992 Barcelona Olympic Games, where the glory of his silver medal—only the second time an American had medaled in two Olympics in Greco-Roman wrestling—was headlocked by the noise of Michael Jordan, Charles Barkley, Magic Johnson, and their Dream Team.

When the Koslowski brothers were in high school, Tim Miles was a loud-mouthed, frozen-pizza-eating basketball gym rat annoying his sixth grade teachers on the other end of the school. One day in class Dennis Koslowski jerked Miles out of class and taught him the fireman's carry. His teacher must not have minded because the two worked on it until Miles mastered the move.

Miles tells this story on the radio at Carlos O'Kelly's to continue his strategy of not talking about the Creighton loss.

"So, I basically ran through districts and regionals as a one-trick pony," he says.

In those days Alyce would wake up early to prepare breakfast, and the beat-up car the twins brought to school would be parked across the street, with the boys inside working out at six o'clock. When her kids showed up in the kitchen, Alyce would point out the window at that disaster of a car and tell them that those boys have nothing, but they're going to outwork everybody else. They have the discipline. They aren't afraid of hard work. Of pain.

Dennis Koslowski's twin brother, Duane, said in an *Aberdeen American News* "Where are they now?" story that "athletics taught me anything is possible with discipline, dedication and a plan."

The Koslowski twins went on to tiny University of Minnesota–Morris. They kept working hard. Going to school. Playing football and wrestling. Then doing damage on the national and international wrestling scenes. Dennis then became a high-profile chiropractor in Minneapolis, working with the Minnesota Vikings, Twins, and Timberwolves. Duane became a financial planner in Virginia.

Alyce says her kids, especially Tim, saw the Koslowskis as an inspiration, a symbol of possibility. She made sure of it.

"I'd say, 'Look at this car out here. They're going to be somebody,'" Alyce says now. "Tim took that to heart. 'I can do any-thing coming from Doland.'"

Being from Doland, you just made do with what you had. Those brothers overcame tough circumstances, was her point, so go out there and be somebody.

Three

Us Always

11

John and Sharon Hanigan lived on a farm across from Blue-stem Lake about a half hour south of Lincoln. The couple was selling the place and moving to a condominium in town. Getting smaller. Sharon had retired from managing the office in the Psychology Department at the University of Nebraska–Lincoln. John was semiretired from the accounting firm he helped establish, but still did financial work for friends and clients.

In August John was spraying weeds on the acreage when he fell. Pain burned through his ribs afterward, and when his brother-in-law, a doctor, gave him a regular check-up in early fall, he ordered some chest X-rays that found fluid in John's lungs. He sent John home with meds.

But John didn't feel any better. By the end of October doctors would diagnose him with something called non-small-cell adenocarcinoma, the equivalent of nonsmoking lung cancer. Doctors cut into John's chest in a procedure called a thoracotomy to take a look. The surgeon found "rice-like cells" of cancer along the chest wall. A biopsy later confirmed the cancer.

"After that," John's son Ryan says, "everything was just a blur."

A longtime season-ticket holder, John had great seats for the first season in the Pinnacle Bank Arena, and despite the crushing loss to Creighton, he was excited to see a game in the new digs and the progress of Miles's team. The next game was supposed to be a laugher against Arkansas State, a low-level team from a midmajor conference. John had a parking-garage space reserved across the street from the new arena and thought he should escape his recliner and catch the game with son Ryan.

...

Practice is edgy the day before that game. Miles makes the goals clear at center court in his prepractice talk.

He looks at Trevor Menke, his scout-team point guard from Beatrice, maybe the smartest kid on the team besides Shavon Shields, the premed major. In two years Menke had learned to run more teams' offenses than anyone. And his pay for that? Two minutes per game in fewer than ten games per year.

"How many days are in a year, Menke?" Miles asks. "Don't say 364. There are 365."

He turns to senior Ray Gallegos. "How many games do we play in a year, Ray? Thirty? Thirty-one?"

Then he turns on Deverell Biggs—who had the disastrous game at Creighton—for the first of many face-offs throughout the next ninety minutes of drills. "Deverell, when people see you on campus, how do they define you? As a cool guy? As a basketball player? . . . That means you have 32 days where you can have an impact on how people define you. And they don't care how [Mike] Peltz practices today. They don't care how the scout team performs. They care that you win. They want to know how are the Huskers going to react after getting their ass kicked by Creighton? Are they going to compete?

"After walk-through, we're just having an hour and a half practice; then we're out of here. I know it's a tough week for you with classes and everything else, but let's go."

They put their hands on top of Miles's right hand.

Terran Petteway: "One, two, three."

Everyone: "Team."

Kenya Hunter in his baritone: "Let's go, fellas."

The practice starts loose. Assistant Chris Harriman, the Australian who recruited Tai Webster, the freshman New Zealand point guard, is still amazed the eighteen-year-old can't name half the teams in the Big Ten. And now Webster is lost on half-court team defense, wandering around on the weak side of the court, where he can't protect the basket. Coaches call this defensive no-man's-land "China," a desolate place where players are out of position and can't help protect the basket. Assistant coach Craig Smith shouts "China" at least twenty times every practice.

"Ray, China."

"Shavon, China."

"Dev, you're in China. Get out of there. We need you in help defense. China, China."

Hunter, the new assistant, is still having trouble with this lingo, but tries it out.

"Tai, get in China."

The players and coaches crack up.

Miles keeps a straight face: "Coacher, we don't want him in China. We want him in America. Make him an American."

Then the practice darkens as mistakes don't seem as funny. In a half-court game, the scout team keeps scoring in Arkansas State offensive sets against the Husker rotation. The black jerseys, with Velcroed numbers to represent Arkansas State scorers, keep getting to the rim for layups and lead 12–8 in a game to 15. Black has the ball on an inbounds play, and Miles tells Deverell Biggs, who has the man inbounding the ball, to protect the lane and stop anyone from scoring a layup. Instead, he stands flat-footed and watches the inbounder. Freshman Nick Fuller swoops in to take a pass directly from the inbounder and lays the ball in over Biggs, who never moved.

"Ray, get Dev. Dev, I just told you to stop that."

Biggs barks back at his coach.

Kenya Hunter tries to jump in: "Come on, Dev."

"I don't want to hear your excuses, Deverell," Miles says. He's yelling now. "You stood right there and looked at him, and they scored right on you."

Biggs won't look at his coach, and he mumbles something.

"I don't want to hear your excuses. You don't have any answers. You played like garbage in Omaha [against Creighton]."

The red team gets two points to cut the lead to 14–10, but Miles is staring at Biggs.

Biggs still won't look at Miles. He puts his arms out to Hunter for help, but Hunter isn't offering any. Shields gets a steal, and then David Rivers gets another to tie the game at 14–14. Then red gets another stop, and Rivers pulls in the rebound for a 15–14 win. Miles, though, is still on Biggs.

"Dev, you saw a team come back from 14–8 when you were out. How did they win it? Lots of talk on defense. Not taking chances. That's your problem, Dev. Taking chances and not talking."

Biggs nods at his coach, who isn't yelling anymore. He inserts Biggs back into the next game.

"Come on, Dev," he says.

The rest of practice runs more smoothly. By the end Miles puts in a new inbounds play he's dreamed up for Walt Pitchford. It's Friday the 13th, so he decides to call it Freddy, but the players point out Freddy Krueger was in *Nightmare on Elm Street*, not *Friday the 13th*. They rename the play Jason.

"I don't care what you call it," he says. "Run it right."

The game follows the same flow as practice. As John and Ryan Hanigan watch from the northeast corner of Pinnacle Bank Arena, about twenty rows up behind the Husker bench, Walt Pitchford hits his first two shots, and then Ray Gallegos hits two three-pointers. The Huskers jump ahead 15–2 and stretch the lead to 50–27 at halftime, but just before the half Pitchford hotdogs his way in for a layup and misses. Miles is peeved. Rather than joining his coaches in a strategy room with a conference table and blank notebooks to talk game plans for the second half, Miles follows Pitchford all the way through the locker room to the player film room to hammer Pitchford and Tai Webster.

"Get locked in," he screams at them.

Back in the arena John decides he's too tired to stay. He hasn't said much in the first half, except to complain about turnovers. He's seen enough. He loves the arena. He likes the way Miles stays on top of his players. But he's got to go home to his recliner, where he can sit or sleep without the fluid in his lungs causing him to cough. On the way home he hears Husker Sports Network announcers Kent Pavelka and Matt Davison describe an ugly second half. Deverell Biggs earns a technical for yelling at an Arkansas State player who fouled him. Then Terran Petteway and an Arkansas State forward earn double technicals for some shoving. In the end Arkansas State's senior-laden team battles back to close the gap to twelve, 79–67, and most of the energy is sucked out of the arena.

In the locker-room classroom Miles delivers one of his longest postgame speeches of the season. He rips his team for what he calls "keeping score."

"Who knows what that means, 'keeping score'? Mike?"

Mike Peltz: "A guy scores on me. He did this. I got to do that."

Miles says the issue is poise and focus. Instead of keeping score, and getting technicals, he wants his team to move on to the next play. Just keep playing. He sees these same issues within the team, too.

"'Well, he didn't pass me the ball. Well, I'm not gonna pass him the ball. Well, that guy hit me here, so I'm gonna hit him there.' You know what I mean? We can't keep score. You don't see Kobe Bryant keep score. And I don't see LeBron James keep score. I don't. They might run their mouths, you know, here and there, but they don't get into it with people. Magic Johnson?"

It's an issue of intensity, he says, and they'd better bring some in the next five games, because after playing the Citadel, the schedule turns brutal. The Huskers will go to Cincinnati and then start the Big Ten schedule on the road, too.

"We gotta work to get better," Miles says. "At Cincinnati, at Iowa, at Ohio State [osu], at home against Michigan, at Purdue. There are a billion people in this world who think we go oh-for-five in that run. . . . We saw what Creighton did to us when we don't practice well. We saw when we practice pretty well how we can start. Then we saw we can mess it up. And that just is what it is."

Miles figures the smart people in Las Vegas will make the Huskers underdogs in their next six games, actually. If they were to prove Vegas right and lose those games, they would be sitting at eight wins and nine losses, and 0-4 in the Big Ten Conference, with all conference games left on the schedule. Things could get uglier than last year, when his team went 5-13 in the Big Ten with no expectations. Miles was still trying to calibrate his own expectations of this team.

"Everybody's gotta look [in the mirror] tonight and think about, [to Petteway] 'How'd I lose my poise?' [To Shields] 'How'd I lose my intensity?' [To Webster] 'Why'd I travel three times?' [To Biggs] 'Why'd I overhandle it a couple times?' [To Gallegos] 'How come my jumpers fell one half and not the next half? What is it?' [To Leslee Smith] 'Why'd I miss defensive spots?'

"I think we should've beat [Arkansas State] by thirty, but we screwed it up. And we can't let that happen in a Big Ten game. We can't let that happen in the rest of our schedule, because, my friends, let me tell you this: Shavon, David, Benny, Ray? Is there a break on the schedule when you get into Big Ten play? No, sir. No, sir. There is no break. It's like playing Creighton every night, only quicker, stronger, faster. All right? We gotta be up to it, because I want this team to make the NCAA Tournament. I want Ray's senior year, Mike's senior year, to be the best they can have. I want to be in the postseason. But it's gonna take a week's worth of practice. So start with film on Monday, and we're getting better from there. So any questions or comments from you guys?"

He gives them no time to answer.

"All right, let's take a knee."

They pray. They need answers. Can they make do?

Miles: "Team on three."

Petteway: "One, two, three."

Everyone: "Team."

Hunter: "Let's go, fellas."

12

A week before Christmas, Coach Tim Miles is selling his program. The previous night, he'd been selling it to a high school player in Wisconsin and returned on a late-night flight. In the morning, he was digging into film and numbers. He believes in the coaching aphorism that the team you have in November and December is never the team you have in February and March. The team can gel and improve, or it can clash and nosedive. The change occurs during the holidays and through January. Despite the high stakes of this point in the season, though, he's still selling the fan base and the future.

At eleven thirty he works with his media-relations guy, Shamus McKnight, on a forty-five-minute live fan chat via Twitter at #askCoachMiles. The coach doesn't worry about spelling or grammar, and his media man doesn't screen the answers.

Fans want to know personal details about his life. Did he like the Jay Z concert at the arena?

@CoachMiles: Excellent . . . until the smoke alarms went on.

What's his favorite Will Ferrell movie?

@CoachMiles: I think I'm already tired of seeing Anchorman 2 promos

And what about the new Dumb and Dumber To movie coming out?

@CoachMiles: Too little too late

Do you actually Tweet at the half or does someone else?

@Coach Miles: Famous Shamus . . . He types & edits.

Why won't he free forward David Rivers from the doghouse?

@CoachMiles: . . . he's 9th man in rotation—great kid Hustler.

What needs to improve?

@CoachMiles: Defensive Rebounding & more efficient offense

His team is near the bottom of the NCAA in defensive rebounding and assists. He tells fans the team needs better point-guard play and more size to win. He knows his players will see his answers. Many follow him on Twitter. All the coaches follow them, too. As do members of the Athletic Department, whose job is to watch all of their social media for anything inappropriate or embarrassing.

One fan wants to know how much he wants to make the NCAA Tournament right now, in his second year.

@CoachMiles: It's a red exclamation point-email joke

Another fan wants to know what a three-year or five-year goal is for the team.

@CoachMiles: Every year we want to be in NCAA Tournament.

A college buddy, who now coaches women's college basketball in Texas, asks about his favorite story from his University of Mary days in Bismarck.

@CoachMiles: Most likely would be getting fired if I told that.

The buddy is Scott Hyland, who often rode the basketball bench with Miles for U-Mary Marauders coach Al Bortke. Miles had been a star at Doland High School, and his family sent him four hours northeast to Bismarck to get a good Catholic education. Even more, they appreciated the scholarship package the school put together by combining academic, basketball, and track scholarships.

But Miles rarely played for the varsity team. He returned from Mary dejected and full of doubt. He also had a plan. What if he transferred to St. John's in Minnesota? It was an even smaller school, and he'd get to play. Bortke didn't like South Dakota kids, he told his father, and only played homegrown North Dakota players or Minnesota guys.

His dad urged him to sit down with Mr. Bortke. Tip Miles still refers to the retired coach as Mr. Bortke and respects the man's integrity, even if he never played his son. He also feared a St. John's tuition with no scholarship help.

"See if you can work something out," Tip told his son.

Bortke had a system for dealing with upperclassmen who didn't make the seven- or eight-man rotation. They could become student coaches and learn the business by leading the freshman or junior varsity (jv) teams and assisting on the varsity bench.

"Let's face the facts. That was really our cut process," Bortke recalled. "As far as being an outstanding player, Tim wasn't. I didn't want to call him up in the last few minutes of a game and him not want to go in. It would be an embarrassment."

But Miles didn't see things that way. He made a condition: he'd agree to the student-coaching option only if he could sit in on Bortke's practice-planning meetings. He never missed one. And he took Bortke's coaching class with eleven other students who never got a chance to talk.

Bortke finally told him, "I'm not going to call on you anymore, Tim."

"Coach," Miles said, "I just want to learn."

By the end of the next year, Bortke ignored his jv team and let Miles run the show. Miles even stood up and called his own time-out in a varsity game when the team was falling apart. Bortke was livid. He stared down the bench at Miles and remained in his seat.

"Oh, I forgot I wasn't coaching jv," Miles said.

"Hey," Bortke yelled, "you called the time-out. You talk to them."

The team got blown out, which Bortke thought was going to happen anyway.

Another day Miles asked Bortke to give him some tips on building team chemistry.

"I told him it's okay to make a fool of yourself," Bortke said. "I'm going to tell you the truth. When the team's getting ready for practice, all you have to do is take a crap, sit with your notebook in there, and you'll find out who's training hard and who's fighting with his girlfriend, and when you open the door of the stall, you'll see some shocked faces."

And no matter how hard you push them, how much you yell at them, how much you make them run, always leave practice with everybody smiling.

"Everyone's going to get their butt chewed," Coach said. "But leave it on the floor. Come back another day."

By the end of college, Miles learned he wouldn't make the NBA or represent his country at the Olympics as a hurdler. But he could coach. His family says Tim Miles learned humility in college. He was a cocky kid in his eighteen years in Doland, where he was a three-sport star, making two-inch-tall headlines in his parents' newspaper. He may still resemble a cocky kid, his siblings admit, but now he knows what it's like to lose, not just basketball games, but also his confidence, or something bigger in life.

Once he became successful at coaching, he was often asked about his mentor, and though he won't deny that he learned from his high school coaches, Bortke, and his bosses in grad school at Northern State, he almost always answers the question like this: "Losing was my mentor."

After the Twitter fan chat, he eats lunch with the coaches, who usually either go out to downtown restaurants or make lowest-ranked staffer Teddy Owens pick something up, sandwiches or pizza. Then Miles digs into more film and practice planning. By 3:35 he's in the Hendricks practice gym attacking the treadmill. Rather than using his headphones and iPhone, he orders the managers to crank up some hip-hop into the gym.

"We'll crank this pretty loud before we go to Michigan and Michigan State," he explains while running. "We'll do it some today, too, [to prep Cincinnati] in practice. We want them to try to communicate on the floor when it's loud."

Petteway makes fun of Miles for his choices, mainly gleaned from his kids' music. Miles has been a Top 40 guy since middle school days, a Casey Kasem devotee. But he isn't one to say music was better back in his day. Miles fights back by making fun of Petteway's dreadlocks. Very old school.

Once he's done with the workout, his last sales pitch of the day is to sell his team on saving the season. He started that in yesterday's practice. Miles is a numbers guy. Besides reading coaching philosophy books, he'll read numbers books, such as Dean Oliver's *Basketball on Paper*. Miles's copy is annotated with his ideas on how to put the numbers to work for him.

His favorite numbers, though, belong to Ken Pomeroy, whom some experts consider the Bill James of college basketball. Bill James developed statistical principles that led to the Oakland Athletics' resurgence in the early 2000s and spawned the book and movie *Moneyball*, starring Brad Pitt as A's general manager Billy Beane. The A's had a low payroll and used James's ideas to find affordable players who excelled in unsexy stats that added up to wins, even against large-market teams such as the New York Yankees and Boston Red Sox. The movie painted Beane as a wizard, thwarting traditional baseball scouting and conventional wisdom to build teams of nobodies that repeatedly made the playoffs despite their disadvantages against their richer competitors.

Pomeroy has a site called kenpom.com, where coaches, players, fans, and gamblers can, for a price, access college basketball analytics that Pomeroy thinks allow him to predict success, or failure. More important, he says, he's trying to show coaches areas where they can focus to improve their teams. Most veteran coaches are set in their ways and happy with their systems, which is fine. But younger coaches looking for breakthrough success will often be open to anything that could provide an edge. Miles contacted Pomeroy early in his Colorado State career, when his teams were struggling through the 0-16 first Mountain West season and twenty-plus losses in each of the first two years. He needed answers.

With Nebraska sitting at 8-3 and about to face, after the Citadel, the toughest part of its schedule, Miles found himself digging deeply into Pomeroy's numbers. What he saw was scary. And he had several choices in how to react to them, how to use them.

Pomeroy admits that college basketball analysis is much less of an exact science than baseball, where the emphasis is on the individual and the numbers are more discreet. The coaches who best use his site are able, he thinks, to figure out how to exploit what the numbers tell them their teams do well and how to exploit what opponents don't do well. Sounds simple, he says, but that's where his numbers stop. The coach has to figure out how to translate the information into strategy and action.

At the end of December, Miles would tweet something that would hold Pomeroy's attention for the rest of the season: "@ kenpomeroy I'm breaking up with your computer!" He then added a screenshot from his iPhone of kenpom.com predicting the Huskers would lose their first ten games of the Big Ten season, starting with Iowa on New Year's Eve.

"In that tweet he was joking about what I was forecasting because a lot of people don't use that kind of information constructively," Pomeroy said. "They just build a chip on their shoulders. They get angry. But Miles just figures there's some reason that my numbers are working out the way they are, and he found a reasonable way to act on them."

His strategy starts with the first practice after the sloppy Arkansas State win. Miles finds more Pomeroy numbers showing that thirteen out of the last nineteen games on the Huskers schedule would be decided by six or fewer points.

"That's two possessions," Miles says in the coaches' locker room while building his practice plan. "Each game is within two possessions. We're picked to go four and nine in those games. So how do we turn that into eight and five, or nine and four?"

That's the difference, Miles figures, between this team sneaking into the postseason and this team fighting to keep fans in the seats.

He has a two-part approach to the problem. First, he pulls out a sheet of scribbles and shows it to his numbers guy, Teddy Owens, on his way onto the Pinnacle Bank Arena court. They are set plays he dreamed up three years ago for late-game situations at Colorado State. Miles wants his teams to play a motion offense that offers players choices based on reading defenses. But this team has shown it isn't mature enough offensively to run an offense on basketball IQ and instincts. Instead, he'll put in these set plays during the next few days, with concrete directives his team can follow, and save them for the ends of games.

"This is gold. I'm telling you, this stuff is gold," he says to Owens at the scorer's table while his team warms up. He grins at the crinkled piece of paper until his face looks like a five-year-old's and then grins at Owens, who breaks up laughing.

Second, he scripts a practice in which the bulk of the head-to-head scrimmage will be one-minute games that simulate end-of-game scenarios. Student managers will put the white team, or the top eight players, on the court with a two-point lead, a two-point deficit, or a tie with one minute remaining on the scoreboard clock against a red scout team. Miles will referee as he figures Big Ten officials will call the last minute of a game, which is to say they won't call much.

The scout team includes David Rivers and Benny Parker, both of whom haven't played much lately. It also includes Ray Gallegos, who started last season but had his minutes slashed in half this year, partly because of his suspension.

Game 1: Tied 53–53. The white team misses a free throw to seal the game, and the scout team misses a three to win. White wins by two.

Game 2: Tied 55–55. Guard Deverell Biggs nails a seventeen-footer and adds two free throws to give white the lead, but the scout team comes back to win, as Terran Petteway misses a desperation three-pointer to tie.

Between games Miles draws up his new plays on a portable whiteboard with his Husker rotation in white. The break is supposed to be as long as a full or thirty-second time-out to simulate real games. But Miles holds his team long after the student manager blasts the gym's horn. Harriman, coaching the scout team, shouts at his head coach a few times, arguing that long breaks defeat the purpose of the drill. Usually, that griping goes the other way, as scout-team coaches huddle with their players and Miles gets impatient, taunting, "Come on, Belichick." Miles grins without acknowledging his high-strung Australian assistant, who leans forward with his hands on his knees, glaring into some unknown space, like an obstetrician waiting for a baby to come into the world.

Game 3: Tied 60–60. Biggs hits a fearless, and maybe illogical, three-pointer with a man in his face to take the lead late. Petteway misses free throws, and Gallegos hits a three to tie the game in the last second. 63–63.

Miles's white team wins three of the next four games and ties the other.

Before game 8, Miles mixes the teams up for balance, and Harriman goes nuts because turnovers and missed free throws dominate the final three games. Despite all that, Miles slow claps the team to the middle of the gym and swears they got something done today. Then he hops on a plane with assistant Craig Smith to get his recruit.

Before practice the next day, fresh from the Wisconsin trip and the live tweet chat, he's ready for a long afternoon, starting with a seventy-three-minute film session. He starts by having video coordinator Greg Eaton show clips of last season's San Antonio Spurs playoff series against Golden State. Many college coaches view Spurs coach Gregg Popovich's system as the closest thing to emulating a perfect team concept. Miles wants his point guards to watch Spurs point guard Tony Parker start the offense and keep the ball moving, keep his dribble alive through the lane if nothing is there. He wants them to see Manu Ginobili, a perennial All-Star, accept his role coming off the bench, keeping his head up to look for open guys and finish off screens to free up his teammates. These players are All-Stars who do the dirty work to win, Miles tells his team. And they stay cool under pressure.

Then he shows the contrast of the sloppy Arkansas State win.

"Look, we lose our minds once we get up ten or twelve," he says.

Smith jumps in: "Play the same way whether we're up ten or down ten. Whether it's scoreboard, good or bad calls, the crowd: stay level-headed."

Then Miles drops Ken Pomeroy's analytics on the team. He tells them Pomeroy has done all the number crunching and has the Huskers at ninety-second in the country and eleventh out of twelve teams in the Big Ten, just above Northwestern. And that's the good news.

He tells them they're picked to lose to Cincinnati. And when the Big Ten season starts on New Year's Eve, Pomeroy has picked the Huskers to lose by fifteen at Iowa and by sixteen at Ohio State. Then lose by four to Michigan at home. At home.

Then lose and lose and lose, he tells them. Thirteen straight. He tells them: If we play like we've been playing, they say we'll lose thirteen in a row and start the season 0-12 in the Big Ten. That means we're last in the Big Ten, behind Penn State, Northwestern, everyone. We weren't that bad last year.

"So let's get to work," he says. "We have thirteen games that will be decided by two possessions or less. We have to play well under pressure. We have to steal games."

Back on the floor he starts them off with layups from the top of the key with body shots and arm hits from Woody and coach Kenya Hunter. Miles jumps on guys for walking back to the back of the line, for having jerseys untucked, for not playing with pace.

A half hour into the workout, he breaks into a new drill called "Full Chaos." He splits teams evenly and has each defense press all over the court, trying to trap the ball with two defenders. They play two on offense against three defenders in the back-court, then play three on offense against two defenders in the frontcourt. The idea is to smartly get the ball across half-court against pressure and then make the defense pay on the other end by scoring layups and dunks or driving and dishing for open three-pointers.

After every score, Miles screams at everyone to get going the other way. Get the trap on. Get the ball inbounds. Move the ball to the open man. Don't celebrate. Talk to each other.

"Hey, get off our knees," he yells at Walter Pitchford. "What are we trying to accomplish? Eat them up. You never let up. Never quit on a play. Box out. Create a frenetic pace. Citadel's gonna do it. Cincinnati's gonna do it. Minnesota is gonna do it. Attack it with some poise and some pace."

His cocaptain Terran Petteway feeds off this pressure. He's talking to everyone. Getting on people after mistakes. Moving people to the right spots, even when he's not in the drill.

Biggs drives through the lane and jumps in the air before throwing the ball away against a double-team.

"Dev, what's your error?" Miles asks, not really shouting yet. "What would Tony Parker do?"

Biggs is speechless.

"Keep dribbling through there. That's patience."

Then Pitchford gets trapped at half-court and throws the ball away in a panic. He complains that the double-team went against the rules of the drill.

"I was already across the line," he screams.

And he's right. But the coach isn't buying it. Sometimes things happen in a game that aren't fair, like a shot rimming out, slipping on a wet spot, a terrible call by an official. You can't throw the ball and scream that things aren't fair in this world. The theme? Just keep playing.

"Walter, don't complain about the rules," Miles shouts. Then he speaks to him more softly. "Walt, Cincinnati doesn't care about the rules. They're going to cause chaos."

Freshman point guard Tai Webster takes charge and gets his team to move the ball through the full-court defense without dribbling. When he gets the ball back, he blows through the lane and misses.

"Make that layup, Tai," Miles says, but he's happy, mostly with himself, he admits later. "Get a quick drink. Great drill. Great drill. Full Chaos, baby."

Next is an even team scrimmage. The message here is that nobody has a protected spot. Earn your place in the rotation every practice. Coach Hunter's red team jumps up on coach Smith's white team right away.

"Okay, Smith, it's 11–2," Miles says after he calls a foul. "Why do you think that is?"

"Well, we're tentative. We're playing slow."

Miles stares at him and waits a beat. "Okay, just checking."

The team cuts the gap to three, but can never catch up.

Usually, this would be the end of practice, but Miles wants more defensive drills. Petteway lunges for a steal on a screen-and-roll drill and gets caught out of position, and his man scores.

"Terran, you go to the white team," Miles says.

Petteway turns away and smiles. Miles then makes him play every play with his hands up in the air so that he won't just go for steals, as was his instinct in high school, when he could take the ball from anyone. But that won't work in two weeks against Iowa's Roy Devyn Marble, Ohio State's Aaron Craft, and Michigan's Nik Stauskas. Soon, everyone has to play with hands in the air. Webster, who along with Petteway has never played a Big Ten game, is tired and frustrated. He stomps in circles between plays with his hands on his hips and his elbows out. He scrunches down his eyebrows. He battles against Biggs, who keeps trying to take him off the dribble, or keeps hacking him when he shoots. He fights through atomic screens from the 255-pound Leslee Smith. He takes repeated verbal shots from Miles and Hunter. He blows layup after layup. Then backup to the backup point guard Benny Parker blows by him for a layup of his own.

"You let a five-foot-five guy get by you, Tai," Miles screams, then smiles.

Miles walks to the top of the key to face a grinning Parker, who rarely shows any emotion in practice or games. Soon, Miles is inches away from the one Husker player he can look down on in a literal sense. "How tall are you? Five-five?"

Parker: "Five seven and a half."

Miles smiles and nods. "Yeah, right."

Miles lists Parker at five-foot-nine on the roster. He's going to need that kind of optimism going into the holiday and January. His brain knows Parker must be five-foot-five, but Parker sees himself two and a half inches taller, closer to reality, and Miles's public persona claims Parker is five-nine. It's a symbol for how he has to treat this team, which is supposed to lose its next thirteen games. By the end of that stretch on February 16 at Michigan State, where Ken Pomeroy has them getting blown out by fifteen points, they would be 9-14, if the numbers hold true. They'd have no chance to make any tournament, much less the Big Dance. So he's worked them over with a nearly four-hour practice. He's humbled them down to 5-foot-5 with how bad they are and how hard they must work to overcome their badness. The analytics prove it. Publicly, he tells his Twitter followers and radio-show listeners that they're striving for the tournament. They're not waiting on some four-year program. The truth is somewhere in the middle.

Then, like University of Mary coach Al Bortke taught him, Miles decides to take them off the court with a smile. Even a grin from the stoic Benny Parker, who is buried on the bench.

Miles knows what that feels like.

13

Before the Huskers can deal with those next thirteen games of being underdogs, often-heavy underdogs, they have to host the Citadel. The Bulldogs from Charleston, South Carolina, are ranked 345th out of 349 NCAA Division I programs in the country. The coaches didn't spend much time scouting them, with Cincinnati coming up later in the week. In the locker room Miles paints the theme of the game in harsh colors of aggression: red and black dry-erase marker.

The pregame, halftime, and postgame routines are always the same, as long as circumstances—national media game constraints or special occasion games, such as senior nights or legends nights—don't disrupt the drill.

The players show up an hour and forty-five minutes before a home game. They get taped and filter out to the floor to shoot and get stretched out by strength coach Tim Wilson. Assistants stay in the coaches' locker room to start dressing up. They often talk last-minute strategy, such as defensive matchups or inbounds plays. Other times, if they're loose, like tonight, they just tell stories. Smith talks about a recruit he needed when he had the head job at Mayville State, but Miles poached him away to North Dakota State.

"For four days," Smith says, "I'm puking my brains out because the guy is so good and we had him signed and everything."

During the story Miles, as usual, pretends he's not listening while he works on his game cards, a set of color-coded notes mostly for running in-game offense. He's still wearing his futuristic Adidas sweats while his suit hangs in his locker. But he can't help smiling now at Smith's version of the story.

"So Miles calls me again," Smith says, looking over at his head coach. "He says, 'You know what? You know, we were late on him. He wants to come here, but you know what? We're done with him. We're not gonna pursue him. You got him, blah, blah, blah.' So we got him."

Miles argues with Smith about some facts in the story, and then he picks on Kenya Hunter, always the best-dressed coach, for using cheap shoe polish on his loafers. "That your juco shine?" Miles asks him before most home games. Running gag.

The players then return to the film classroom with thirty-two minutes left on the pregame clock and wait silently for Coach to deliver his game theme. Miles leads the coaches through the door between their locker room and the classroom.

"Here are the keys," he says. "Play with aggressiveness. Every second you're out there . . . Attack on all phases of the game and compete your ass off. Show me what you got for forty minutes."

He talks about rebounding and defending, as usual.

Then he closes hard.

"If you're not hustling and busting your ass tonight, don't expect to play. You guys have a chance to go out there and set the tone. We didn't finish the job last time out there against Arkansas State. . . . We wanna be a postseason team, right? We have to work every night we get a chance to get out there and compete and get better and do the right things so we're the kind of team we wanna be. You don't get better by accident. You don't get better by hoping you get better. You get better by mental capacity. Right? You get better by how hard you work, and how you handle stress, how you handle competition, how you handle coaching, how you handle officials, how you handle a bad night. Right? How you handle distractions. Right? Outside influences. If you have the mental capacity to go out and compete your ass off, if you have the edge to compete in all phases of the game, we're gonna be in good shape. Lock in, concentrate, and let's win this damn game. Any questions? Let's go."

The players shoot as the crowd of nearly fifteen thousand starts to fill up the arena. Not bad for school being out.

Until the clock ticks away to twelve minutes before the game, coaches keep telling stories and getting dressed, except for Miles, who is buried in his game cards. The assistants, who went out to the court without wearing their suit jackets, talk about how the team always wants senior Ray Gallegos to launch the first shot in warm-ups. He missed that first one tonight, but "he hits the next thirty," Harriman says. Smith says the first-shot superstition started last season with leading scorer Dylan Talley. They tell stories about last season. The players return to wait for their second pep talk. Miles leads the coaches in again.

"One of two things happens tonight," Miles says. "I don't know much, but I promise you that at the end of the night, your basketball team is either gonna be 7-4 or 8-3, and it's completely your choice, right? On how you play, how you execute, how we compete. . . . Let's go out and earn it. Let's take a knee."

All coaches and players kneel silently for eleven seconds.

"Let's go, Huskers," Miles says, but doesn't yell his customary high-pitched "Woooooooooo." Not for Citadel.

"Team on three," Petteway says when everyone's hands are in the circle, Miles in the middle, assistants on the outside with hands on players' shoulders. "One, two, three."

Everyone: "Team."

Hunter: "Let's go, fellas."

Miles dresses in a hurry, picking a tie that looks like a winner, a literal winner, as in "I can win a game in this tie." He always has to be the last man to leave the locker room, and he does that with 3:27 left on the scoreboard, which is electronically synched to a small digital clock in the coaches' locker room. He won his first game at Mayville State when he left the locker room at 3:27. The digits are connected to some of his past track times and other superstitious coincidences. He tries to nail that exact time every game, even though he hasn't won every one. He'll wait under that clock as it ticks down: 3:30, 3:29, 3:28 . . .

The first half is a mess. Nebraska jacks up outside shots and can't get offensive rebounds. Citadel guards drive right by Tai Webster, Deverell Biggs, and Benny Parker to get in the lane and lead 32–25 after a Raemond Robinson three-pointer. The Huskers score the last seven points of the half to tie the game and calm an uneasy crowd. Miles is livid. He's somewhere between shouting and screaming in the locker room's classroom.

"They're dying to beat a team like us. You mention Citadel, which is 345th in the RPI, beating a Big Ten team? You know what that would do for them? They just blew a seven-point lead, right? They're gonna come out and believe they can win. You put them in a position to believe they can win. You cannot be tentative."

He implores them to get to the rim. To defend. To outrebound them. He doesn't want to win this game by out-talenting Citadel, which is what they did to tie the game. He wants to outplay them, outhustle them, outsmart them. Because in the Big Ten, this team won't out-talent anybody.

"We showed you the Spurs this week," Miles says. "Yet we go out and we don't do any of it. You think we're cutting tape for our health? You think it's just fun to sit there and try to find new and innovative ways to try to show you guys how to play the game the right way? . . . That ain't good enough. That's not gonna beat Citadel, Cincinnati, Iowa. That's not gonna beat [anybody]!"

He drops the volume now.

"Unless you go out there with the mentality that you're gonna fight for it every possession you're there. You be on attack, mentally on attack, doing it every play. Let's go."

The Huskers, mainly Terran Petteway, play a solid second half, but much like Northern Illinois, Western Illinois, and Arkansas State wins before this one, they simply out-talent a weaker opponent to win 77–62. Petteway finishes with twenty-seven points to carry the offense. In a game where he should have been able to clear his bench and let his scout team get some glory for most of the second half, Miles plays only nine guys. His team won't out-talent anyone else on its schedule. After the game he wants answers from his team and himself, so he goes into Miles the Elementary Education Major mode:

Miles: "Okay, guys, listen up. I think we know the lesson, but

I want to hear it from a different vantage point. David, what did you see tonight?"

David Rivers (who didn't get into the game): "Ohm, we weren't aggressive on defense."

Miles: "They were the aggressor, weren't they? Trevor."

Trevor Menke (zero minutes): "We didn't have much urgency."

Miles: "Tai."

Tai Webster (sixteen minutes, two shots, two points): "Yeah, just a little bit of, uh, I think we slacked a bit, got behind in the beginning. Got behind and let them get ahead."

Miles: "Serge?"

Sergej Vucetic (zero minutes): "Not trying to contest shots."

Miles: "Yeah, especially early. Michael?"

Mike Peltz (zero minutes): "Not as much intensity, but also on another note I think we need to have more fun. I don't think anyone, from what it looked, had much fun at all."

Miles: "Yeah, it's hard to have fun when you don't perform to your abilities, right? To your potential. And, uh, Nick, what'd you see?"

Nick Fuller (Miles has chosen to redshirt him): "Those guys really came out flat and just . . ."

Miles: "Are you doing the freshman take? Just say what I say? Listen, you guys, you know what happened. I mean, they were the aggressor. The aggressor always wins. I don't know what your mind frame was going into the game. I do know this. Any time I'm sitting in that locker room with the coaches before the game, and I come in here and I hear a lot of talking, right? I know it's a bad night. . . . This is a bad comparison, but it's a realistic one: When a soldier goes to war, when a warrior goes to battle, how do they prepare? Well, they don't sit around and chitchat with Grandma and Grandpa, right? They get quiet. They concentrate on every scenario that could happen, that might happen, that they may encounter. And when you get a team that comes in from warm-up and you're all sitting, you're all talking, regardless of what it's about, you know, it might be something about the game, but it's not a team talking mentally. It's not a team that's focusing through all scenarios they'll encounter tonight."

He stops to lock eyes with each player, even the scout-team guys in the second row. Miles and his coaches were joking and chitchatting before the game, too, which may lurk somewhere in his mind, but he's not mentioning that. He'll beat himself up later when he watches film. For now, he'll return to teaching.

"And hopefully tonight's a lesson that way, you know?" he says. "When you look at how you approach every night out, the aggressor always wins. We said that before this game. You have to play with an edge. What's our edge over our opponents? What's our edge over Cincinnati, Shavon? What's our edge over Iowa, who will be nationally ranked probably? And what's our edge over Ohio State, the No. 2 team in the country? And we damn well better figure out between now and the time we play all those guys. And the first thing it's gotta be is we gotta be together, and, like Mike says, we gotta be able to enjoy each other and play together and have fun together, but that doesn't happen unless we're all on the same page, we're all bringing the effort. It doesn't happen unless all those things happen, right?"

He pauses again, but the question is rhetorical. Players know better than to answer him, even if they have the right answer.

"That's enough. I want you guys to get a good off day; we don't get many days off. The good part about basketball, you go for months and months and months, so take some time, forget about basketball for a while, enjoy it, all right? Enjoy your time off; we know we have to come back Christmas night. I'll get you back in shape. We'll do our part to make sure we're good, but just enjoy your time with your family. Enjoy your time with whoever you're with, and just take some time off and be a kid for a while. And I don't know that I've met anybody who could possibly get in trouble over Christmas, so I think you'll stay out of trouble. . . . All right? Let's take a knee. Bring it in, Huskers. Merry Christmas break, get it in here."

Petteway: "One, two, three."

Everybody: "Merry Christmas."

Cincinnati would be waiting three days after Christmas. They were bigger, stronger, more experienced. They were supposed to win big. Then the Huskers were picked to lose their first twelve Big Ten games.

Merry Christmas.

14

Pat Schneider knows about losing. Growing up in Turton, South Dakota, he caught his right arm in a grain auger. The spiraling metal tore through bone and muscle to leave him with a stub just below the elbow and barely any bicep. He was three years old.

He attended Doland Elementary across the street from Tim Miles's house, and the two of them became quick friends. They shared a competitiveness, he remembers, that few other kids showed on the playground. In fourth grade, as Pat fought off any grief he might be getting about having a prosthetic arm, he found himself in a fight with his friend. Pat nailed Tim with a punch that knocked him to the ground, skinning his elbow. Tim popped up and returned the favor, skinning Pat's good elbow. Pat walked away to sit on the merry-go-round, where an older and bigger kid told him he wasn't welcome. Get out of here.

"And from behind me, there was Tim, sticking up for me," Pat Schneider says forty years later. "That was Tim. We'd just been in a fight, and here he is sticking up for me."

Pat shakes his head at the memory while sitting on the tailgate of his pickup on his ranch. Along with a buddy named David Troske, he and Tim grew up playing sports together, sharing rides to Clark for legion baseball games and dances on the Red Runway Bar's sunken floor. They even sank some lines in the water together, though Tim never really liked fishing. Pat and David got held back in seventh grade, but they still ran all over the county together and fought to win games for the Wheelers together.

In Tim's senior year Pat was a sub-six-foot B-teamer trying to scrounge for rebounds. The coach was Don Greenfield, a first-year coach for Tim, who played for four coaches in four years of high school. Greenfield had just finished a successful fall girls basketball season when the town's newspaperman, Tip Miles, came to the school for a visit. Greenfield feared the worst, an angry parent before the year even started, but the father pleaded with the new coach to try to have a winning season, even just a game over .500, because Tim and the other boys had never won anything in organized basketball.

The team started 1-3, and Greenfield promoted his one-armed forward to varsity, where he scrapped for every rebound and loose ball. With Corwyn Wipf running the point, Tim Miles running the baseline as a six-foot small forward, and Pat Schneider doing the dirty work, the team took off, winning its last fifteen games and the first two games at the district tournament. The Wheelers had to face Clark, the host team, in the finals for a shot at regionals. With a seven-point lead in the second half, Wipf fouled out, and the Wheelers fell behind.

Usually, when the coach wanted Tim's attention, he'd call him "Sally"—even today, he won't say why—but he didn't call him Sally this time.

"Miles," Greenfield screamed, "take control of the game."

The first-year coach wanted Miles to drive the baseline on every possession, with that quick first step of his, to blow by the bigger, slower Clark players to score or get fouled. But Tim wouldn't take over like that. He kept running the offense. Finally, he hit a fifteen-footer on the baseline to tie the game at the end of regulation. Then, in overtime, he fouled out. In the second overtime Pat Schneider got hammered just before the final buzzer. He had two free throws with the Wheelers trailing by two, though he was confused and thought they trailed by just one. He hit the first free throw but missed the second. Clark players and fans went berserk. And one player, who had been a summer baseball teammate, got picked up by a teammate in celebration.

Pat ran up to the guy and showed him the middle finger on his good hand. Then he showed that finger off to the entire Clark crowd.

"It hit pretty hard," he says now, remembering the game play for play. "I said, 'Screw this. I'm not playing baseball with those guys next summer.' Of course, Tim did."

That year Tim and Pat took a shop class with the new football coach.

"We took it as a screw-off class," Pat says.

They finished a project for the first semester, but they just talked the whole second semester as the basketball season played out and then kept screwing off into track season. With a week left in school, the teacher told Tim he wouldn't graduate if he and Pat didn't finish a project in class. They threw some one-by-sixes together, stapling them last-minute into something that looked a little like a trophy case. At Tim's graduation party Pat presented the case, cracking himself up more than Tim. The next year, when Pat finally graduated, Tim returned from Mary College with a huge, awkwardly wrapped gift.

The trophy case.

Four years later, when Pat finished a college long-jumping and triple-jumping career by graduating from Northern State, Tim gifted him that case again.

Since then they lost David to a car wreck. Pat married his high school sweetheart and started ranching with his dad. And Miles became some kind of basketball coaching phenomenon who ignored his high school coach's advice to start small with a Class B high school program, then move on to a Class A school, then maybe go back to college for a master's degree.

Instead, Miles skipped high school coaching altogether and made his way to the Big Ten in twenty-three years, rising through nearly every level of college basketball.

"Tim told me he'd replace Dean Smith at North Carolina one

day," says Greenfield from his stool in Greenie's Short Stop gas station in Clark, where he works days before opening Greenie's Tavern in Doland each night. "He said if he ever made it as a coach like that, he'd hire me to be his assistant. Don't think I haven't thrown that in his face a time or two."

Pat still texts Tim after big wins, and they get together when Miles returns to Doland.

"He's still the same guy," Pat swears, but he also swears he knows what he's giving Miles if the Huskers ever win a national championship. The trophy would look great inside that crappy class project inside Miles's $750,000 home in South Lincoln.

Dan Dakich learned basketball under Indiana University coaching legend Bob Knight. Playing with guys such as Steve Alford, Randy Wittman, and Winston Morgan in the early '80s, Dakich never averaged more than 5.6 points per game. He wasn't a Hoosier star, but he made a name for himself by harassing North Carolina's Michael Jordan all over the court in an upset win in the Sweet Sixteen in 1983 as Alford shot lights out to score twenty-seven points. Dakich stayed on with Knight as a graduate assistant after his senior year and went on to coach ten years at Bowling Green in the Mid-American Conference. He took over for Kelvin Sampson in 2007–8 as a seven-game interim coach after Sampson resigned amid allegations of recruitment violations, the low point of Hoosier basketball. Since then he'd developed into an Indiana talk radio star on ESPN 1070: The Fan and a national ESPN color analyst.

As the grad assistant coach at Indiana, Dakich's job was to soothe players after Knight berated them. His missionary trips from practice gym to locker room after Knight kicked players out of practice are well chronicled in John Feinstein's best-selling book *A Season on the Brink*. But later, as a member of the media, he gained a reputation as a hard-nosed analyst, not afraid to call out players and teams, including Indiana's beloved Hoosiers, when they played horribly. And Nebraska played horribly as Dakich watched from press row December 28 at Cincinnati.

In a pregame conversation with Miles, Dakich picked up on the coach's desire to toughen up his team mentally, and he carried that theme into his broadcast with ESPN play-by-play man Mark Neely.

The Huskers trailed by eight at halftime, as Terran Petteway sat most of the half after two quick fouls. Forward Walter Pitchford struggled shooting his three-pointers and gave up offensive rebounds. Cincinnati, the biggest and most aggressive team the Huskers had played so far, consistently drove into the lane, and if the Bearcats missed, they easily put back rebounds at the rim.

At the half Dakich broke down a Bearcat driving through the lane to go by all five Huskers, who stood straight up to watch him go by. After his teammate missed the layup, forward Justin Jackson swooped in to hammer home a rebound and dunk. No resistance.

"Tim Miles wants toughness from his team," Dakich said. "But that's not about physical toughness. It's about this."

Petteway returned to the court in the second half and started scoring on one-on-one plays, hitting shots with hands in his face or driving through multiple Bearcats to hit tough shots. He cut the lead to four right away, but Jackson posted up and missed his shot and then rebounded the miss as Pitchford stood under the basket.

"Pitchford just can't guard Jackson," Dakich told the national television audience. "You're taught in fifth grade to get between the ball and the basket. Fifth grade."

Coaches pulled Pitchford, and Leslee Smith gave up another basket to Jackson. The Huskers continued to have nonproductive possessions on offense. At one point, point guard Tai Webster threw the ball in the stands, well over Petteway and his head coach, who stood with his hands on his hips, elbows out. They couldn't replace Webster with Deverell Biggs because Miles had left Biggs at home for showing up late to a film session. But

Petteway and Ray Gallegos kept hitting three-pointers to keep the Huskers close. After Petteway created another three for himself by taking his man one-on-one and hitting the tough shot to cut the lead to 47–44 with less than ten minutes left, Dakich still wasn't impressed, hammering the Huskers for not being together as a team on either end of the court.

"Cincy has it," Dakich said. "Nebraska doesn't. They're still trying to find that."

The one-on-one play on offense caught up with Miles's team. Down fourteen points, Petteway hit a free throw, and Dakich was still talking toughness and togetherness.

"This is what I mean by a connected team," Dakich said as Petteway waited for his next free throw. "Petteway makes that first free throw and reaches back to slap hands with Webster and Gallegos, and they aren't there. It's a small thing. But connected teams do that. They always congratulate each other on free throws. Always."

Dakich had picked up on the nonverbal messages coaches had been talking about the last two months to players.

Cincinnati pushed its lead to seventeen points and wound up winning by fifteen. The Bearcats were unranked, but would make a run late in the season and make the NCAA Tournament. Losing to them on the road wasn't an embarrassment, but the coaches were embarrassed by how the team played, particularly by not competing on defense and resorting to playground basketball on offense.

"Nebraska became a stand-around team trying to score one-on-one, and that's not gonna work against Cincinnati," Dakich said in his final indictment.

When Tim Miles came to Nebraska, he guaranteed the media, the fans, and his bosses—in his first press conference in the spring of 2012—that his team may not win right away, but it would play the right way. At this point this year-two team had delivered on only the first promise. They weren't winning.

The Huskers had parked themselves at 8-4 going into the

New Year's Eve's Big Ten opener at Iowa, which was at least one game worse than where Miles figured they'd need to be. He wanted 10-2, or 9-3 at worst. Ken Pomeroy had picked them to lose big to Cincinnati, and he was right. Now, he was picking them to lose the next twelve. Miles could joke publicly all he wanted on Twitter about breaking up with Pomeroy's computer. Privately, he and his coaches had some decisions to make. Something had to give.

15

Brad Bigler showed up in 1997 at Southwest Minnesota State University in Marshall as a freshman point guard. A coach's son from Iowa, Bigler was quiet and relentless, known for battling for loose balls against quicker guys and rebounds against bigger guys. He had been offered a five-hundred-dollar scholarship by Perry Ford to play for the Mustangs.

By the time Bigler showed up for classes, Coach Ford had left town for a job at Augustana College in Sioux Falls, and Bigler found himself in a film room with the new coach, who was about the same size at less than six feet tall and 150 pounds. Everything else about Tim Miles was foreign to Bigler.

In a film session Miles started going through one of the team's first practices when Isaac Bay, a junior college transfer from Utah, smacked the teammate next to him in celebration of his basket. He started complimenting himself when Miles stopped the tape, turned around, and blasted him.

"Do you think this is a rap session? What do you think we're doing?" Miles screamed.

Bigler remembers looking around that room at all the different personalities and thinking he had gotten himself into a mess. While Bigler's dad had taught him to let his actions speak louder than his words and to keep his emotions in check and play with his brain, Miles wanted constant intensity and vocal leadership out of his point guard. Bigler played his freshman year as a backup, though he admits he wasn't ready. He fell off a ladder the next summer, hurt his wrist, and had to redshirt the next year. His sophomore and junior years he had been beaten out by the talent of other guys Miles brought into the program. The team was simply getting better. Miles brought on three Koenen brothers from Clara City, forty-five minutes northeast of town if you push it, and the two younger ones should have played NCAA Division I basketball. The Mustangs were winning. But not all the time.

Bigler remembers one of Miles's toughest losses to his nemesis, Greg McDermott, who was at Wayne State (Nebraska) at the time. Miles was so keyed up that he broke the door into the locker room at halftime by slamming it too hard. With a one-point lead and the ball with just a few seconds remaining in the game, his star, Scott Koenen, the middle brother, couldn't get the ball inbounds and simply stepped over the end line under his own basket and handed the ball to Bigler, which resulted in a turnover. Pure panic.

Wayne State inbounded the ball in the corner to its sharpshooter, Brad Jones, who waited for a Mustang defender to fly by him and then calmly hit the winning three at the buzzer for the 67–65 road win.

"The gym just went silent," said guard Jacob Fahl, who wound up being SMSU's all-time leading scorer.

The team marched to the locker room for its lashing, but couldn't get through the broken door, which refused to open after Miles's halftime slam. Last to reach the door, the coach was confused by everyone standing in the hallway.

"Miles had that look of just utter disappointment in us," Fahl says. "Man, that look. I'd hate to be his kid and get that look."

In 2001, Miles's fourth and last year at SMSU, the team started out 2-4, and the most memorable of the four losses was the championship game of the University of Wisconsin–Stout tournament against the host team, a Division III program while the Mustangs played Division II. The halftime speech was essentially, as Bigler recalls, Miles getting directly in front of each player, pointing to his chest, and telling him what he thought of his manhood in language he couldn't bring home to Doland and language Bigler couldn't repeat. The team lost by ten points.

"The next week in practice, he just killed us," Bigler says. "He broke. It started with the seniors and on down. As a player I wasn't aware of this, but he went into practice saying, "I'm going after Scott Koenen all practice.'"

Miles would ride Koenen for not hustling or for missing open teammates, anything. He'd made the decision before practice. And even though his eyes met only the chest of his six-foot-seven forward who scored eighteen points per game, he made sure Koenen looked him in the eye. Miles would even get on his tiptoes to get in that face. He would claim he may not be big, but he was "wiry tough" or "wiry strong," so Koenen had better pay attention, which made the team internally crack up and try not to show smiles. It also made them do anything to avoid being the next target. Practices ran like the printing presses back in Doland. Fifteen years later Bigler gets what his coach was doing. What he respects most about his coach is probably Miles's ability to hold players accountable, for the screwups, for their attitudes, and for their talent. Bigler refers to this skill as "calling a player's bluff."

"When you light up your best player all practice, he lights up and starts going hard, and everyone lights up," Bigler says. "For two weeks he went after Scott Koenen every day. Then others. And we went on a run."

Miles rode Koenen by design for weeks, just like he would ride Terran Petteway for his defensive errors in 2013–14. But in games he turned Koenen—and Koenen's frustrations and the collective angst of his entire team—loose on opponents. They won seventeen in a row and twenty-six of their last twenty-nine, winning the school's first Northern Sun Intercollegiate Conference title and first NCAA Division II regional to make the Elite Eight and launching Miles to his North Dakota State job, where he replaced Greg McDermott.

Jacob Fahl and Brad Bigler admit they cried the day Miles called them to his house and told them he was leaving for Fargo. Miles had helped Bigler through his parents' divorce, pulling him into a classroom when he saw his point guard about to break down in a hallway. Miles had made him a tough leader after he had been buried three deep on the bench. All those lessons would be important later, when Bigler would become a husband, a father, and the Mustangs' coach in 2009.

Bigler says he'll never be the communicator or marketer that Miles is. Heck, he can't even try to coach with Miles's style or bravado or sense of humor. Bigler is a Christian, a quiet man who has little aspiration to coach in a huge market, and claims he isn't all that interested in the high-pressure, million-dollar lifestyle of a big-time college coach. But he's found a way to use those lessons of how to hold his Southwest Minnesota State players accountable, how to show a team it can always work harder, how every win and loss matters when you're trying to win a conference title or make it to nationals. But Bigler isn't scared of losing basketball games, or even his job.

In 2011, coming off a losing season, Bigler finally relented to his mother, who had been bugging him about kayaking together. They launched at Hawk Creek near Sacred Heart, Minnesota, but not until after he told his mom that his wife, Heather, was pregnant. They hit some rapids as they turned a corner. His mom went under while being pulled down by a tree. Bigler said in an interview with ESPN that just before submerging, his mother said she didn't want to die. Bigler tried to pull her back above the surface, but couldn't. She drowned at age fifty-five. Right in front of him.

He returned to coaching three months later. And baby Drake came soon after that. Then came a win in the Northern Sun Interscholastic Conference Tournament title game, something Miles didn't even do.

Four months later, in late July, a drunk driver hit the family SUV as it was about to arrive at a lake cabin in Starbuck, Minnesota.

Brad had a bruised brain, a concussion, broken bones all over, and was in critical condition. The rest of the family was okay, but Drake didn't survive. The family said good-bye to the five-month-old boy in the emergency room while Brad was silent.

Miles had just taken the Nebraska job. He arrived in Lincoln that spring to find a home for his family, organize his office, and build a coaching staff. When he heard the news about his former point guard, he dropped everything and drove five hours to Marshall.

Bigler woke up from a painkiller-induced nap a few days after the accident to find Miles in his hospital room talking to the rest of his family.

"It meant a lot," Bigler said later. "You know, sometimes actions speak a lot more than words. He didn't have to say anything. Just his presence, being there, was uplifting. He was perfect for the moment."

Of course, Miles—the coach who had once questioned his point guard's toughness and leadership skills—said all kinds of things. He talked directly to Bigler and his wife, Heather, giving advice and offering methods of coping. He joked with Bigler. Everyone wound up laughing in a reprieve from the stress and pain.

He eventually asked Bigler how he felt.

"You know, Coach," he said through the pain meds, "I'm wiry strong."

Miles cracked up.

16

Chris Harriman is the only assistant coach who can match Miles's intensity. He celebrates harder than anyone in the gym, and he's harder on guys than anyone except his head coach. He has that glare.

The Australian came to America to play college basketball at Augusta State, a Division II school where he was a hard-nosed guard. Tough. You had to earn your points against him. He met his wife, Cheryl, there, and she was as country as they come. She followed him back to Australia, then to Fort Lauderdale, where he coached at Nova Southeastern University for Gary Tuell, who'd coached him at Augusta and became his mentor.

Through Tuell he met basketball guru Rick Majerus, who spent rare vacations from his St. Louis University job at a celebrity weight-loss clinic in Florida. Tuell and Harriman would visit him there to help him through the boredom. They talked basketball constantly. Harriman was learning.

Eventually, Majerus hired Harriman and put him through hell.

"I figured I was going there to get my basketball PhD," Harriman says. "That's how I sold it to Cheryl."

They had a two-year-old boy, Avery, and Cheryl was pregnant with their daughter, Kacee. That first year Harriman was miserable. He thought he was tough and detail oriented. But Majerus demanded perfection from his players. He never allowed the slightest "slippage," as Harriman calls it.

Majerus called out players in practice, and he called out his assistants, who were on call at all hours of the day.

"He was not afraid to embarrass you," Harriman said. "For me, you were on your toes at all times. It was the greatest thing for me. So it taught me how to do things right. If he calls you in for a meeting, you better have your recruiting calendar, you better have your schedule, or practice schedule, your recruiting list, a white notepad, to talk about stuff, a yellow notepad."

Majerus lived in a posh St. Louis hotel. He had no family with him. Only the team.

"He's relentless and it's twenty-four hours, seven days with him," Harriman says.

After surviving the year he grew to love the coach. As hard as Majerus was on his assistants, he treated coaches' wives like royalty. He regularly sent flowers and food to Cheryl, who also grew to love him. She still has notes of encouragement the coach wrote to her.

Then Avery got sick. He had leukemia. And Harriman learned

a new lesson in toughness. Through all of it, Majerus acted like a
father to Harriman, whose own family was literally half a world
away. The team rallied around Cheryl and Avery, who eventually willed his disease into remission with all the medical, family, and team support.

In his fourth year at St. Louis, Harriman had become the
longest-tenured assistant with the Billikens, now coaching along-
side Majerus and veteran coaches Jim Crews and Jim Whitesell.
Two-thirds of the St. Louis players were Harriman's recruits,
the kind of guys who would ask how Avery was doing every day.
Late in the season Majerus, who had his own health problems,
messed up his complicated dosage of medications and felt woozy
on the bus to Palumbo Center in Pittsburgh for a crucial game
against Duquesne. St. Louis needed the game to secure a spot
in the NCAA Tournament and to nab a No. 2 seed in the Atlantic 10 Conference tourney.

"Harri, you're coaching the game," Majerus said at the arena.

"Okay, Coach."

Harriman wasn't going to argue with his coach, who was a
mess, really out of it.

Majerus was rushed to a hospital, and Harriman looked at
the fifty-something assistants in the coaching office of the visitors' locker room.

"I'm not coaching the game," he said.

"Why?" Crews and Whitesell asked.

"It's disrespectful to you guys. It looks bad on you."

Harriman didn't want the tight-knit coaching world to see
that Majerus would trust the team to a young nobody of a coach
rather than these two guys, who had both already run their own
programs. Harriman had never been a head coach of anything.
But they refused to take over. The kids know you, they said.
They respect you.

"Coach the game," one of the Jims said.

"We've got your back," said the other.

Harriman walked into the locker room to tell the team that

Coach was gone, but it was only precautionary. He'd be fine, Harriman said, and Majerus would be back in a few hours.

"I'm coaching the game. Anybody have a problem with that?"

"Let's go," they yelled.

Harriman smiles at the memory.

"So I'm like, all right, here we go. This is going to go one of two ways. They're going to rally and play their ass off, or they're going to play too hard, too emotional, and lose by twenty-five."

This was the Billikens' last road game of the year, and the Dukes were having Senior Night in their gym. And they never had a chance. St. Louis won 75–60 in a game that wasn't even that close.

Duquesne fired coach Ron Everhart the next day, and when Harriman ran into him at the Atlanta airport the next year, he bought him a beer.

Harriman learned meticulous scouting from Majerus. He learned to allow no slippage. He learned every screen matters on offense and every rule of positioning on defense. He learned that if you give players a chance to say it's okay to make mistakes, then it is okay.

"But hey, it's never okay," Harriman says, imitating his mentor. "We'll do it again and again until we do it right. And every practice let's get better at one or two things. It may be overkill, but if we teach the right way, and take the time to do it right, we'll get better at those two things, rather than being okay at thirty-five things.

"No matter where I go, that's important to me as a coach," he says.

Those four years with Majerus were tough. Getting his family through Avery's leukemia was tougher. And Harriman loved those four years. He says he learned to live day to day. His motto with Cheryl was "Get through today."

Then he met Tim Miles.

After the Duquesne game the Billikens made the 2012 NCAA Tournament and then upset Memphis in the first round before getting clipped by No. 1 seed Michigan State, 65–61. At the Final Four in New Orleans, Harriman drank coffee with Porter Moser, a former colleague at St. Louis, at a sidewalk café. Here came Miles down the street, grinning in his new University of Nebraska polo. He knew Moser, so he stopped outside the short fence enclosing the café tables.

"I need some assistants," Miles eventually said, "and I have the money to get really good guys."

Harriman leaned over the fence and stuck out his hand.

"I'm sorry, can I introduce myself? I'm Chris Harriman."

They met two days later in a hotel for coffee. The meeting was supposed to last thirty minutes. Instead, they talked for more than two hours and forgot to order coffee. Harriman didn't mind the coach's frenetic pace, his philosophies all over the map, his constant texting and tweeting. He learned that this guy made it to the Big Ten, Harriman's favorite conference, the gentlemen's conference, filled with gentleman coaches at historic universities. And he'd not made it because of his connections, because he had been in the North Carolina coaching tree, or had played fifteen years in the NBA. Miles had earned the job by turning around programs as a tough, small-school guy. Harriman could relate, and he wanted to learn how to do that.

The problem was Cheryl, who adored Majerus and the doctors and restaurants in St. Louis.

The problem was Majerus, who had taught him everything he knew and trusted him with his team.

Telling Majerus was the toughest thing Harriman ever had to do, outside of Avery's leukemia. Majerus said he understood the decision, but he didn't know Miles, what kind of coach he'd be. And he said Harriman had better be sure, because there would be no coming back to St. Louis. Harriman understood what this really meant. If he was in Majerus's inner circle, he was like a son. But if he left, he would be shut out of the coach's life, as past assistants had been. That was just the way the man worked.

Harriman came to Nebraska to visit. Saw the facilities. Ran

some drills. He ate three orders of pizza rolls and washed them down with beer at Old Chicago on P Street in Lincoln before he got the offer from Miles. And he took it without waiting for Cheryl's consent. He called her.

"I took it," he said sheepishly.

"Oh, yeah?" she said.

"Are you coming with me?"

"Uh, we'll talk about it."

Cheryl had been doing her own homework on Miles. She knew he had kids, and that was important. Maybe Harriman wouldn't have to work all night, every night, if the coaches all had kids. But she had to be convinced that the Lincoln and Omaha hospitals could help Avery if his leukemia reappeared. On a smaller note, did it have good restaurants? She drove with the kids from St. Louis. Between Kansas City and Lincoln, on Highway 2, she called Harriman in a panic.

"What have you done?" she screamed into her cell phone. "Where am I? There's nothing but cornfields. What are we going to do?"

She was going to come. She'd been watching and rewatching Miles's press conference on YouTube when he took the job. She wanted to know if she could trust her family to him, just as she trusted Majerus. Eventually, she decided she trusted him.

That was important. Because on October 27, right before Miles's first season was to start, Avery went to the Children's Hospital and Medical Center in Omaha to meet with an oncologist for a checkup and to have his port taken out that fed him his medicine. On the way home to Lincoln, they got a call from the oncologist. Avery had relapsed. He would need a bone-marrow transplant. The Harrimans would have to fight again, during the season.

"Tough day," Chris Harriman told the Big Ten Network when it came to feature his family on *The Journey*. "You've been through the fight and struggle and felt like you beat it. It was really tough. We didn't know where to turn."

He didn't have to reach out to find help.

"People just came out of the woodwork here," Harriman says.

Tom Osborne's wife stood by Cheryl's side through it all. And current athletic director Shawn Eichorst's wife helped, too. Then football defensive coordinator John Papuchis's wife. All the assistant coaches' wives came together for Cheryl. Even Creighton coach Greg McDermott was instrumental in getting the Harrimans in contact with Omaha doctors and experts.

Chris watched film overnight from Avery's Omaha hospital bed. He scouted teams there and looked for slippage in Husker practices.

Avery pulled through to beat the cancer again in what Harriman called a community effort.

"Yeah," Harriman says a year later, "my wife loves it here now. It's the people."

And Miles was different from anybody he'd ever been around. His philosophies differed from Majerus's, and Harriman was getting his second PhD. This time in converting a culture of losing. Of having fun while he was doing it. More important, he could trust Miles with his family.

Miles learned, too.

"Life is how you handle it," Miles told the BTN cameras. "And watching how the Harriman family handled it, their strength, was amazing."

17

In January of that first season in Nebraska, as the Huskers suffered loss after loss, ESPN ran a story called "Bigler's Way," which chronicled Brad Bigler's multiple tragedies and how he coped with them through faith and reaching out to people. While that moved viewers across the country, the Huskers were helping Harriman get through Avery's illness. And Miles had life-and-death issues of his own.

A few months earlier Miles answered his door on Halloween

to find Dr. Richard Thompson, a cardiologist who had graduated from Columbia University and Duke, out trick-or-treating with his kids. Miles wanted to talk with Thompson about his father. Tip, eighty-six, needed open-heart surgery because a valve wasn't working and he had blockage everywhere, but he was refusing to undergo the surgery his family doctor and cardiologist had been saying was inevitable.

"My brother had done a triple bypass," Tip says. "He told me the cemetery didn't look too bad after going through open-heart surgery, so I was scared of it."

The family was also scared that he refused. Miles brought his parents down for a house call in his living room from Dr. Thompson. Eventually, the doctor said a double bypass, valve replacement, and pacemaker implant were dangerous, but essential. At Thanksgiving Tip called a family meeting and wanted everyone's opinion.

"We told Dad," Miles's older brother Kevin says, "'Do you want to live for three months, or do you want to live to see Tim win a national championship?'"

Tim worried he had talked his father into a surgery he might not survive. He had Catholic guilt about it, his brother Kevin and sister Karin said, and he had his mother's pessimism on top of that. He was a wreck after his dad's surgery. The Huskers had lost their first five Big Ten games before freshman Shavon Shields scored twenty-nine to beat Penn State on the road by four. With Tip unconscious on a respirator in the recovery room from the Monday-night surgery he might not survive, Illinois came to town Tuesday. For the first time in his career, Miles didn't want to coach a basketball game.

Dr. Thompson told the family that Tip's was the most difficult surgery of his career. Tim's siblings, wife, and mother took turns at Tip's bedside at Bryan East in Lincoln. He was unconscious for a long stretch and then intentionally tranquilized into sleep because he would rage whenever he woke up, pulling in a panic at wires that kept him alive.

Illinois won by twenty points over the home team.

In March that year the Big Ten Network's program *The Journey* ran a story on Miles and his father, and in the interview Miles cried, explaining that his father asked him to solve his problem, and when Tip didn't come out of the surgery right away in perfect condition—his heart, his health, his smile—Miles thought he'd failed him. He could solve problems on and off the court for his teams. He'd had players in all kinds of trouble, whether they had put themselves in the path of the train or been put there by others. But his dad's health was out of the coach's control.

On the fourth day after the surgery, Tip opened his eyes and couldn't muster speech, but he was calm and locked eyes with Karin, his oldest child. She asked him if he knew who she was.

Tip nodded.

She guided Alyce up to the bed and asked Tip if he knew who she was.

Tip nodded again.

Then she pointed to Tim, his baby boy who had more than seventy thousand followers on Twitter, the selfie king of Nebraska, and asked the same question.

Tip looked confused.

Karin took her little brother out into the hallway, preparing a strategy to keep her brother from losing any kind of hope. When they got to the elevator, Tim turned to her.

"This is great," he said of his father's apparent amnesia. "I'm going to rewrite my history. I'm going to tell him I was a straight-A student. I'm going to tell him I won championships."

Kevin swears to this day that Tip, who can't remember much of any of this moment, just didn't want people asking him any more questions and four days after life-threatening surgery wanted to pull a prank on Tim to keep him in his place.

Tim's wife, Kari, a physical therapist, put up Tip and Alyce in their home. She forced Tip to do his exercises, and by the time the Huskers played Iowa a month after surgery, Tip was behind the bench in a wheelchair.

The Huskers upset the Hawkeyes 64–60 when guard Dylan Talley nailed a twenty-five-foot three-pointer right over a defender. With 2.9 seconds left in the game, *Lincoln Journal Star* photographer Ted Kirk captured a shot of Miles directing his defense to get back, while Tip shows an I-cheated-death smile behind his son and the Gatorade water cooler.

Miles knew about losing games and was closing on 250 losses in his career. He had seen Brad Bigler lose his mother and baby son. He'd seen the Harrimans almost lose their boy. Losing was his mentor. But he hadn't lost his father.

Miles gave a framed print of Kirk's last-second photo to Tip for Father's Day.

Tim Miles was never more scared of losing his job than he was after losing seven of his first nine games his third year at North Dakota State University in 2003–4. His athletic director, Gene Taylor, hadn't hired him, but he was supportive, to the point that after Miles's second year, he wanted to extend Miles's contract three more years. The real issue was that the school had decided to move from NCAA Division II to Division I. Miles refused, saying they could figure it out after the season.

When he got the news that the Bison were moving up to the toughest competition in college basketball, Miles called every coach in his phone for advice.

"They all said it was a death sentence," he said. He would lose and lose and lose. Miles had come through on that prophecy. He told *Fargo Forum* sportswriter Jeff Kolpack he surely was going to be fired. He called Craig Smith, who was coaching at Mayville State, to say he thought Taylor was going to move him into some administrative role.

Smith argued with Miles. "No, you're a coach. You're going to win."

And he was right. The team reeled off a school record eleven straight wins and finished the season at 16-13. Miles got his contract extension from Taylor.

But Miles was more scared at 2-7 that season than any other point in his career, even more than he would be at Colorado State. And Smith claims Miles had good reason to be scared at Colorado State. After many players left and others had to be kicked off that first year in Fort Collins, the team was in trouble with the NCAA. Schools are graded for academics by a system called the Academic Progress Rate, or APR, which rewards schools for keeping players eligible and retaining them in school. For every student-athlete who fails in the classroom or transfers, the program takes a hit. The Rams, through attrition and player scandal, lost three scholarships in two years.

Smith was an operations guy in Miles's first year at CSU, when the team went 0-16 in the Mountain West Conference, but won the miracle game in the eight-versus-nine play-in game at the conference tournament over Wyoming, which Smith calls the Toilet Bowl. But in the second year, still suffering from scholarship loss and trying to build a program, Miles lost 71–67 to Air Force, a team that hadn't won a conference game, in the same play-in game. Embarrassing. Miles cried in the shower after that game. Year two at Colorado State had been worse than year one, when he was winless in the conference. He'd finished by losing the Toilet Bowl.

"People always remember the good times," Smith says. "People don't understand how dire that time was, how dire that situation was. They forget the heavy lifting involved to get players in. Not only was our roster depleted. Then the APR. The scholarships. Then we lost to two Division II schools at home. Man, it was brutal."

After that first season, though, CSU athletic director Paul Kowalczyk gave Miles an extension. Miles told his boss to call it a do-over, not an extension. And after he got out of that postgame shower at the Thomas & Mack Center—losers of the play-in game of the Mountain West Conference Tournament—thirty-year equipment manager Mike Biggs put his hand on the coach's shoulder and said the wins would come. And they did.

Again, Miles claimed losing to be his mentor, his motivator. At Nebraska he'd won his 300th game, but he was also closing in on 250 losses in his career. They were piling up like Tetris blocks.

After the Cincinnati loss, the Huskers were beaten soundly at No. 22 Iowa, 67–57, on New Year's Eve. They trailed by twenty in the second half before cutting the lead to five, but came no closer. Five nights later third-ranked Ohio State blew them out, 84–53, in a game that felt like the Creighton loss. Ohio State guard Aaron Craft led a 7–0 run at the end of the first half to give the Buckeyes a ten-point lead, and osu kept the hammer down to the final buzzer, outscoring the Huskers 44–23 in the second half.

On January 9 Nebraska finally got to play at home, and though Michigan wasn't ranked at the time, the Wolverines were loaded, with three guys who would be drafted by the NBA six months later. The team would eventually make it to the Elite Eight in the tournament before getting clipped by Kentucky.

Kevin Miles came down from Sioux Falls, South Dakota, for the game, and wound up watching it over and over at his little brother's house over Coors Lights long after the last buzzer went off. What the brothers saw was a team that could play with Michigan's speed and length. Michigan freshman Derrick Walton hit a half-court shot to give the Wolverines a 33–30 halftime lead. But every time Michigan built the lead to five or six points, Deverell Biggs would make a play, or Terran Petteway. Guard Ray Gallegos was hitting his threes and hit his fourth with 4:32 remaining to tie the game at 63–63. The Pinnacle Bank Arena fans, even those who could afford lower-level season tickets, were on their feet each time Michigan coach John Beilein called a time-out.

Miles switched to Kenya Hunter's Georgetown zone and packed up the middle. Leslee Smith blocked Michigan center Jordan

Morgan at the hoop on a fast-break layup, swatting the ball out of bounds. The crowd erupted again.

Petteway and Nik Stauskas traded hoops before Petteway put back his own miss to tie the game again, and Ray Gallegos stole the ball from Stauskas to lead to two Petteway free throws.

"In pressure situations, Terran never misses," Smith said later. Petteway made the first shot for a 70–69 lead with a minute left, but front-rimmed the second shot.

Walton, who had hit the half-court shot, then drove from the right side to put up a wild shot, running over Leslee Smith. ESPN announcer Sean Farnham said Smith arrived too late, but Miles's family, particularly Alyce and Tip, went nuts in the stands. Craig Smith would say later that the call would be a charge nine times out of ten. But the real issue was that Petteway, whom Miles calls his emotional perfectionist, was frustrated with himself for missing the free throw and forgot the team was in a zone, and Walton took advantage. The shot fell in for a 71–70 Michigan lead with 21.8 seconds left, and Smith got called for the blocking foul. Then Walton missed the free throw.

With 9.3 seconds left Miles called time-out and drew up the play that had worked all night, his "chin action." He put his best scorer, Petteway, on the left side of the court and had Leslee Smith, his biggest body, set the screen. Petteway blew through three Michigan defenders, as he had all night, but he couldn't get deep enough into the lane, and he had to lift a long scoop toward the rim. Leslee Smith rolled to the basket from the left and charged up over two Wolverines to tip the miss, but it also bonked off the rim before the buzzer sounded.

Michigan 71, Nebraska 70.

"It was just really more disappointing for the players than anybody," Craig Smith said. "But personally, after doing all the scouting and prep work for Michigan, I knew how good they were. I, frankly, thought we outplayed them. It gave me confidence in our team that with a tweak or two, we could be pretty good."

Miles's boss was quietly ecstatic, too. Athletic director Shawn

Eichorst had seen nearly every big basketball venue in the country, and he liked what he saw from both the team and the crowd.

"You know, there was a grittiness in some ways to our approach," he said. "To see the fans respond and connect with the team like that, and how electric it was . . . I was like, 'Wow, this place could be really electric.'"

Especially if the team had won, which it hadn't. As much as Miles answered the mentor question with "losing," he more often was asked about his goals for his team, and that answer was "winning." What did he want from a holiday tournament? "To win." What did he want in year two? "To win." What did he want to do at Nebraska? "To win."

Now, the team was 0-3 in the Big Ten. It needed a win. And Purdue wouldn't give it to them on a Sunday afternoon. In West Lafayette, Indiana, Tai Webster stole the ball and scored a layup, followed by a Petteway free throw to give the Huskers a 58–55 lead with six minutes remaining. But Purdue's veteran guards took over from there, and the Boilermakers won, 70–64, in Mackey Arena. Ronnie Johnson got through the lane repeatedly to score fourteen points, and center A. J. Hammonds owned the lane to score eighteen. Worse, the team crumbled in the final minutes when it had a shot to win a Big Ten road game. With a team that wanted to establish a gaudy home record and win when it could on the road, the game was a missed opportunity.

At 0-4 in the Big Ten, the season was starting to feel like Colorado State year two all over again for Miles and assistant Craig Smith. The schedule had worked against the Huskers and wouldn't get any better. They were fulfilling stat guru Ken Pomeroy's prophecy, losing game after game. And Ohio State was coming to town next, to kick off another month of being picked to lose every game.

Assistant coach Craig Smith calls Tim Miles a basketball-coaching machine. Always selling the program. Always devising a play that exposes an opponent's weakness. Always playing with team chemistry. Always trying to solve problems. But sometimes the coach can crack.

As a graduate student at Northern State in Aberdeen, South Dakota, he met Kari, a sprinter who grew up in Aberdeen. Their first dance was to the B52s' "Love Shack," and she says she knew right away that he was going somewhere in coaching, probably big-time college basketball or the NBA. They married while Miles started his coaching career at Mayville State. The couple planned a weekend night reception in Aberdeen over the Christmas holiday in 1996. Afterward, Miles joined his best friend, David Troske, for a beer at a local bar. Troske was the kind of guy who would start a story, accidentally knock his glasses down into his beer, return them to his face, and finish his story without wiping them off or even pausing. The punch line mattered more.

Three nights later Troske died on the highway between Aberdeen and Doland in his Honda compact. He'd forgotten his gloves in a blizzard and tried turning around to get them at home near Turton when a white semitruck hit him.

Miles still remembers getting the call in his Mayville apartment that day after Christmas, which was also Troske's father's birthday.

"I just sobbed forever," he says. "I remember seeing him in his coffin as a pallbearer. We were in our late twenties. . . . I remember just feeling like life was so fragile."

But Mayville had road games to play. They ate their Hardee's specials on the way to the Black Hills to lose 67–64 in overtime to South Dakota Tech and face Black Hills State the next night. Smith says Miles loved beating teams like that, especially schools that had turned him down for jobs before Mayville took a chance on him. Those schools included the University of Mary, his alma mater, a job he really wanted more than any other. He even got turned down by Miles Community College in Miles City, Montana. Miles tells that story when he needs to prove how far he's come as a coach. That story's punch line: "I mean, are you kidding me? That job had my name written all over it."

He'd told Smith that Black Hills State was a pretty place with resources, a place where you could recruit, unlike Mayville. At that point in his career, he considered the Yellow Jackets a great NAIA job, where he could win on a national level.

Black Hills was ranked eighteenth in the NAIA national rankings at the time and had a center Mayville couldn't handle, but the lead changed hands all night. In the end the center hit a hook shot with two seconds left for the win.

Miles and Smith followed the Comet team into a long hallway that led to the locker room.

"I look over at Coach, and he's killing himself, pulverizing himself, so pissed at himself," Smith says. "It was a combination of that game and everything prior to that. Usually, he's so good at fighting through all that stuff. Not letting stuff get to him. I remember thinking, 'He's human. Not a machine.'"

When he has to deal with what he calls "personal stuff," his mind drifts in the office. He thinks too much. He plays out worst-case scenarios—for his dad's surgery, for Chris Harriman's family, for the Troske family—which his brother Kevin says comes from growing up in the Catholic Church and his mother's home.

Alyce Miles's philosophy may have been to fear the worst. But Miles had many philosophers in his journey to the Big Ten. At Northern State, when he was a graduate assistant, his athletic director was Jim Kretchman, who used to say, "The three biggest demotivators in life are fear, worry, and doubt. How you manage those will determine how successful you become."

Miles also coached at North Dakota State with current Jacksonville Jaguars coach Gus Bradley, who was then the defensive coordinator for the Bison football team. In Bradley theory the worst thing coaches can do is create anxiety, especially about things they can't control. Instead, they apply pressure toward a high goal that's attainable.

"Any time I feel something is out of my control, of course, I'm a mess," Miles says.

With a winless team in the Big Ten, Miles could use some philosophy. Or a new way of thinking about his own philosophies. Or maybe even a new philosopher.

18

Jon Gordon thinks of himself as a problem solver. Nebraska athletic director Shawn Eichorst thinks of Gordon as a positivity maven.

Gordon lives in Florida, where he writes books, creates online content, and hits the road to speak to business and sports entities about changing cultures. Eichorst is a fan of Gordon's book *The Energy Bus*, in which Gordon lays out his philosophies of organizational connectivity and the dreaded "energy vampire," who can suck all the positivity and connectivity out of a group. While Gordon is an outgoing, emotional pep talker, Eichorst is a reserved, deliberate, constantly calculating leader. Don't invite either man to a poker game. Gordon will distract you from your cards, and Eichorst will never show his, to a fault. He's a lawyer and gets criticized by local media for being too quiet. Area journalists have complained that he sometimes takes days to answer reporters' questions and at times answers them only via e-mail through his associate athletic director for community relations. As different as Gordon and Eichorst are in practice, their philosophies about running programs are nearly identical. So much so that Eichorst bought *The Energy Bus* for all his staff at the Husker Athletic Department, and without knowing his men's basketball team would return to Lincoln reeling at 0-4 on Sunday, January 13, he hired Jon Gordon to speak to all Husker athletes Sunday night and then meet with coaches Monday morning.

Gordon challenged athletes to give more of themselves and be better teammates.

Gordon's comments fed Miles's maxim that you don't win until you win the locker room first.

After the second talk Miles went directly to Gordon to break down the message, to apply it to his team. Part of the reason he sought out Gordon is obvious: anything for an edge. But Miles also knew Gordon had worked successfully with Chris Harriman and Rick Majerus at the University of St. Louis, and his friend Gus Bradley, the National Football League (NFL) coach, had used Gordon the previous year when he had an 0-8 team. The Jaguars went 4-4 in the second half of the season. At 0-4 in the Big Ten, going .500 in the remaining conference games seemed pretty unlikely.

Gordon had a lunch scheduled with the athletic director, who invited his basketball coach to join them. The three of them talked more about connectivity. They talked about the players about whom Miles was most concerned and what to do with them.

"Tim is very driven and seems to want to do whatever it takes to win in a positive way," Gordon would say later. "He was willing to sit down with me at lunch, and that was great. One of the things about the great coaches is they want to get better. The great ones want to get better."

The stat guru, Pomeroy, had said his numbers are useful only if a coach can analyze them to turn them into strategy and action. The positivity guru, Gordon, said his work is useful only if a coach can reinforce and embody the philosophy—take it beyond happy talk—and carry it through every practice, every game, and every interaction with his team. "Live and breathe it."

Assistant coach Craig Smith said Jon Gordon's visit, and that lunch, may have changed the season.

Miles held no practice the day of the lunch. Then he flew to Texas and Wichita to recruit Tuesday, while players had individual meetings and workouts with assistants.

By Wednesday he's itching to go. He has a plan that includes numbers and philosophy and basketball, and he hasn't shared it with his coaches. Ohio State is coming to the Pinnacle Bank Arena in five days with a three-game losing streak and will be ready to destroy his Huskers if they don't make some changes right now. But first, he has an announcement. Assistant Chris Harriman's wife, Cheryl, has just given birth to a baby girl. Miles has a scholarship certificate for Elsie Louise. Harriman scoots around the players to grab the framed document.

"That's binding. What year is she?" Miles says.

"She'll be 2032," Harriman answers.

"So track us all down and make sure the money's there. Good luck."

Miles smiles at Harriman all the way back to his seat. Then he uses a closed-mouth smile on his team, locking eyes with each of them, making them wait for what would come next.

"First of all, everybody saw Jon Gordon on Sunday night, right? Raise your hand."

His eyes move to forward David Rivers in the second row.

"You didn't?"

"I did. I just didn't raise it in time."

"I got you. Okay. Hey, man, it's okay. I got issues, too."

In a way, that's his message today: We've got issues. I've got them, and Lord knows you've got them. But Miles has chosen to start in elementary teacher mode today and asks his players about their thoughts on Jon Gordon. Rivers has singled himself out by not raising his hand, so he's being picked on first.

Nothing.

Miles doesn't wait long for an answer, as usual. He starts talking about Gordon's influence on the Jacksonville Jaguars. Maurice Jones-Drew, the Jaguars' veteran running back, who was an all-pro in 2011 and had played on winning teams, said the 4-12 season was his favorite year of professional football. In other words, this could be a defining moment if we want a defining moment. We need one.

"So, what did you take from it?"

"They had us write down three things," says cocaptain Terran Petteway, who was leading the team in scoring. "I wrote, 'Make every day a quest to get better. Wake up every day to challenge yourself in some aspect.'"

"Leslee?"

"Stay positive," Leslee Smith says. "I think most of it is staying positive and being a good teammate and stuff like that."

"Mike?"

"A lot of it was about your overall perspective," says Peltz, his senior from western Nebraska, who hadn't played much lately. "How you view . . ."

"What is your perspective?"

"Try to do your best. Be the best person you can be. Don't get too low or too high. Because there's always going to be ups and downs. It related to a lot of things, basketball included."

"Family. Basketball. Work."

"So, David?"

"One that stood out to me was staying connected as a team. That was good," Rivers says.

"Are we on the high end or low end of being connected during games?"

"At the beginning of the season it was pretty low, but I think we've been much better," Rivers says.

Miles pulls his lips into his mouth and then bulges out his cheeks by filling them with air. He isn't so sure he agrees with David Rivers. They have lost five straight.

"So, we're improving?"

Scout-team center Kye Kurkowski says he liked how Gordon has lived his positive philosophy, rather than just "going around talking about his stupid theories." He relays Gordon's story about being a negative thirty-year-old, which almost cost him his marriage and kids. His wife had threatened to leave him. So he stopped complaining about everything.

"Did he tell you complaining is like puking?" Miles says. "Makes you feel better but stinks for everybody else?"

Miles asks everyone in the front row to speak. Walter Pitchford. Deverell Biggs. Ray Gallegos.

"What did he call a negative person, Ray?"

"An energy vampire."

"What is that to you, Sergej?"

"Someone who sucks energy from the team. Cannot help. Don't screw your team."

Sergej Vucetic is his seven-foot center from Serbia who won't play any meaningful minutes this year. But Miles is bringing out this core concept through Sergej, who sits in the second row. Miles is looking at Sergej, but he's being direct with everyone, some more than others. Between them, in the front row, sits Deverell Biggs.

"Yeah, you ever play with an energy vampire? Any of our guys energy vampires at times? Be honest. Because I'm going to say yes."

"Yeah, sometimes."

"Okay," Miles says. "That's very politically correct. Maybe sometimes."

Miles puts two fingers, like the peace sign, over his mouth. He does this gesture so often in games that his son, Gabe, has developed a serviceable impression of it. The Thinker pose.

After a few seconds, Petteway speaks up again.

"I like at the end, when he said his family picked a word at the end of every year of what they like to work to get good at."

Gordon then had asked the athletes to pick a word that would be their focus for improvement.

"I picked mine to be *attitude* to change things in basketball and in life," Petteway says.

Miles is big on credos. He has molded his own since his early coaching days with Bortke, Kretchman, and Bradley. He's had nine core concepts, then eleven, and for this team he's shaved them to four. They show up on posters in the locker room, whiteboard game plans, and social media. Attitude fits in well with Miles's credos.

"That was good," he says to Petteway. "That was my word, too."

He asks a few more players for their words, but he's ready to move back to attitude and to his next step in the dance.

"Yeah, I thought about the one-word thing, and we've got the four [Colorado State] Rams principles, and the first one is attitude. If I have an attitude that craves improvement. And Tai, if I just commit to you that I'm going to come in every day to make our team better. I'm going to try to work harder than I'm already working every day. I'm going to try to outdo myself every day. Do you think I'd be a better coach?"

His freshman point guard, Tai Webster, nods.

"All right. Can you make the same commitment to me? Can you have the same attitude that says 'Every day I'm going to try to outwork myself to be a better player'?"

Webster nods again, but that's not good enough for Miles, who needs his freshman to start taking over the team.

"You have to verbalize this."

"Yes."

"Okay. Could you also make the commitment to say that 'I will work harder to be a better teammate'? What more would we need to be successful? Because if I just said, 'Chris [Harriman], I want you to outwork yourself for the betterment of the team. All right? Be a better coach. Just find a way to be a better coach for this team and work harder than you did yesterday.' . . . As a player I would ask you to just outwork yourself every day to get better and make our team better, but also I'm going to be a better teammate."

He pauses to look around the room. His hands are on his hips, over the bottom of his red Husker polo and his gray Husker sweats.

"I can't think of one negative thing that would happen if we just simply picked that one word, *attitude*, and just say, 'My attitude is I'm going to outwork myself from yesterday, and at the same time my attitude toward my teammates is going to be that I'm going to be a better teammate than I was yesterday.' If we all do that and we all commit to that, all right, we should be in good shape. When I think to myself, it's honestly that simple."

He tells the team that every time he's on them, every time he's asking something of them in practice or games, he's just asking them to be better than the day before. For that to happen today, they're going to blow off the Purdue game video. Instead, what's important is attitude. He asks them to agree that *attitude* is going to be the key word for the team. He points at every player and makes them audibly agree with a "Yes."

Then he points up to the third row of coaches: "How about you bastards?"

The team cracks up as the coaches say "Yes."

Miles launches into an ESPN *Sportscenter*-style highlight package of his lunch with the athletic director and Jon Gordon from two days ago.

"So, what's the problem with the team?" Gordon had asked.

We lost five in a row.

"That's not the problem," Gordon said. "What's the problem with the team?"

We're young, immature, undisciplined. We're not always together. We get mad at a teammate, and it costs us a possession here, a possession there. If our team chemistry is on a one to ten scale, we started at a two, and now we're a five.

"It needs to be a ten," Gordon said. "You're in the best league in the country. You're young. If you're not a ten, you have no chance. So the process has to be most important to you. Don't worry about losses or mistakes. The process of team chemistry is more important. If you're not a ten when you're young in this league, you're not going to be successful."

He lets that sit for a second. Then he turns to cocaptain Shavon Shields in the front row: "So the most important thing is the connection to each other and the trust in each other. What does *unconditional* mean, Shavon?"

Shields: "No terms come with it."

Miles: "No terms. Your sister. Something goes wrong. Say

she's in drug rehab. She's pregnant with the wrong guy. How do you feel about her?"

Shields: "I still love her."

Miles: "Yeah. You're mad. You're upset. What's going on? But you accept her. You're going to try to help her any way you can, right? Same thing, you know?"

Then he looks over the entire team.

"Well, we're different because we're not brothers," he said. "We're not brothers, but we have to act like brothers."

He launches into a war metaphor about how soldiers build foxholes. He mentions *Saving Private Ryan, Lone Survivor,* and *Zero Dark Thirty.*

"Have you guys ever seen a war movie? What, are you just playing Candy Crush all the time?"

Miles says there's always a point in these movies, and in life, when guys have to trust each other. Then he explains his version of the term *fragging* while drawing foxholes on the whiteboard.

"If there was somebody they didn't trust in the platoon, that they thought was going to get them killed, they'd let him lead one mission out. You know what they'd do when they got out there? They'd shoot him in the back and kill him. They'd rather kill their own than trust somebody they knew they couldn't trust. . . . The Mafia, the Mob, used to do that. Soldiers used to do that. It was life or death. That guy can't be trusted. Send him out. Bang. Got no problems now. Addition by subtraction. 'I don't know what happened. Sniper got him,' you know?

"Look, we're a young team. We're picked last in the league. We've worked our way to where now? We're last. Tied with Penn State. So, we worked our way right down to where they said we were gonna be. Is that good enough for you?"

He says a tough schedule is no excuse. Two games, Michigan and Purdue, were right there for them in the final minutes—if they had trusted each other and executed.

"I'd say our number-one issue on our team is . . . ," Miles writes the next two words on the white board, "*togetherness uncondi-*

tionally. It that spelled right? I won't worry about it. Does anybody disagree with that?"

The theme is clear. We're not a team. What he doesn't include yet in his *Sportscenter* highlights from his lunch with Gordon and the athletic director are the epiphanies that came to him when discussing individual players. But that will work its way into this speech, too. First, he wants to back up the theoretical framework of his plea with numbers. He wants to show how unconditional togetherness translates into a formula for winning, or how a lack of it is a formula for losing, mathematically. Again, men lie, women lie, but numbers don't lie, even though sometimes they do.

"Let's look at where we are right now," he says.

He hands out an eight-and-a-half-by-eleven-inch sheet of white paper he's annotated in four colors. The sheet is gridded up on two sides with tables from a Teddy Owens database.

"This is a huge math thing," he says as they pass the papers through the rows, "and not even someone in the actuary department can figure out all this math, but I'm going to talk you through it, okay?"

Some players scoot down in their chairs, while others, including all coaches, lean forward into the sheets, looking for their names and numbers. The front side is an "Individual Offense Review," and the back is a "Team Defensive Summary." On the offense sheet, he's highlighted three troubling categories in yellow: effective field-goal percentage, field-goal percentage on two-point jumpers, and percentage of two-point jumpers. He's highlighted four other categories in pink and one in orange. He's also made notes in red pen and red Sharpie. All of these categories are what Ken Pomeroy and other Miles-approved basketball economists believe are crucial to scoring efficiently. They're more important than raw shooting percentages and assist totals that matter to the general public and old-school coaching staffs.

These numbers show him that his Huskers aren't taking enough shots that they're good at making. They shoot 64 percent when they are within three feet of the rim. They shoot 34 percent from behind the three-point line, which translates to 51 percent when you consider the extra point per make. But in two-point jumpers his team shoots just 30 percent, 6 percentage points below the national average. Worse, they take 6 percent more shots from that range than the national average. In other words, you take too many shots you can't shoot well. Get to the rim or shoot the three, where you're better or at the national average, but avoid contested two-point shots, where you're terrible.

"I would tell you most of those shots happen early in offense, by the way," the coach says. "Taking a quick, bad shot just by driving. Tai, you're picking the ball up too early. What's your percentage, Tai? The yellow column all the way down."

Tai Webster: "16.7."

"What's yours, Dev?"

Deverell Biggs: "28.6."

"Yeah, our two point guards are 17 percent and 29 percent in twos. Is that good offense or not?"

They both say "No" and look back down to their sheets, but only after the coach does the same.

Another example Miles mentions: When Terran Petteway couldn't get to the rim for his last-second shot at home against Michigan and scooped the ball from five feet, he wasn't giving himself enough of a chance. The percentages weren't good, at 36 percent, which is what he shoots in that category. And the shot was contested by three guys. Leslee Smith, of course, had a tip-in at the rim, where his are a meteoric 80 percent, though he still missed. And they lost a big opportunity.

"I am going to tell you this," he says. "If we're average in our league, Nate, how are we going to be? What number is our league in the country out of thirty-two conferences?"

Freshman Nate Hawkins: "Number one."

"One," Miles says. "So if we're just average as Division I, is that good enough?"

He doesn't wait for an answer, because that's not the worst of the news here. Miles argues that these two-pointers are mainly contested jump shots or drives into the lane when his perimeter players take on three bigger players and miss. His proof is that less than 24 percent—11 percent below the national average—of those two-pointers come off of an assist. In fact, the team is in the bottom 10 of the 349 NCAA Division I teams in assists.

"So what does that tell you?" he asks, getting louder now. "I already wrote it down for you [in red pen at the top]. It's a lot of 'hero basketball.' A lot of one-on-one hero basketball. What's the number-one problem on our team? Togetherness. For us, you can relate that to shot selection on the floor. Are we together? Do we trust?"

Webster, Biggs, and Petteway all have more turnovers than assists. And Miles reminds them of that now, before summing up the offensive findings.

"That's what our offense is right now," he says. "Can you guys see that and see the math of it right there? Is there any confusion on this? Create for your teammates. Nobody's driving to create. All right, flip it to the back page."

On to the defense, with two spreadsheets marked up in pink and yellow highlighter, with circles in red pen over the most egregious numbers. He also has hand-drawn a third chart.

His takeaway is that his team does a good job of forcing many two-point shots, but they don't contest them well enough, and opponents are making them.

"So why are they making them?" he asks. "Are we not contesting well enough? Is it that's what's available because of a breakdown because we didn't switch up? Or we got lost or confused, or our screen-and-roll defense wasn't good enough? Why are opponents so far ahead of us?"

The numbers are becoming brain scalding for the players. And he's losing some of them. A few have hands on their heads. Most are almost lying down in their seats.

"Now, here's something that really stumped me," he says, pointing his finger to a category called "Start of Possession."

"When we shoot and miss, those numbers aren't terrible. Look at what happens when we score: when we score, their numbers are better. They don't shoot as many, but their numbers are better."

On almost every kind of shot, at almost any point in the possession, opponents shoot higher percentages after the Huskers score than when they don't. Conventional wisdom suggests they would get more easy drives and baskets after misses, especially long misses or bad misses. But the numbers show the opposite.

"Why are we letting down after makes?" he asks. "You know what I would tell you? It's discipline. It's attitude. 'I just scored. I can relax a little bit.' What are we thinking? A dominant mentality gets stops every time. . . . But there's something in our mentality that really lacks after we score. Do we understand that?"

He looks at his premed power forward, Shavon Shields.

"What would you prescribe if you were a doctor and you wanted to cure this ailment?"

Nothing.

"What do you think the issue is, Deverell?"

Silence.

"You don't know? Kye [Kurkowski, the scout-team center], you sit there and watch a lot. Are we celebrating? I don't think we're a huge celebrating team because we don't like each other much, so we're not high-fiving or anything."

"I agree with what you say about what the problem is, but I don't know why," Kurkowski says after using his agricultural engineering mind to analyze the ninety-five percentages on the page before him.

"To me it's mental discipline," the coach says. "It's mental toughness. We scored. Go to hell. You're not scoring. Instead, we trot back and hey. Like you're all that. And you shoot 28 percent on twos [pointers]—you're not all that. We just can't have it. That's a lack of discipline. It's the wrong attitude. What should your attitude be after a make. Terran?"

Petteway: "Go get a stop."

"On a shot attempt, what should your attitude be? Every time the shot's up?"

Terran: "Get the rebound?"

"It's a miss. It's a pass to me."

He writes his next words on the board, finding space between *attitude* and circular foxholes: "They are passing to me."

He's starting to get loud again, and he's parked himself in front of Petteway and Biggs in the front left corner of the room.

"What's your attitude about ball handling? What do you think of when you think about ball handling?"

Biggs, Petteway, and Webster get singled out. They answer quietly.

"You know, it's funny," the coach says. "I said 'ball handling,' and three guys answer 'Dribbling.' And you know what I was thinking? 'Pass to the first open man.' It's ball handling. Pivoting, passing, dribbling. And you all thought dribbling. Do the best offensive teams do that? Pass. When you have the ball, it should be pass to the first open man. Just keep hitting the open guy. And here I am at the rim.

"What about shot selection on offense? What should your attitude be? Benny first."

Benny Parker draws a blank.

"Oh, surprised you, huh? Because you never shoot, so I'd like to know your attitude on offense."

Benny: "Take the best shot possible."

"Trev?"

Trevor Menke: "Take what teams give and create, or take a shot, or just keep it hot and move it."

He moves around the room and gets to Shields.

Shavon: "Don't force it."

"I would change that thought, honestly. I'd just say, you'll know when you're wide open. You've played enough basketball that you know what a wide-open shot feels like. So when you get the ball, if that's not there, what Trevor said—it's can I create for somebody else? . . . Eyes to the rim. Keep it moving. Keep it moving. Keep. It. Moving."

Back to defense.

"When we miss or turn it over, what do we think? Terran, what do you think?"

Petteway: "I'm angry."

"Deverell, what about you?"

After a few seconds assistant coach Kenya Hunter helps him out: "I got to get that back. That's our mentality. If I turned the ball over, I got to get that back as far as helping my teammate. I got to make a play at the other end."

Miles leads his witness: "Kenya, do you mean gamble to make a play? That's got to be what you mean."

Hunter: "No. Rebound. Take a charge. Make a play on the other end.

"Make a teammate play," Miles says, then writes the rest of his nouns on the board: "That's a raid. That's a charge. A rebound. What am I missing? A tip. A deflection, maybe."

Assistant coach Chris Harriman has been sitting on the edge of his third-row chair, and now he stands, which he's been on the verge of doing for the past hour.

"Coacher, I think when you say *attitude*, and you say *discipline*, and we talk about all these things, I think a big part of that, too, fellas, is your body language," Harriman says, trying to bring everything back to Gordon's speech. In his previous stop he saw the young St. Louis Billikens transform from a middle-of-the-road small-conference team to a force that had the confidence to beat up on Memphis in the NCAA Tournament, then nearly upset No. 1 seed Michigan State. He wants to keep the coach on message and remind the players of the stakes. He wants to offend them. He keeps talking.

"Whether you make a shot, miss a shot, whether you foul, or whatever it is, that's part of togetherness. You know, I got a lot of friends who watch a lot of basketball, and I know a lot of coaches who watch a lot of basketball, and it's interesting to hear a lot of perspectives on our team. And you get defensive, you know? They say nothing but bad things, and you take it as if they're saying bad things about your brothers. You know what I mean? Like, 'Man, I watched your team play the other day. What's it like coaching those guys? They look like they just aren't playing for each other.' Then you get a bunch of calls after the Michigan game, and they say it looks like your guys are really starting to come together. Playing hard for each other. 'That was fun to watch. I enjoyed that.' I mean, body language. If you don't play with an energy and enthusiasm and you don't live with an energy and enthusiasm, then you're an energy vampire. And you cannot be an energy vampire and be successful. And I don't know how that fits, Coach, but I think that's part of it."

If he has fired anyone up, it's Miles, who looks straight from Harriman down to guard Deverell Biggs, his first recruit, the offensive machine from Omaha Central High School. Miles and his program have a ton riding on Biggs's success.

"So, and I'm not trying to call you out, Dev, on this, but you beat yourself up more than anybody. Look me in the eyes. You take a shot. Or you do something wrong. And you'll hit your head like this when you're walking down the court. You've got your head down, so your body language is terrible that way. You're beating yourself up. You won three state championships, right? Three or four? I want to hear it real loud."

Biggs: "Three."

"Three state championships. There had to be a certain attitude you had to win three state championships. Are you bringing that attitude to us? Are you helping us be that winner? Or are you too worried about mistakes you made that you can't uphold that image you had when you were that state champion? . . . Make some lamebrain plays and walk around, and you can't get past it. It may take you fifteen seconds, and I want you past it in three. That extra twelve seconds doesn't do anybody any good. It sucks the life out of you, sucks the life out of us coaches, and sucks the life out of the team. All right? But if you're a true champion, then why aren't you bringing to us what you brought to Omaha Central [High School]? What you brought to Seward [County Community College in Kansas]? . . . Well, why don't we get that, Dev? There had to be a different Deverell bravado, energy, intensity."

He turns to his other point guard, freshman Tai Webster, and tries to change the tone a bit, but with the same message. He explains that his son, Gabe, asked him a question during the weekend: "Is Tai any good?"

Some players smile.

"He's nine, okay? Don't blame the kid."

Some players laugh out loud.

"If you take it out on him, I'll have your nuts," Miles warns with a smile. "I said, 'Well, let's check.' We get on YouTube, and we start watching you for New Zealand, and we see you canning threes against Angola, and we see you spike a volleyball, and we see your three-on-three championships, and he says, 'He's really good.' Then he says to me, 'What happened?'"

Miles says he explained to Gabe that progress takes time, and Tai isn't facing the same players in NCAA Division I basketball. The competition is better.

"But are you bringing the same attitude when you were kicking ass there? Are you bringing that to us? Why not? Why don't we deserve that attitude?"

Webster: "You do."

Now, Miles is in a place in this team meeting that he hadn't planned. Maybe Harriman got his blood flowing. Maybe Harriman reminded him of frank discussions from his Monday lunch he hadn't planned to share. But now he's yelling in an intimate room of twenty-five people. He's somewhere short of losing control, but not too short.

"That's what I don't get. We've got two guys, point guards, who are underperforming when you look at the stats. Both champions in their own way, and what attitude are you bringing to us?"

He paces now and the volume rises. Players now sit up in their seats, careful to meet their coach's eyes.

"Now, I could go through the room, here, there, and there. But I can tell you Benny Parker brings us an attitude. He needs to score better and score more so that guys respect him and guard him that way, but do you think that Benny brings a defensive energy that nobody else brings to our team? We all agree with that. We've always agreed with that. That's a heart of a champion."

He screams the last sentence. The text is that his diminutive third-string point guard plays hard. The subtext is that nobody in the top-eight rotation plays with an urgency like that. He then calls out all his starters, one by one, before pulling everyone into his doghouse.

"I could go around to everyone if I want to. You two guys [Biggs and Webster] got it today. You guys are champions. Why aren't you bringing that to us? Why don't we deserve that?"

He takes a five-second pause. Thick seconds.

"You owe us that. This program. Your teammates. Us coaches. Our fans. You owe us that attitude. Bottom line. You've had it. I see it. My kid sees it. . . . What championship attitude are we getting out of you two guys? And I could go guy to guy to guy to guy."

Miles feels himself moving past a crescendo. He sums up.

"Today, I am going to be the best player I can be," he says, calmer now. "I'm going to outwork myself from yesterday, and today I'm going to be a better teammate than I was yesterday. I'm going to work harder at coaching you guys. A lot of thought went into all of this. Two days of sleepless nights on this, right? Because I care. And it's not just winning and losing. It's about the way we are perceived, like Chris says. How much fun are we having? Is this a blast for your senior year? Is this the way you want to go out, Mike? Ray, are you having fun? Honestly, no? And winning won't solve that. It'll help. We'll feel a little better. But we'll still have shitty practices if we're not together. If we don't solve these things. We'll still have this problem and that

problem and get grumpy with each other and all those issues if
we don't bring the right mentality.

"So all you champions out there, right? Don't you owe it to
us to bring the same attitude only better because we're in the
elite league, top conference in the country? Don't you think you
have to try harder? Do better? Because if you're scared, you're
not going to succeed, or you're worried that I'm not as good as
I was, well you've already answered that question. . . . You don't
know how many people say to me, 'I thought you were going to
[start winning] this year' . . . and I say, 'You know what, we're
just not where we need to be right now.' My only concern is get
us ready for Ohio State and Penn State, and I don't even know
who we play after that. I might not even be right about that. Is
that who we play?"

Hunter: "Yeah."

Miles talks about how he has nineteen team photos on his
office walls. Eventually, he'll have forty before he gives up on
coaching. He asks them what they want to remember about
that team when they look at that photo twenty years from now.

"Mike, how many games are left for you in your career?"

Mike Peltz doesn't have to think or do math. With no hesitation, he answers, "Fifteen."

Miles repeats the number and looks around the room, locking eyes with every player before continuing.

"For something to talk about the rest of your life, you get one
crack at it. You'd think you'd want to have fun doing it. You'd
think you'd embrace the guys that are here because it ain't changing. LeBron James is not walking through that door, is he? James
Young [a high school senior who had just signed with Kentucky]
isn't walking through the door. It's us or it's nobody."

He tells a story about bouncing around in a small airplane
next to assistant coach Craig Smith on a recruiting trip. Miles
was in freak mode, complaining about every bump and jostle.
Smith, Mr. Positive and Mr. Superlative, smiled at his head coach
and said, "My grandpa told me one time, 'It's just something

1. The Miles family's Christmas photo taken in the fall of 1966, two months after Tim, the youngest, was born. *From left*: Kelly, Tip, Tim, Alyce, Karin, Kevin, and Paula. CREDIT: MILES FAMILY ALBUMS.

2. Tim Miles, age five, plays nose tackle against his older brother, Kevin, and friends in 1971. CREDIT: MILES FAMILY ALBUMS.

1 double team
2 team work
3 throw the ball
to Timmy and Karla
4 Don't foul
5 If someone is
open throw the
ball to them
6. Get a big lead
and keep scoring
if you can.
7. Get the rebound
8. Get opened
9 Don't always shot
if there is
someone open

3. (*Opposite*) On an envelope from his parents'
weekly newspaper, the *Times-Record* in Dol-
and, South Dakota, a ten-year-old Tim Miles
wrote down a game plan for his gym class
team, the Super Jocks, in 1976.
CREDIT: MILES FAMILY ALBUMS.

4. (*Above*) A thirteen-year-old Tim Miles
opens presents on Christmas Day 1979.
CREDIT: MILES FAMILY ALBUMS.

5. Wheeler High School senior Tim Miles hits a baseline jumper to send the 1984 district championship game into overtime. During the extra period Miles fouled out, and rival Clark High School, the host team, won the tournament. CREDIT: TIM MILES.

6. As an assistant at Northern State
University in Aberdeen, South
Dakota, Tim Miles coached under
Bob Olson, who here runs a Wolves
timeout in 1991 with Miles standing behind him. While working
there for six years, Miles met his
wife, Kari, a track and cross country
runner for Northern State.

7. Tim Miles scored his first job at Mayville (North Dakota) State University, where he turned the Comets from back-to-back 2-22 teams to national NAIA contenders while making less than $30,000 per year.

CREDIT: MILES FAMILY ALBUMS.

8. Tim Miles, 34, and his wife, Kari, and daughter Ava pose for a photo after the press conference announcing him as North Dakota State's coach in 2001. Miles had turned around programs at Mayville State and Southwest Minnesota State by that point, but NDSU would soon jump to NCAA Division I, which he didn't know when he took the job.

CREDIT: MILES FAMILY ALBUMS.

9. (*Above*) Tim Miles begins most speeches to new audiences by talking about his Doland, South Dakota, roots, including pointing out that one sign heading into town claims 306 residents while this one, on the other end of town, reads 297. CREDIT: TIM MILES.

10. (*Opposite*) Colorado State University coach Tim Miles greets Duke University coach Mike Krzyzewski before a December nonconference game in 2011. Duke won 87–64, but Miles went on to take that team to the NCAA Tournament in what would be his last season in Fort Collins, Colorado. CREDIT: TIM MILES.

11. (*Opposite top*) University of Nebraska athletic director Tom Osborne welcomes Tim Miles at the coach's initial press conference at the Hendricks Training Complex lobby after Miles got the Husker job in 2012. Osborne and Director of Basketball Operations Marc Boehm made the hire after interviewing Miles in Atlanta, Georgia.
CREDIT: SCOTT BRUHN, HUSKER ATHLETIC DEPARTMENT.

12. (*Opposite bottom*) Alyce and Tip Miles greet their son at the Hendricks Training Complex after his first Nebraska press conference in April of 2012. The couple hadn't seen him since he had accepted the position. Since then they've traveled to multiple Husker home games every season.
CREDIT: SCOTT BRUHN, HUSKER ATHLETIC DEPARTMENT.

13. (*Above*) Tim Miles meets the University of Nebraska media in spring of 2012 at the Hendricks Training Complex.
CREDIT: SCOTT BRUHN, HUSKER ATHLETIC DEPARTMENT.

14. (*Opposite top*) In his first season at Nebraska,
Tim Miles brought his son, Gabe, on the road to
historic Assembly Hall at the University of Indiana
in February of 2013. The No. 1–ranked Hoosiers
won 76–47. CREDIT: TIM MILES.

15. (*Opposite bottom*) Tim Miles holds up the game
ball after his 300th victory, a 62–47 home win
over Western Illinois at Pinnacle Bank Arena on
November 12, 2013. Six months later Miles hired
Western Illinois coach Jim Molinari as an assistant
coach. CREDIT: BRUCE THORSON.

16. (*Above*) Nebraska coach Tim Miles talks to forwards Shavon Shields (31) and David Rivers (2) during a 67-58 win over Illinois on February 12, 2014.
The victory set up a season-defining game at Michigan State University four nights later. CREDIT:
BRUCE THORSON.

17. (*Opposite top*) Nebraska guard Shavon Shields (31) looks to pass the ball past Ohio State's guard Aaron Craft (4), forward LaQuinton Ross (10), and guard Lenzelle Smith Jr. (32) during the second half of a January 20 game at Pinnacle Bank Arena. Craft played an integral role in three games against the Huskers during the 2013–2014 season. CREDIT: BRUCE THORSON.

18. (*Opposite bottom*) Nebraska coach Tim Miles watches his team during the second half against Ohio State at Pinnacle Bank Arena. Nebraska entered the game winless after four Big Ten games, but the Huskers won 68–62. After the game, students rushed the court for the first time at the Pinnacle Bank Arena. CREDIT: BRUCE THORSON.

19. (*Above*) Nebraska coach Tim Miles and forward Terran Petteway (5) hug after defeating the Indiana Hoosiers 60–55 at Pinnacle Bank Arena on January 30, 2014. The Huskers swept the Hoosiers during the 2013–2014 season. CREDIT: BRUCE THORSON.

20. (*Above*) Tim Miles reacts to a first-half foul call during a February 20 game against Penn State, which Nebraska won 80–67 at Pinnacle Bank Arena. The game avenged what the Nebraska coaches saw as their worst loss of the season: a 56–43 loss to Penn State in State College, Pennsylvania, on February 7. CREDIT: BRUCE THORSON.

21. (*Opposite*) Nebraska coaches (*from left*) Chris Harriman, Tim Miles, and Craig Smith cheer on their players with forward Leslee Smith (21) in the closing seconds of a 76–57 win over Purdue on February 23, 2014. The Huskers lost just one game in season one at Pinnacle Bank Arena. CREDIT: BRUCE THORSON.

22. Nebraska coach Tim Miles watches the No. 9 Wisconsin Badgers make a run at his Huskers during the second half of a 77–68 regular season win at Pinnacle Bank Arena on March 9, 2014. CREDIT: BRUCE THORSON.

you're going to have to accept. If you're going to die in a plane crash, there's not a helluva lot you can do about it. So what are you worrying about?' I'm like, 'Yeah, he's got me on that one.'"

Some players laugh.

"It's the same as our team. What are we worried about? Ourselves? Everybody back home talking about you? The noise? Or are we going to accept each other and figure this out together and celebrate each other? And like Chris said, 'No vampires.' And like Gordon said, 'Hey, take a picture of your prick every week, every day. Just have your ops [operations] guy, when Terran is acting up and being an energy vampire, post it in the locker room. And just keep posting them. Post a picture every day. Maybe it's Peltz one day. Maybe it's Shavon another. Maybe Walt's flipping out on me."

He mentions catching Walt Pitchford tweeting until two the night before Ohio State beat the Huskers by thirty-one.

"See how many guys are the same guys up there over and over and over. How would you like to live with that?"

Then he lightens up.

"Smile, Dev. Let's go. Walt. Come on, Benny. What are you going to bring to the table? What attitude are you going to bring? . . . If you don't know what to do, just work harder. If you don't know how to act, just try to get better. If you don't know who to listen to, at least listen to your coaches because we are going to tell you the truth."

Miles says his mother, Alyce, lies to him regularly. After the heartbreaker loss at home to Michigan, Alyce texted: "THOSE REFS TOOK IT FROM YOU. IT WAS TERRIBLE THOSE REFS." Miles texted back: "Did you see the one-incher we missed? You didn't see the thirteen layups we gave up in the second half, Ma?"

"Not that many, maybe seven," he says, grinning about the toughest loss of the season. "Wide-open layups. She's not counting those. That's not Timmy's fault."

He uses the story, and a few more, to explain the difference between what fans, friends, and parents say versus what coaches say.

"Here's the thing about coaches: I honestly don't care if I send you home in a little bit of a bad mood because you're not playing the way I know you can play. I really don't care if I challenge Terran and frustrate him to a point where he might punch the wall because I am going to challenge him. I am going to make him better. I'm going to decide today what buttons I'm going to push. And I got to use nineteen years of experience, twenty-five years of college experience, to decide what we need now. [He points to players.] What that kid. That kid. That dude and this team need right now. Sometimes I screw it up; a lot of times I'm right. But I don't really give a shit if Tai walks out complaining about me. I really don't care. Because I don't really care if Tai likes me. I want to make Tai a better player. I want to make Tai a better person. I want him to reach his goals. If I do that for him, he'll respect me. And that's enough for me. I don't have to sit here and be Mr. Nice Guy. Because I'm not yelling all the time, don't mistake kindness for weakness."

He's going off on tangents here, and he knows it. So he brings back the main point, and he calls it his main point because he doesn't want anybody to miss it.

"My point is, we're all in this together. We're all cut from the same cloth. We all want to win. Sometimes we get frustrated, and we don't know what to do. Sometimes we feel sorry for ourselves. Sometimes we listen to people who make us feel better, but that doesn't make us better. Who makes you better, Benny? Your friends or your enemies?"

Benny Parker, his heart of a champion: "Your enemies."

"Your enemies every day of the week. We got an enemy coming in next Monday, then Thursday, then another one and another one and another one. And they want to step on our throats and crush us. And the only way we're going to do it is if we can have an attitude that I'm going to be the best player I can be. I'm going to be better than I was yesterday. Be a better teammate than I was yesterday. And I'm going to coach better than I did yesterday. [He's pointing at players now, and then the coaches.] And he's going to coach, and he's going to coach, and he's going to coach, and they're going to operate. That's a joke on the ops guys. We all have to be on the same page."

Players are moving forward in their seats, preparing to launch themselves out to the practice court. They've been sitting in the film room for seventy-three minutes of part calculus class and part manhood challenge.

"So maybe we should have watched tape today, but I had something to say. Now, I agree with Terran's word. And if I would have gone across, we would have gotten that word three or four times over. *Attitude.* And it's the first thing when you look at the locker room. I want to have an attitude that craves improvement. If we can do that, we'll be in good shape."

He tells them to stretch because he's going to run the hell out of them after two days off. He smiles big, but they leave quietly, no joking around. As soon as the door shuts on the last player, Miles turns to the assistants milling around him in the front of the room.

"Did we do it right, boys? Yes? No? Maybe? What would you have added? Taken away? Cut out half of it?"

The assistants swear they aren't afraid to speak up to Miles, to offer ideas or straight out disagree with him. He comes to each of their offices often to bounce ideas off them. He calls himself the Big Dog, and that confidence is there, but he wants to hear more than just affirmation from his assistants, even his first-year guys, such as Hunter.

"We all came in with no ego and being selfless," Hunter would say later in the season. "I've been on staffs where it's not that way."

Craig Smith has been with Miles the longest, and he remembers a time early in the Colorado State mess, in the middle of that horrible second season, when Miles was trying to recruit better and better athletes, but not what Smith would consider Miles guys, who had high character but would do anything to win. Chip-on-their-shoulder guys. So Smith pulled out video-tapes of Mayville State wins and North Dakota State wins and said, "'These are the kids you won with. Let's find your types of players. You know the recipe for success. Let's get back to where you were.' Then we got his kind of guys, and that's when we really took off at Colorado State."

After the come-to-Jesus meeting with his Huskers, Miles wants to know if he took things too far.

After some mumbling among the assistants, Teddy Owens speaks up: "I don't think numbers do anything for them. I tried to look at some of the guys when we started giving the numbers, and guys started dropping their heads a little bit. I just don't think they can engage with that."

Miles argues: "Certainly, you got to see that we're 20 percent below the national average on assists on twos and at the rim. They have to understand that, right? Because that's kind of the main point?"

More numbers. Owens smiles at him.

Harriman jumps in: "You know I wanted to kind of say somehow . . ."

"I know, I know. You told me to just do three things, but I just couldn't do it."

19

That day, the Huskers had one of their most crisp practices of the year, and then they practiced well the rest of the week. Before Monday night's Big Ten Network game against Ohio State, Miles stuck with the "better player, better teammate" theme in his two pregame speeches. He warned them that the Buckeyes, who had lost three in a row since beating the Huskers by thirty-one, would probably turn up the pressure all over the court. Then he told them how to approach play after play, no matter which direction the game went.

"Be a better player, be a better teammate. We'll be better coaches. No matter what happens, stick with the process. Tonight is a night where we run out of time. We're so focused, you look up and you're surprised there's seven minutes left in the game. You're up by eight. You're up by eleven. It's gonna be one of those nights."

Back in the coaches' locker room, Craig Smith raved about Ohio State guard Aaron Craft's toughness. How a few games ago, Craft had simply dove and tackled the basketball to get a steal from a Michigan State guard. Miles, though, wasn't talking hoops. He pulled out a red and black tie.

"My mom gave me this," he said, grinning. "I told her, 'Mom, I don't want just another tie from JCPenney. She says, 'Okay, Okay.' When I looked at it in the box, sixty-five bucks. So it's a good tie. So I wear it for important games."

With 3:27 left in warm-ups, he left the locker room. Students roared for him from behind the bench as he entered the arena. He shook hands with officials and some Ohio State assistants, then he walked out to center court and right up to Aaron Craft.

"My niece is married," Miles said, "but she has a huge crush on you. The rest of us call you Aaron Crap, though."

"Yeah, I get a lot of that," Craft said.

"Yeah," Miles said, again grinning, "but we really mean it."

He slapped Craft on the back, and the guard laughed.

The Huskers had the crowd in the game from the start. The Nebraska football team had upset Georgia, 24–19, in the Gator Bowl on New Year's Day, so the fan-experience team showed the ninety-nine-yard touchdown pass to wideout Quincy Enunwa on the scoreboard at the first time-out with the Huskers already ahead. Then Enunwa and running back Ameer Abdullah spoke to the crowd with teammates all over the floor. The time-out ended and they kept talking, but the Huskers didn't lose any rhythm.

Shavon Shields repeatedly drove the right side of the lane and over people to score or get fouled to give the Huskers a 27–20 lead. Then Leslee Smith stole the ball at the top of the key and drove the length of the court for a layup. Petteway scored as he was fouled and hit the free throw to put Nebraska ahead by two touchdowns, 34–20 with 2:17 left in the half.

Ohio State doubled down on its full-court press, forced turnovers from Petteway and Deverell Biggs, and cut the lead to 34–25 at the half. Shields had ten points, while Biggs and Smith had six each off the bench.

In the locker room Miles started talking calmly, but that didn't last. He implored them to take care of the basketball. He warned them to move the ball with passes rather than dribbling, just like the four-on-five full-court drill they had been practicing well all week. Petteway had five of the Huskers' seven turnovers, so Miles told him to stop that. "Just stop that." And keep the ball moving until it gets to the rim, where the Huskers were shooting ten for twelve, versus one for six from the three-point line.

Then he went a little manic, speaking in fragments: "Attack. Poise. Attack. Poise. Team, team. Get better. Share it. Come up with loose balls. The whole deal."

He knew they had an opportunity here, so he gathered himself for the big-picture talk, and in raising the stakes he also raised his voice and challenged them.

"We've got to be men," he said. "This is a men's game. A large-caliber game. All right? And it's for forty minutes. We got to be on top of it the first ten minutes. We got to kick their ass the first ten minutes of this half. It's a large-caliber game. You don't bring a small-caliber bullet to a game like this. Whatever's happened doesn't count. It's 0–0. We got to do whatever it takes and beat their ass. And send a message that the Huskers are for real. We do it by sticking with the process. Be a better teammate, look out for each other, play for each other, take care of each other."

Then he remembered a moment from the first half, and he turned to his leading scorer. Petteway had looked to the arena roof when he got pulled during a routine substitution and stormed off the court, the kind of body-language felony Harriman had mentioned in the meeting the previous week. Now, Miles glared down upon Petteway, who sat in his usual spot on the right side of the front row.

"You're better than that," he said. "It's simple. Hold it in yourself. [If] you're not playing well, create for others for a while. Be calm. Get fouled. Play. Let's go. Players make plays. Let's go."

The whole team started clapping to pick up its cocaptain before doing its team chant and returning to the floor.

On the Huskers' first two possessions of the second half, Petteway lost the ball out of bounds and threw a lob pass over everyone and into the stands. Tai Webster gave the ball away. Shields scored. Biggs lost the ball twice.

Miles called time-out, then Biggs traveled, Benny Parker missed a layup, and Petteway got picked clean.

Nine possessions, two points. And Ohio State was scoring layups off those turnovers on the other end to lead 38–36 after two scores by Craft. The Buckeyes had gone on an 18–2 run. But the crowd was still in the game, even if the Huskers were losing their cool against the press. In a time-out Miles remained positive, but honest.

"They're bringing the fight to you, but you're not fighting back. All right?" he yelled over crowd noise. "You're finding excuses. All this crazy stuff . . . But we got to play. Bring it. Bring it. Bring it. Bring intensity. Bring attitude."

Shields and Petteway continued to drive to the rim to score, but officials whistled Petteway for his fourth foul with 7:22 left. The lead kept changing hands.

With 3:38 left, Biggs got a steal and scored a layup right over Craft. The crowd erupted, and Petteway returned during Ohio State's time-out. David Rivers recorded a key blocked shot, Benny Parker an assist.

The crowd remained on its feet for the balance of the game as the Huskers rode Petteway, Shields, and Biggs to the finish for a 68–62 win, sealing it by hitting seventeen of twenty-one free throws in the second half. In the final minute students flooded the four corners of the court to wait for the final buzzer, which sent them sprinting across the floor. Security didn't even try to stop them. Fans took selfies with the coach, who never refuses. One of them with a student would go viral.

"It was just one of those things that happened," Miles would say later. "You know, I love our fans. I love to see them happy. Your fans can make such a huge difference in the game."

In the postgame locker room, Walt Pitchford poured water on his own head while dancing with Tai Webster, and the team greeted Shavon Shields with cheers after his postgame interviews.

"Welcome back, man," assistant coach Kenya Hunter said to him.

Miles let the players and coaches enjoy the moment before he took over the room. His team had proven Ken Pomeroy wrong. They wouldn't lose thirteen straight. They wouldn't start the season 0-12 in the Big Ten. He took a deep breath and blew air out before starting a speech about perspective.

"Now, we had a good week of practice. We talked about what we can do together. We played more guys than we played in months, and they all helped out. It was really huge. You [Benny] made a big assist, and Dave comes out of nowhere to block a shot. Good plays from guys who haven't played in a while. You really stepped up to the plate, and I'm really proud of you. But listen, it only counts as one. All right? That counts as one win. We're not .500. It only counts as one . . . but when they come, they come in bunches. If you stay with the process, they'll come in bunches. In spurts. But the only way we're gonna do it is if we're mentally good. We're ready to go tomorrow by saying, 'What do I got to do to be a better player, better teammate?'

"So, congratulations, well done, but remember, we travel Wednesday and play Thursday; we come home, we play Sunday. Three games in seven days. So there's no time for messing around. You go home, watch it on rebroadcast, beat your chest, and be ready to go tomorrow."

Even Miles would later find it implausible that one word (*atti-*

tude) or one theme (be a better player today, a better teammate) could make the thirty-seven-point difference from when Nebraska played the Buckeyes sixteen days earlier and lost by thirty-one. Ohio State's downward spiral played a role. The venue could account for some of it. Maybe Shavon Shields just played better. Miles was right when he said "It was just one," because the Huskers hadn't solved their problems. Not yet.

Three nights later the team flew to Pennsylvania on a high. Penn State came into the game at 9-10, having lost its first six Big Ten games, two by three points and one game by just one.

The game was a grind. The Huskers couldn't get loose balls, couldn't get rebounds, and they fouled all night long. The coaches felt like they were back in Charleston, South Carolina. Tai Webster found himself buried on the bench most of the game after getting run over repeatedly by Nittany Lion guard D. J. Newbill. Webster's replacement, Deverell Biggs, couldn't handle the Penn State guards, either. Despite that, the Huskers built a lead to nine points and led 51–47 with 2:24 left on a Biggs basket that gave him nine points off the bench. The Huskers were 144 seconds from a road win in the Big Ten.

Penn State hit a free throw and then pressed the Huskers with a small lineup. Leslee Smith missed a post move badly, and Ray Gallegos air-balled a three-pointer at the shot clock. Petteway shook his fist and spun around, shouting to his teammates as he returned on defense.

Penn State missed a wide-open three-pointer that Smith couldn't grab with two hands, and psu's Donovan Jack went right over him to take the ball away and put it in to cut the lead to 51–50 with 1:20 left. Seconds later, with Petteway wide open on his left and Shavon Shields wide open on his right, Biggs tried to dribble through a double-team and lost the ball to Tim Frazier, who fed Newbill for a dunk as Shields fouled him. Newbill hit the free throw for a 53–51 lead and 65 seconds left.

Penn State had found ways to lose these kinds of games all season. But Walt Pitchford missed a three on a set play, and Penn State hit one to go up five. Terran Petteway then took the ball inbounds and dribbled straight to the three-point line, jumped over Frazier, and hit a three.

Miles called time-out to figure out how to win the game. The Huskers were down 56–54 with 11.4 seconds left. The Nittany Lions had the ball.

Miles did all the talking. He had his Huskers face-guard the three Penn State guards, and the Nittany Lions threw the ball away with 10.4 seconds left. Miles called his play as Shields inbounded the ball beside him, near the bench. The players bunched together at the free-throw line, and Biggs came off a double screen. He took the ball with no pressure on him and waited for a Pitchford ball screen at the top of the key. When the Penn State defenders switched the screen, Biggs tried to cross over to split through them both and lost the ball. Penn State tied him up on the floor. Penn State ball with 2.7 seconds left. Game over.

Petteway opened his arms toward Biggs and then pulled at his jersey and bared his teeth at the bench. Biggs had made a move to the lane, where four defenders were waiting, and Petteway, with fifteen points on the night to lead the team, never got to touch the ball.

Penn State made two free throws to win 58–54. In the handshake lineup, Biggs trailed at the back, where freshman Nate Hawkins put his arm around him and tried to buck him up. Biggs had turned the ball over twice down the stretch, and the team had fallen apart against the last-place team in the league.

If beating Ohio State could be called Miles's biggest win at Nebraska, he may have followed with his most difficult loss. For the coaches, this was rock bottom.

Four

Planting Two Feet

20

Tim Miles focused on playing a game he knew he would win after four of the most chaotic days of his coaching career. With Minnesota coming to town in three days, he agreed to be a guest on Minneapolis–St. Paul sports radio. Sell. Sell. Sell. Make people laugh.

KFAN had a fascination with Miles since his days at North Dakota State—more specifically, its 9:00 a.m. to noon program featuring Paul Allen, who later went on to become the voice of the Minnesota Vikings. Allen had tried to goad Miles on the air to come to Minnesota for the Gophers job when Tubby Smith had disappointing years or late-season meltdowns.

Monday's fill-in host for KFAN's afternoon drive-time show, *Bumper to Bumper with Dan Barreiro*, was Justin Gaard, who asked Miles if he'd recovered emotionally from the Penn State loss. Miles's answer was his classic evasion, followed by his self-deprecating tactic of underselling in the hopes of overdelivering later.

"You know, it's a beautiful day in Lincoln," he started. "It's about forty degrees, the sun's shining, it's clear skies. . . . You know, the Big Ten is a brutal league. I mean, it just feels like I sound hoarse, and the reason I sound hoarse is not from yelling at our guys, even though they deserve it. It's from somebody stepping on my throat for the last month, and it looks like it's going to continue for another month and a half."

He summarized the Penn State loss the best way he could without swearing or being too brutally honest. "Against Penn State we were solid, but we weren't good enough to win. When we had a chance to build a bigger lead, we didn't, and then when we had a chance to really win a tight game, we didn't. We made every mistake we could, and then eventually we lost the game."

Then he sent a clear message, though, that he expected to win, because he has to expect success. He has to get his team to expect success. And that would begin with beating up on Minnesota on Wednesday, January 26.

So, the first thing he did later that day was ask his players to list the four core values of the program, and the only one they could name was the first one—an attitude that craves improvement. He instantly banned them from their posh locker rooms at both the Hendricks Training Center and the Pinnacle Bank Arena. Instead of using stainless-steel bathroom stalls with TVS showing ESPN's *Sportscenter*, they'd have to ask Woody, the student manager, where the nearest public restrooms were located. Instead of piping their iTunes playlists from their locker-room iPads directly to their shower stalls, they'd have to shower at home.

Miles has this idea: throughout the season, you have to constantly change the stimulus to get the team's attention. He'd been looking for a reason to shake things up anyway, and when nobody on the team could get past the word *attitude*, the word he'd made the focus of his Jon Gordon talk, the word that his leading scorer, Terran Petteway, had chosen for a team theme, he went berserk. Core values are important to Miles. His four for the Huskers were:

1. An attitude that craves improvement. Miles explains the concept like this: "Come to work every day, dying to get better. Dying to get better."

2. Build your team. "Without cliques and adverse personalities. Meaning, unconditional to each other. Fearless communication. Communicate without fear."

3. Compete at your highest level every day. "John Maxwell wrote a book that said 'Today matters.' The very opening chapter it says, 'What's a good day to you? Would you even realize it if you had one?' And I stopped the CD or whatever it was, and I started thinking, what is a good day to me? So I said you have to be able to compete at your highest level each day. How do

you prepare yourself for practices and games and workouts? Or are you just going through life and trying to survive?"

4. Find a way to win. "What happens is, every game is different, and every practice is different, and every day kind of becomes different because things happen to you. You're thrown. You have this idea of what today is going to be like, and all of a sudden five different things get thrown at you. How do you handle it? How do you find solutions? How do you problem-solve? And I say it's easy. You focus on the process. On the fundamentals. Focus on your attitude, focus on together, and focus on competing your ass off."

So when the team got the first one right, Miles said, "That's our first principle. Give me our other three." Somebody weakly said "Team," and the rest were silent. Miles dropped his head.

"We go through this two or three times a year over a hand-out. We got it posted in your locker. And you don't give a shit because you got an iPad and you can get on Facebook."

Miles called out to Teddy Owens: "Teddy, go to the janitors, get the trash bags, and clean out their lockers. They're out of here."

The players had an idea of how practice was supposed to work. They come to the locker room and hang out. They shoot around and relax. They go to film. They practice. But that routine was losing games. Now, they had no locker room. How were they going to handle it?

"Man, when the guys got kicked out of the locker room, there was a lot of pressure," new assistant coach Kenya Hunter said later. "It came down to our core values. For the team not to know their identity that late into the season, it was a little shock. A lot of pressure."

Hunter was already under pressure anyway. He was still fig-uring out how to scout opposing teams the Husker way. To focus on personnel. To plan what would work on both ends against Minnesota. And he knew Coach yearned to beat the Gophers, the Big Ten team Miles watched as a kid, as much as anybody.

Not only that, but the guy Hunter replaced on the Husker staff, Ben Johnson, now coached for the Gophers and would use his knowledge against his old team.

"It was one of those things where I wanted to do a good job," Hunter said. "And for us to get the win was important."

Hunter and Owens made sure Woody and the other student managers grabbed black garbage bags and hauled the players' stuff out to the gym during practice. They would just have to live out of their cars until things changed. Hunter had been through this before when he worked for Herb Sendek at North Carolina State. Sendek ordered the players to no longer wear any gear with the North Carolina State or Wolfpack logos on them. They didn't deserve to wear program gear. Their effort and play were offensive to fans who loved the university and gave it money willingly. And the strategy worked. The Wolfpack made three straight NCAA Tournaments. Hunter thought the stimulus change was necessary with this Husker team, too.

"We [assistants] didn't say much to each other when it happened," he said. "We needed it. It was warranted. The fellas didn't understand the importance of what we were trying to teach. We agreed that was the right thing."

Despite the pressure of the Minnesota scout, and now the trash bags and his overheated coach—was Miles steaming or calculating?—Hunter decided to own the moment. He made the theme of his scouting report this phrase: "Win back the locker room."

Every time Kenya Hunter shared his theme privately with coaches, or publicly with the team, Miles would make a big scene of saying, "No way. Never."

To win back the locker room, the team would have to show they understood all four core values. And it might have to beat Minnesota as a gift to its coach.

They dressed in the Hendricks gym for two days. On the third day they dressed in the stands at Pinnacle Bank Arena. Winter coats and duffels were strewn throughout the first three rows behind the scorer's table. Before practice, though, they had to get the big sell from Kenya Hunter on Minnesota. In the team classroom Miles started the film session with a quick reminder of what needed to happen before his team stepped on the court the next night.

"I have some questions for you guys," he said. "One is, we got to get better today, right? Eyes up, T [Terran Petteway]. We got to get better today, right? Two is, tomorrow, this one's the shirt you wanted."

He held up a red long-sleeved warm-up shirt with "Us Always" splashed across the chest. Adidas had printed and shipped the shirts for free to equipment manager Pat Norris. At the home loss to Michigan earlier in the month, the players had liked the Wolverines' blue- and-gold warm-ups that said "WE WORK" on them. The previous year, Michigan had the same design, with "WE ON" on the front. The Huskers had asked Adidas for simi-lar shirts, and the players wanted the two-word "Us Always" on them, but they hadn't played together, hadn't been together in practice or off the court, in the opinion of Miles and, especially, the opinion of the assistant coaches.

One player had threatened to knock another out in practice. A player had shown up late repeatedly. The assistants were tired of the distractions and figured the players couldn't count on each other in high-pressure game situations if they couldn't get every-one working together on a day-to-day basis.

"Us Always?" Miles asked, as if it were a question and not a creed. "Are we getting away with this, or is it fraudulent? What are we doing? Shavon, you're a captain. What do you think?"

"We got to be together," Shields said. "We gotta be 'Us Always.' We can't just talk about it."

"Ray?"

"Yes," Gallegos answered.

"Ray, what if I take you out of the starting lineup? Are you still about us? You shook your head no."

"I said 'yes.'"

Miles had been considering a move that would put the six-foot-two Gallegos on the bench, instead starting the six-foot-seven David Rivers. With Rivers at power forward, the six-foot-seven Shields could move to small forward and the six-foot-six Petteway to shooting guard. By getting bigger at every position, they might hide their lack of what Miles considered a "true big," a traditional center. Plus, Gallegos would provide scoring off the bench, which Rivers couldn't. For Gallegos, that meant swallowing pride and a long distance away from leading the league in minutes his junior year to playing fewer than thirty minutes per game.

Miles stood over Petteway and Gallegos, who were on the left side of the front row of chairs. He looked back and forth between the two, landing on Gallegos.

"A psychologist would tell you that when you shook your head no, that means your body language is saying no. It would upset you [to not start as a senior], but you have to get over it."

"Yeah."

"But you're still about us? With your enthusiasm, with the same attitude even if you don't make five baskets in a row. You're still about us?"

Miles looked to the second row, behind Shields, to his other senior, Mike Peltz, who hadn't played much since the Big Ten schedule started.

"Peltz? You play one game, not the other. You still about us?"

"Yes, sir."

"All right. You're a winner."

Miles met each player's eyes.

"All right, Coach. All yours."

Hunter tells them to grab their scouting reports, which were waiting for them on their seats before they showed up.

"Listen up, fellas," Hunter said. "Minnesota comes in 4-3 [in the Big Ten] with a lot of energy and feeling good about themselves. We've got to do a good job. Obviously, we play our best at home, but after what we've been through at Penn State, fellas, we got to give our best effort, and I know you guys will. Let's forget about—well, not forget about it—but let's move on from Penn State with getting better today, starting with this practice, this film session."

The lights went out. Players flipped through the stapled photocopies of Kenya Hunter's seven-page Gophers scouting report, which was actually one of the smaller Big Ten reports for the year. Hunter believes "if you slow the mind, you slow the feet." Gophers video clips flashed rapid-fire on the big screen—steals and dunks against Michigan State, thirty-five-foot three-pointers against Ohio State, and lob dunks on set plays against Wisconsin.

Hunter launched into a meticulous breakdown of Minnesota's pressing defense and its ball-screening offense and spent most of his time going from Gopher player to Gopher player, highlighting what each did well and what each didn't. Video coordinator Greg Eaton cued up clip after clip, always a step ahead of what was being said, as if his MacBook Pro had wireless access to Hunter's brain. For sixty-five minutes, Hunter implored the team not to lose focus. Listen. This stuff matters.

If they paid attention, they heard some prescient words from their new assistant coach. The Gophers had two one-thousand-point scorers on the outside, the unrelated Andre Hollins and Austin Hollins. But the key to stopping them was new point guard DeAndre Mathieu, who had repeatedly driven to the rim to lead the Gophers with thirteen points in a 63–53 win over eleventh-ranked Ohio State, and, on Wednesday, when Penn State was gut-punching the Huskers, he ripped through ninth-ranked Wisconsin for eighteen points in an 82–78 win.

"Mathieu's No. 4," Hunter said. "When they're good, he's getting numbers. He's attacking the rim and getting shots or kicking out to three-point shooters. We have to do a good job of shadowing him in transition."

All five Huskers would have to find No. 4 each time down court, and once they got into half-court defense, the Huskers would double-team him every time Gopher centers Mo Walker and Elliot Eliason set a screen for him. They called this going "black" on him. They would take the ball out of his hands whenever possible. Make other Gophers beat them.

"I want turnovers out of him," Miles said.

Then Hunter warned they had to pay attention to Malik Smith coming off the bench. Smith was a twenty-four-year-old senior who made the trip up to Minnesota with new coach Richard Pitino. He would have to be guarded all the way to the half-court line.

"He's their dead three [-point shooter]. We have to know where he is at all times," Hunter said. "He has deep N B A range."

From the back row Miles pitched in when he wanted to emphasize the point, or just to change the stimulus.

"Smith's got poise," Miles said. "He's their worst defender, but he's here to show you he's going to score fifteen on five threes."

Hunter and Miles warned them the Gophers would cheat off the guys they were defending in transition to steal the ball from behind. Always attacking. The Gophers led the league in steals.

"Tai, Dev, watch your backside," Hunter said. "If we yell 'Wolf,' pick your dribble up."

"They'll reach on the ball all day," Miles said. "They'll aggravate you. They'll antagonize you. Expect frustration."

"Fellas, let's win back the locker room," Hunter said for the fifth time during the hour-plus session.

Miles sent them out to the arena floor, but he hung back with the assistants. Hunter wondered if maybe they should switch some screens or handoffs.

"We do. And we'll look at it, but I want them in an attack mentality," Miles said, and then he smiled. "I'm just so pissed off at them. I want them to hustle and get over [screens and handoffs]. But we can change it. It's no big deal. They don't remember anything we say anyway."

All the coaches laughed.

"Except for one guy, and that's Shavon," Hunter said.

He wanted to end on a positive with his head coach. He thought practices had been getting better each of the last two days since they had been kicked out of the locker room. They would practice well today, too, the day before the game. But would they win back the locker room?

21

Tim Miles wasn't convinced. Yeah, his players ran drills and scrimmages without many hiccups, and those hiccups weren't felonious, but he still didn't feel ready for Minnesota, so he called an extra morning film session and walk-through the day of the game to solidify plans for beating the Gophers.

Guard Deverell Biggs didn't show up.

The assistants and players tiptoed around their coach. Eggshells everywhere.

Miles immediately suspended Biggs for the game. This wasn't his first offense. The Omaha Central grad had not been allowed to make the Cincinnati trip in December after showing up late for a film session. He'd also been suspended for the first three games of the season for a DUI charge. Miles told the media Biggs had broken team rules. Externally, media and fans knew Biggs hadn't played well down the stretch against Penn State, with turnovers that cost the Huskers a shot at a win. For him to miss any team event after that game looked like bad timing for the junior from Omaha. But the truth was that assistants had urged Miles repeatedly since the Creighton loss a month earlier to do something about the Biggs problem. More than one had suggested he get kicked off the team, but Miles wanted to counsel Biggs through the tough stretch, and he figured the Huskers needed him. Biggs was the third-leading scorer on a team that, on paper, should struggle to put up points. He was talented and had been crucial to the Ohio State win. But he would be gone for this game. Not on the floor. Not on the bench. Nowhere near the team.

Against the full-court pressure of Minnesota, they'd be without their No. 2 point guard, who had regularly played crunch-time minutes. If they blew this game, Miles's decision to suspend Biggs might come under fire from local fans who wanted the local player, the first one recruited on scholarship in a decade, to succeed.

In his pregame talks, Miles doesn't mention Biggs by name, but he's all over the subtext of the message.

"Hey, this is what we play for right here, understand?" he begins. "The guys in this room [not Biggs]. The guys who show up every day with blood, sweat, and tears [not Biggs]. Right? We're going to go out and we're going to be more together than those guys [Minnesota]. That's what we got to do.

"Now, here's what Pitino's done. He walks into Minnesota, and he says, 'I'm Richard Pitino. My dad [Louisville coach Rick Pitino] is the best coach in college basketball. . . . I know a great system. You're going to love playing in it. We're going to go kick everybody's ass. Let's go.' And that's it. He's got them believing they're going to kick everybody's ass.

"They just play fearless. They're going to beat you up on defense. They'll give you easy shots when you handle the ball well, but you have to understand that fearlessness is the greatest attribute a player can have. Playing without any regard. Just compete and play. All right? That's the best thing you can do. And the guys with the short memory are the guys who are the best players.

"And the guys who play for each other usually get it done. If you don't have that, you'll probably struggle. At the end of the day, when I finally look at it, we've shown some of both. Today is a huge step for us. A huge test for us. What's this group going to do? It's a different dynamic. Anytime somebody's in or somebody's out [Biggs], it's a different dynamic. I expect us to bond together strongly. I expect us to play for each other and play our asses off and hustle even harder and just play better.

"No excuses as far as anything that's going on today [Biggs]. We know exactly what's going on."

He walks them through the press breaker one more time. The more they turn the ball over against Minnesota, the more their chances grow slim. He tells them to leave scars on Gopher defenders who try to take the ball away.

"What's the name of the game, Benny?"

"Basketball," Benny Parker says.

"That's the most important thing, then, isn't it? Go get the basketball. Take care of the basketball. Take good shots with the basketball. Go get it. We know their shooters. Smith? We have to pick him up from the bus. . . . What kind of screen-and-roll defense are we doing on Mathieu?"

Everyone: "Black."

"Black. Exactly. We have to get him corralled as much as we can . . .

"Have poise. Eyes up. This game is going to be like four-on-four pickup, one dribble max. The Chaos drill. They're just going to run at you all day. And they're going to lull you to sleep some, then come at you. They're going to always try to change it up. Always stay on the attack. Just ignore them. We've got the ball, not you. . . . Let's go, on the attack.

"Attitude. Our attitude has got to be right. Am I a better player today? Am I a better teammate today? Is it true with 'Us Always'? Am I gonna keep my head when things go bad? When things go great, am I going to beat my chest, or am I going to maintain that killer instinct and put these guys away?

"Those are the things we have to figure out. Let's go out and let's play it right, and let's win this game. Nobody else is winning in this place. This is our place. Team on three."

He claps as they stand and put their hands together with Terran Petteway's on the bottom.

Petteway: "One, two, three . . ."

Everyone: "Team."

Hunter: "Let's go, fellas."

Before they all leave, Miles grabs his captains, Terran Petteway and Shavon Shields.

"Have fun, you two," he says.

Miles had seen Petteway's frustration through every loss. In a private meeting Shields admitted he wasn't having fun playing basketball anymore, partly due to losses, but more so the friction on the team. Miles had pulled these two captains aside to tell them about his Biggs decision and wanted to know what they thought.

"They said, 'Let's go.'" They didn't complain at all, Miles would say later.

Petteway and Shields follow their team out to the floor and a full arena, packed with students wearing suits and sneakers to support Coaches for Cancer. The night is also a push for Husker fans to get signed up for the bone-marrow registry as a way to support the Harriman family, and especially Avery, who had faced slim chances in finding a donor last year, but found the one person in the country who was able to do it. Husker administrators and their wives organize sign-ups in the entrance to the arena, where athletic director Shawn Eichorst and his wife, Kristin, help sign up fans to donate. They promote the event with a #TeamAvery hashtag on Twitter.

Back in the coaches' locker room, Craig Smith puts on a green shirt he says has won many games. Miles dresses in a rust shirt he's left in the closet for two years. But once dressed in his suit and Adidas sneakers, like all coaches in support of Coaches for Cancer this week, he sits with his knees spread wide and with notes all over the floor. Then he looks up to his coaches on the other side of the narrow room.

"I hate these pricks," he says with a grin, referring to Minnesota.

Smith, who has been quiet all week, introspective, answers him: "You haven't said that in a while."

"I haven't said that a lot this year, have I?"

"Maybe not since Iowa," Greg Eaton says.

"Well, that's Iowa. First of all . . ."

Eaton cuts him off: "You said it before the Creighton game."

Miles smiles big now. (He doesn't hate Creighton at all, but he hates losing to McDermott and the Bluejays, both in games and in public opinion.) Both those teams pumped the Huskers. And he doesn't want to jinx the team. Not tonight. Eaton doesn't agree.

"Bring that out. Fifteen minutes before tip."

"We'll see," Miles says and laughs, still loose. It's been a long day of two walk-throughs, and he still has a game tonight.

Assistants go out to the floor to watch warm-ups. Miles works on his game cards.

When the assistants return, he asks about the arena atmosphere, where students are waving, among others, a photo poster of Miles's official Husker photo, which doesn't look all that different from his ninth grade photo from Doland High School.

"It'll be good," Smith says. "Similar to Ohio State, I'd say."

Miles starts burping, rapid-fire.

"You okay, Coach?" Smith asks.

"Hey, Teddy, did you do something to my coffee? Spit in it or something?"

"I hope not," Teddy Owens says. Never a straight answer. Grinning, he asks if Miles needs more coffee, knowing he doesn't. He tells Miles about chocolates that showed up in the locker room from a Gopher fan.

"Not cool," Miles says, jokingly suspecting sabotage, then he stands up and heads to the film room, where players are back from the court, sitting quietly, sweating, staring at the floor. The assistants follow Miles, who goes to the marker board while the rest of the staff fills the back of the room.

He jokes with Tai Webster. He reminds the team to attack Mathieu and not to let Smith shoot. But no more speeches. He sends them back out. Nothing left to say.

Some good news is that Biggs isn't the only player missing the game. Gopher guard Andre Hollins showed up to the arena in a walking boot—an ankle sprain from their upset win over Wisconsin. Miles walks up to him an hour before the game and demands that he play anyway.

"You can still guard us in that thing," he says.

The better news when the game starts is that the Huskers listened to Kenya Hunter and are harassing DeAndre Mathieu all over the court, doubling him whenever the Gophers set a screen for him. He tries to pound the ball through two defenders and turns the ball over every time he tries to drive into the lane. On the other end of the court, Walt Pitchford opens the game with a dunk off a Shields drive and dish, and then he hits his first three. Ray Gallegos hits his threes, and the team goes 7-14 from behind the arc in the first half.

Everything Hunter warned them about Minnesota has been spot-on. Mathieu is the key, and they are shutting him down. He commits four turnovers and two fouls before sitting on the bench midway through the first half. The Gophers pressure everywhere, and the Huskers, though they make some mistakes, are cognizant of the reaching hands and pass the ball more than pounding it. The one area where they fail in the first half is watching for the three-point shooter, Malik Smith, who starts for the injured Hollins and hits five three-pointers to keep the Gophers within five points at halftime, 35–30.

Miles paces the front of the locker-room classroom while he talks. "What is our mentality going to be? Are we sitting in here like warriors getting ready to go out and battle for twenty more minutes, or are you thinking like we played pretty good and we're up five? What is your mentality?"

He mentions Smith's shooting. He warns Pitchford that Minnesota's centers would start trying to dominate him inside.

"Walt, you gotta love that. Bring it on. I want this all day. Keep hustling. You'll be in good shape. You've done it well."

He tells them to block out and rebound. He warns that they'd taken shots at the rim only twice, which wouldn't be good enough. They are making their three-pointers, but that may not last.

"We're good at the rim. Get to the rim. That's how we get to the foul line."

He orders them to sit in silence for ninety seconds to "get your minds right," but he can wait only sixty-nine seconds before giving his final orders. "We're winning this with defense. We're going to win this by converting every time. Let's do it right. We get to start with a defensive stop. Be warriors out there. Team on three."

Petteway takes over, scoring at the rim and scoring in bunches. With six minutes left in the game, he hits a baseline three-pointer and then dunks an aggressive lob from Benny Parker, and the arena rises to its feet. Minnesota uses its full-court pressure to make the game tight, but Terran demands the ball repeatedly in the final minutes and hits eleven of his fourteen free throws, finishing with thirty-five points. The Huskers win 82–78, the most points they've scored in a Big Ten game.

Running out of the arena and into their locker room, the coaches are as berserk as the players in the classroom and the fans who don't seem to want to leave the arena.

Teddy Owens: "Wheeeeeeee!"

Craig Smith: "It was their unlucky day."

Greg Eaton: "How about Terran's shot in the corner?"

Smith: "He made two huge shots."

Chris Harriman: "Monstrosity."

They walk into the classroom, where the players slap hands, but wait for Miles and Petteway to finish their postgame interviews before going all out. Stainless-steel pots simmer over gas flames on the table in the back of the room. Kenya Hunter lifts one as the players settle into their chairs.

"What do we got? Chicken pot pie today?"

Then Miles comes in loud, clapping and yelling "Good job, boys, good job."

He writes on the board: "19 assists."

Shield screams "Yeah!" drawing it out for five seconds.

Everyone cheers.

"Whatever," Miles says "All right. Hang on. No, no, no . . ."

On the board he draws four boxes that represent the team's four core values. Shields can hardly sit down.

"Okay, Shavon, name one," Miles says, pointing a red dry-erase marker at his captain. "Wait, Terran's not here yet . . ."

"Attitude," point guard Tai Webster yells. He can't help it.

Miles writes "attitude" on the board.

"Yeah," Kenya Hunter yells. "We're getting the locker room back, baby!"

Miles grins at Kenya Hunter, who may be his M V P for the game. Hunter's game plan had worked perfectly, and he'd gotten the team to execute it.

Terran Petteway comes into the locker to cheers, sees the board, and immediately understands what's happening.

"Terran," Miles says, "you got one?"

No hesitation.

"Compete at the highest level!"

Petteway smiles wide. Players and coaches all start yelling now. Within seconds they add "build your team" and "find a way to win." They don't name them perfectly, but they have the general ideas, and the win. They go nuts. They've won back the locker room.

Chris Harriman, who has inexplicably left the room in the commotion, returns with Avery in his arms, and the team loses it again, high-fiving the main character in the #TeamAvery campaign.

"Hell, yeah," Walt Pitchford says as everyone calms down.

"You said, 'Find a way to win,' but that's okay," Miles says. "It's actually 'Finish with a flourish,' but that's all right. I'll give you the handout on Monday so we know for sure.

"I'm proud of you guys. You did a heckuva job. But I tell you what: in life, there's nothing better than following it up. And

I would love nothing better than you guys going out and beating Indiana."

The team starts clapping.

"Us Always," Miles says. "Us Always. Take a knee."

Five seconds of kneeling with heads down and eyes closed.

"A little prayer at the end and let's go. Team on three."

22

Monday morning after the Minnesota win, assistant coach Craig Smith was getting philosophical about players and recruitment. He was actually putting together a metaphor in his head for the kind of basketball players the program needed to get.

For years he'd worked with the notion that players came with four personalities:

1. Unconsciously incompetent. These guys had limitations in what they could do on the court, but they didn't know it. They thought they were stars, and that would never happen. These players were never contributing and never happy.

2. Consciously incompetent. They had limitations, but they knew that, and they found ways to contribute by playing to their strengths and working on their weaknesses. David Rivers and Benny Parker had played like these kinds of players, but they hadn't seen the court much. The assistants were trying to make a case for them to Miles, a case that they could be more than competent.

3. Unconsciously competent. They were good, but they didn't realize their gifts and didn't maximize them. Shavon Shields had shown potential to score at will, carrying the team at times as a freshman, like when he scored twenty-nine points in a win at Penn State. If he knew how good he could be, he could be great every night.

4. Consciously competent. This player was a leader and a winner. He played well on a consistent basis and lifted his team to be better than they should be. Ben Woodside was this kind of player at North Dakota State. Dorian Green at Colorado State. And Terran Petteway could be that kind of player, too, Smith insisted. Maybe Shields and others, too.

At Colorado State Smith found Petteway playing high school basketball in Galveston, Texas, and told Miles he had to see him. They traveled from Fort Collins to South Texas together, and Miles was impressed with Petteway, "just a thoroughbred," but also liked his buddy Mike Evans, a six-foot-five brute who grabbed every rebound and did his best to keep up with Petteway's breakaway athleticism.

They tried to recruit both guys, but Petteway stayed closer to home by choosing Texas Tech, where Pat Knight coached. Evans visited csu, but called the coach to say he'd have a better chance making the nfl than the nba. Miles was disappointed, but he agreed. Things didn't work out for Petteway in Lubbock—Knight got fired, and Petteway became most famous for popping University of Kansas forward Connor Teahan in the jaw. Petteway reached out to Smith and Miles and transferred to Nebraska, where as a redshirt in Miles's first season, he often dominated practices with Pitchford, who transferred in from Florida.

Smith saw glimpses right away of Petteway being a consciously competent leader, though an emotionally unstable one. But at this point in the season, Smith is thinking differently and trying to explain his new theory to operations guy Teddy Owens. He calls it the Wizard of Oz Theory of Recruitment.

"You're the first one to hear it," Smith says, his eyes big. "Some guys are scarecrows, you know? They're brain deficient. Some are tin men with no heart. Some are lions with no courage. You can't recruit guys who are two of those three. You may not want many guys who are even one of those three. Maybe it's the older

I get, but I'm getting more interested in players who have these intangibles—brains, heart, and courage—than talent."

"Okay," Owens says, putting his hand on Smith's shoulder in the hallway between the coaches' upstairs offices at the Hendricks Training Center. "I'm going to chart those."

Smith knows Owens is making fun of him, but he also knows he's on to something. Miles is on to something, too. Smith and Owens make their way downstairs to hear Miles deliver his news to the team. News they already know.

Miles faces a loose team in the three-tiered film classroom. They're still excited about the Minnesota win. The coaches are on top in the third row. The scout team and reserve players are in the second row. In the front, from Miles's left to right, are Walt Pitchford, Shavon Shields, Tai Webster, Miles's seat, an empty seat, Terran Petteway, and Ray Gallegos.

"All right, guys," he says, and then he continues more quietly. "Hey, I dismissed Deverell this afternoon. He won't be with us. It's my call. It's never easy to do. I don't like doing it. You know, I'd made the decision before last night's game."

He wants to clarify to them he didn't dismiss Biggs because of anything they did.

"Last night's game, you played great, but that had nothing to do with it. It was my call. It's not him. It's just that you set a certain standard, right? And you have to follow that standard. If you're going to do a job in life, they're going to expect you to do your job, and I just didn't think Deverell was keeping up his end. And at the end of the day when you look at it, we all have obligations in life, whether that is with a job, or to each other, or in marriage, or any of this and that. And when you can't hold up your end, something's got to give."

He paused to look into every player's eyes, even Petteway's and Shields's, who already knew the news.

"You know, Dev's going to need you guys," Miles said even more quietly. "You can't abandon him. You got to look out for him. Talk to him, you know? Because the hardest thing for him is going to not be here every day with you, all right? It's one thing, the embarrassment of tomorrow—I have to make an announcement. I appreciate it if you keep it off Twitter. Keep it to yourselves. You'll get media [asking you questions]. I'm already being hassled like crazy because he wasn't at the game last night. I would prefer that you say 'No.' 'I have no comment.' Whatever. Because you don't want to be involved. I'll handle it, and we'll go from there."

He tells them to refer all questions to Shamus McKnight, the media-relations director for men's basketball. Then he pauses to meet everyone's eyes again.

"Has anybody got anything to say?" he says, waiting four seconds for an answer he's not going to get. "All right. It's a crappy deal, but at the same time, next best action. We move forward as a team. We saw how we can play as a team. We had nineteen assists on twenty-five field goals. Should be pretty exciting for you guys. I didn't clip out everything. I clipped out more errors because I thought, well, you'd be beating your chest today like you're all that."

Players and coaches laugh.

"Let's watch the last 6:16 [of the game], where we completed our first lob dunk in two and a half months, so nice job, Benny."

Miles sits down, and Petteway, who made the dunk and didn't get mentioned, laughs out loud. He knows his role.

"Yeah, Benny," a few teammates yell, and everyone is loud.

"Go, Benny," Kenya Hunter says from the back row.

"Benny, and he made two jumpers," Miles says. "I said to Ben, 'What's up?' and he said, 'That's what I do.' Old Benny was one for two throwing lobs. The first one hit a cheerleader in the leg [out of bounds]."

"That one was really dangerous," Webster says in his thick New Zealand accent.

"That happened to me. It was out of bounds," Petteway says.

"Terran," Hunter says, "you could have gotten that ball."

"What?! No!"

"Yeah, you could have," Shields says.

"No, I couldn't have," he says, smiling and burying his head in his hands.

Craig Smith from the back row, "Mike Evans would have gotten it."

Miles smiles big, thinking of his high school teammate who would soon get drafted in the first round of the N FL draft. "Yeah, Mike Evans would have gotten it, but don't compare him to a guy he can't compare to."

Petteway has his head down to his knees now: "I couldn't."

Smith: "Well, he's a lot faster."

Miles: "Way more. Stronger. Faster. Way more athletic."

Petteway sings the next words from a high pitch to low: "Yeah, yeah, yeah. Yeah, yeah, yeah."

Miles: "Mike will probably end up in the N BA."

"Oohs" from the team.

Two minutes from an announcement that they'd lost their third-leading scorer for the year, they're relaxed and enjoying each other.

Through the film session Miles goads players, who laugh. On the screen Leslee Smith turns the ball over when he's not ready for a pass.

"Leslee, what's the error?" Miles asks.

"I don't see it," Leslee eventually says.

"Laziness, it's called."

"I think I was looking at you," Smith says softly.

"Don't look at me on offense," Miles says. "I called five plays all last night. I told you I was going to let you guys play."

Then he sees Shields join the defensive end late.

"Oh, Shavon's tired," Miles says. "Coach Smith wouldn't let him out. I was yelling at Coach Smith to get him out of the game. What was the deal, Smith? Why wouldn't you let him out of the game?"

Smith: "He just had to play. He had to get through it."

Kenya Hunter: "Some guys can't play through fatigue, Shavon."

Miles: "He was just trying to make Shavon mentally tougher. I just like guys who play hard and play good."

Players start laughing at David Rivers, and Miles doesn't know why. He forgets what's coming onscreen.

Onscreen, Rivers hits a free throw.

Miles: "Okay, he made a free throw. Big moment."

The players lose it again.

On the Hendricks court Harriman walks through Indiana's offensive sets. The Hoosiers come to town in three days. As happy as everyone is now, they still know they are just 2-5 in the conference and need the wins to come in bunches, as Miles promised they would if they play the right way. For now, Miles lets Harriman run the show while he answers phone calls and texts about Biggs on the sideline. He has his bosses' support because they think he's done his homework and due diligence. He's checking with coaching peers about how to proceed, but he knows how to proceed. Marc Boehm, his boss, advises him to just "be honest" with the public and "stay the course." Eventually, Miles works with McKnight on a press release, which came out Tuesday:

"I've made the very difficult decision that Deverell Biggs will no longer be a part of our basketball program. We have consistently emphasized accountability for our student-athletes on the court, off the court and in the classroom. Individual accountability affects the entire group. As a basketball program, we are moving forward and perhaps a fresh start for Deverell may be beneficial to him as well.

"Deverell will still have access to all of our academic resources to maintain his eligibility and progress toward graduation. Deverell is good young man. My hope is that he remains at Nebraska and finishes his classes this spring and finds another program where he can flourish. We wish him all the best."

The decision wasn't easy for the coach, but it was over. His team was together.

"He was my first recruit here," Miles would say after the season was over. "But we couldn't align. I really wanted him to be successful. Whether that's me not being able to reach him or him not being able to step forward . . . I just couldn't get there with Dev."

Craig Smith has been through attrition with Miles, like when they had to clean house at Colorado State in that first season. Other coaches would have given up on Deverell Biggs much sooner in his eighteen months in the program.

"He's such a bleeding heart," Smith said of Miles. "And I mean that in a good way. . . . He's also always met things head-on and not shied away from truth and controversy. Sometimes, you gotta walk through a river of shit, right? And that's just the truth when you're rebuilding things. Do you like it? Nope. Is it embarrassing at times? Yes. But it's the facts. You have to do it. Just like you expect your players to do it."

Way back in Smith's first year at Mayville State, he also learned another truth from Miles: "If there's an issue between one player and the program, the program is always going to win."

23

John Hanigan had set up camp in his recliner in the living room of the couple's one-story South Lincoln townhome. Getting up often required too much work, and lying down required too much coughing, which was work in itself. He slept in the chair.

Because of chemotherapy treatments, he'd spent his Husker basketball games there at home with his two boys around him, which allowed his wife some respite time to run errands, or just some time for herself, away from lung cancer.

He'd been disappointed in the Huskers' start against Creighton in December, but appreciated that the team fought back in the second half. He'd also grown a closet appreciation, as awkward as it felt, for Creighton basketball. He liked the discipline the Bluejays showed offensively. Their Player of the Year candidate, Doug McDermott, aggressively wore out opponents, and they didn't make mistakes, on or off the court.

He liked discipline. He was always a strict father who didn't have to say much to make his point. He just had to give a look, or snap his fingers, and the kids would stop what he would call their "antics." He didn't like "antics" from his sports teams, either. That's also why he supported embattled Nebraska football coach Bo Pelini, who'd had a roller-coaster 9-4 season that fall and had faced questions about his future with the program. But John Hanigan liked Pelini's no-nonsense style and that his players were rarely in trouble. He saw the same thing in Miles, especially when the coach removed Deverell Biggs from the team. He believed fans didn't know everything that happened behind closed doors, and he trusted Miles had his reasons. The team seemed to understand how to work, which was more important even than knowing how to win. And now, it was figuring out how to win.

Before the season he'd thought that a National Invitational Tournament bid would be success for this team. An invite to that tourney seemed reasonable progress. But now, something else was going on with the team. And in that South Lincoln townhome.

The boys gave away most of their game tickets because of the chemo. They didn't feel right about going to all those games without him. And in Dad's living room, they felt something special happening. During game action they wouldn't say much. Dad might grumble at officials, or give a "Pull your head out" when Leslee Smith missed a shot inside or Tai Webster turned over the ball, but mostly they were quiet. Then, at time-outs, they talked about the possibilities for the team, so much so that the women in the house—Mom and daughters-in-law—would leave the room, do something else. What the Nebraska basketball team had given the men was something to talk about other than the cancer. Growing up, the kids talked to Dad about sports, and later, when they were adults, about sports and financial advice. They didn't talk about the big stuff. Didn't talk about emotions. And now, they didn't talk about cancer. They talked

Huskers and how John might have a chance to see them win some games that mattered on the national level, just like he did with his boys in the 1990s.

In the Big Ten teams play an imbalanced schedule. In other words, they play some of the twelve teams once and others twice. In Miles's first year at Nebraska, the 2012–13 season, Indiana throttled the Huskers by twenty-nine points in Bloomington in the only meeting of the two teams. The loss hurt Miles as much as any that season, not just because of the score, but because he'd been embarrassed and angry. Things happened that weren't fair. He took the night personally.

With Indiana in the Huskers' new building, Miles feels a minor chance at some redemption. Put simply, redemption feels good. He has two shots to beat the Hoosiers and coach Tom Crean this season, and one starts in forty-five minutes.

"Some days," he says at his locker, "I just love this job."

Fifteen minutes later he tells his players how to beat the Hoosiers:

"Make it a half-court game. We'll win.

"Rebound with all five guys. We will win.

"Whether the ball goes in the hole or not, we maintain our poise. We'll win.

"We win the hustle game—energy, enthusiasm, attitude. We will win."

Then, with his volume increasing each sentence, he tells them why he is in such a good mood.

"Do you think these guys respect Nebraska basketball?" he asks. "Maybe they're going to play great. But you know what? It's our job to take them out of it. It's our job to make them uncomfortable and know that when they come into Pinnacle Bank Arena, when they come to Nebraska, they're walking out of here with a loss. Because we're going to be the toughest out in the league. Everybody understand that? Let's go."

By now players and coaches are yelling and clapping.

"Ready? 'Attitude' on three."

Miles is in such a good mood he almost blanks on one of his latest last-minute rituals.

"Forgot my drawers," he says to Kenya Hunter, the only assistant left in the locker room.

Hunter knows what this means, one of many Miles superstitions. He hasn't forgotten to wear them. He's forgotten to remove them. One of his sisters had once told him to stop pulling on his bottom during games every time he stood at the bench, but his underwear kept running up on him. His solution: don't wear them. And they won. So he kept not wearing them.

He runs out to the floor to join his Huskers, who do none of those things he said they'd have to do to win. They miss open shots. They take quick three-pointers and get beaten down court. They get hammered on the boards.

Indiana, despite early turnovers, launches a 15–0 run, and Terran Petteway has to drive through three Hoosiers to convert a three-point play just before the half to trail 32–19 at the buzzer. Just nineteen points. Tim Miles isn't loving his job.

He runs straight for the team rather than waiting to talk to coaches.

"This is Penn State all over again," he screams. "I've never seen a more tentative, hapless group."

He hammers Leslee Smith for pulling in zero rebounds in nine minutes. Tai Webster for pure panic. Then he goes after the whole team for its attitude.

"You're scared. Once you confront that, 'I'm scared. I can't compete with these guys,' you know what? When you're like that, you just have to say, 'I'm gonna try my hardest. I'm gonna work harder.' It's amazing when a guy just works harder, what can happen. Just plays better defense. Box out. Set a screen. Post up where I belong. It's amazing what can happen."

He reads from the stat sheet: they had eleven turnovers and nine baskets, just four assists.

"That's one way to empty your crowd. There won't be seven thousand left the last five minutes of the game if you continue to play like this embarrassment that you've played."

Then he looks at Indiana's stats and can't believe the names he is seeing who saw minutes in the first half of a Big Ten road game, evidence his team didn't deserve the respect he told them to earn from Indiana in pregame.

"He's playing kids he hasn't played all year," says Miles, who knows this because he looked at hours of extra film before this game. "That's what you want to be?"

He is asking them if they want to be irrelevant.

"We have every excuse because we're scared. You can't be scared, boys. Just go out and outwork your opponent. Concentrate on defense. Block out. Rebounds. Let's go get a good shot. Let's go get it done."

They start clapping and rising to their feet. Petteway doesn't wait for his coach to give him the signal.

Petteway: "Team on three."

Team: "One, two, three. TEAM."

"You got to fight for it. No cowards," Miles yells at them as they run out to the arena for the second half. "You can't be scared. You got to compete."

Four minutes into the second half, Petteway and Ray Gallegos have the Huskers within four points with a barrage of three-pointers. When Petteway, fighting foul trouble, hits a shot from the elbow to pull the Huskers within one at 40–39, the arena erupts, and the game is on.

With 3:25 left, Gallegos steals the ball from Indiana's Yogi Ferrell and walks it up with a one-point lead. Miles directs traffic and even puts his hand on Shavon Shields's back while he delivers instructions into his right ear. Miles pushes Shields forward, and official Gene Steratore smiles, even though he's had two run-ins with Miles in the game already.

Shields, who has just missed two wide-open jumpers, immediately cuts to the left side of the court, where he receives a pass on the move and drives across the teeth of the defense at the free-throw line. He sweeps to the right side of the rim for a layup and an Indiana time-out.

Petteway then hits a step-back three-pointer to move the lead to six points. At the end of the game he could fly in for a dunk. Instead, he dribbles the ball out to half-court to wait out the last seconds and dribbles over to his bench and his coach. The two of them do interviews with the Big Ten Network before joining the rest of the team in the locker room.

Right away, Miles jokes with Tai Webster and Leslee Smith, the two guys he ripped the hardest at halftime.

"Who was that team in the first half? Anybody want to explain that to me? I mean, do you want that? Is that what you like?"

He grins at Smith now and then takes in his entire team with his eyes.

"Because you suck after days off, you'll be back tomorrow," he says. "I just want to tell you I'm proud of you. . . . Now, I've been waiting for this game since the last time we played them. All right? Our focus is Michigan. If you want to send a message to anybody, you go to Michigan and win."

"Damn right," Hunter says.

After that Wednesday win the national news started paying attention to Nebraska basketball, for various reasons.

Joe Haack, a local advertising guy, contacted Miles via Twitter to get some help proposing to his girlfriend. On his phone Miles filmed a video in his office to set up the proposal at Zen's Lounge in downtown Lincoln.

The Big Ten Network's Jimmy Jackson had asked Miles about the video before the Indiana game.

"It only took two takes," Miles said. "She said 'Yes,' so everybody wins."

The story got picked up by college basketball websites nationwide, along with ESPN, Yahoo! Sports, and USA Today.

Planting Two Feet

But ESPN also wanted to talk about what was happening on the floor. Andy Katz, the network's college basketball insider, used his weekly 3-*Point Shot* online video to talk about the Huskers becoming a legitimate threat in the Big Ten with how well they play at home.

And ESPN numbers guy John Gasaway was on his way to Nebraska to get a closer look at what was happening at Pinnacle Bank Arena. He'd actually planned the trip in December, when the Huskers looked like they'd be the same Huskers they'd been for sixteen years.

"My bosses couldn't believe I wanted to go to Lincoln," he said. "But I had a feeling about them."

Thursday night the student managers beat up on the guys who serve as the scout team for the women's basketball program. The win was satisfying because the women's scout team had just been featured in the *Lincoln Journal Star*. Student manager Brad Shaw bragged about the win at Friday's practice, where Miles ran the show himself because his assistants were out recruiting.

"Hitch [Jordan Hitchcock] did all the scoring, but I had a big second half," said Shaw, a family science major from Fargo, North Dakota, who, like Woody, wanted to be a college basketball coach. "They were talking a lot of trash."

At Saturday morning's 10:00 a.m. practice, everything changes. Six players show up late. Well, not technically late, but they wander in eight minutes before start time, not dressed, not taped, not ready to go.

Harriman rants. Before Miles can come down from his office with his practice plan, Harriman lights into the team. If he were running the team, he'd run them into the ground. Then they'd come in the next day at 9:00 a.m., then the next day at 8:00 a.m., and get run into the ground again.

At 10:15 Miles descends to give his pep talk. He's thinking big things. He has dreams of the NCAA Tournament he wants to share. He wants his team to believe in itself and its chances to do something special. He's a human Jon Gordon positivity book, an *Oprah* closing segment.

"It's Saturday morning, and we can't sleepwalk through it. If we want to make the NCAAS, we have to go on a run. We have to win on the road. We have to beat the bluebloods, the Michigans, the Wisconsins."

Harriman grumbles: "The Michigan States." He's already started to work on scouting the Spartans, still four games away.

Miles tells them they're sitting at seventh in the Big Ten, but just two games out of fourth. Their strength of schedule is 13th in the nation and will only get better as the Big Ten season moves along. Their RPI is at 64, and they'll have to win some big games, like this upcoming one at Michigan, to get them to the 30s or 40s, which is where they could get an at-large tournament bid at the end of the season. That's what they'd done at Colorado State. And this team can do that, he tells them.

"Every win moves you up," he says. "Every win . . . So we can't sleepwalk through today's practice. I really believe we can beat anyone now. But that starts today. How can I be a better player today? How can I be a better teammate? If I take care of that . . ."

He nods.

"Okay, let's go. Team on three."

Petteway and the team give a quieter version of their "team" chant.

As they run shooting drills, strength coach Tim Wilson sneaks over to tell Miles about the late start to warm-ups. Miles blows his whistle and pulls everybody to center court. He's not yelling.

"Somebody tell me team policy. What time are we supposed to be here for practice? Thirty minutes before, right?"

He's still not yelling. He locks eyes with everyone. He doesn't care exactly which of the five or six players were late—he'll find out later, but that's not the point. He blames them all. He thought he fixed the Us Always thing last week.

"Okay, we're going to pay a price for that. You disrespect your coaches, your teammates. You don't take off a Saturday. If I did that, I would be out of coaching. . . . We can beat Indiana. We can kick Michigan's ass. But you don't do that, a guy trying to break into the lineup, but shows up five minutes before practice. I mean, why isn't Deverell here? . . . And I like him. I want him to succeed."

He shakes his head, then talks about how Ohio State is struggling in the Big Ten after starting out ranked second in the country by winning its first fifteen games. Since then OSU has lost five of six. The Buckeyes have three McDonald's All-Americans, but they can't play together.

"Let me ask, are you [Leslee Smith] a McDonald's All-American?"

Smith shakes his head.

"Are you [Shavon Shields]?"

Shields shakes his head, too.

"No. Peltz? How many Division I scholarships were you offered?"

Mike Peltz answers him verbally: "None."

"He practiced like he wanted something for weeks. Then I give him a scholarship, and he walks around. Is that what you want?"

Peltz again answers a question that's supposed to be rhetorical: "No."

"You don't need to answer me. We know the answers. . . . So what are we about? This morning we're about nothing. We're not about being something special, making something special happen. . . . Let's go. On the baseline."

He runs them until they're gasping for air and coughing. Then he takes them back to October's defensive shuffling drills. Petteway and Peltz sprint to get in the front of the line. Student managers, joking and clapping each other's backs for their big win over the women's scout team the previous night, now clap and shout for each player zigzagging the length of the court and back in defensive stances. Even Walter Pitchford is getting his six-foot-ten frame down close to the court.

At the scorer's table, operations guy Teddy Owens laments

that he thought they'd be out of the gym by 1:00 p.m. today, but no way that's happening now.

Miles shouts at them to get their hands off their knees between rotations. He tells them to imagine Michigan's Nik Stauskas or Glenn Robinson coming at them off a screen.

"This is not punishment. This is how we play late-game defense with a lead so that we can kick somebody's ass. Get up in them and turn them."

He implores Tai Webster to try to dribble past Benny Parker, who's so low in his stance his chin is below Webster's waist.

Miles has again hired referees to check for fouls in drills and a scrimmage against Chris Harriman's scout team. He tells the refs, "Big Ten is letting more contact go."

The gray scout team, mainly Leslee Smith, starts eating up the starters in red. Miles moves Smith and David Rivers back and forth between teams. Peltz hits an open jumper for the scout team, and Harriman is all smiles.

"Hey, scout-team all-star," Miles says. "Try hitting a shot in a game sometime."

Peltz is oh-for-the-season in games.

But Miles starts riding his red team as the drill moves to a full-court game that stresses getting back on defense. Peltz keeps getting steals and scoring. The red team runs twenty-two-second sprint punishments, down and back twice. As red players get frustrated, Harriman claps up high, right in their ears as they go by him.

"Good job, gray! Good job, gray!" he screams. He's grinning at red-team guys, but he isn't happy. He's still livid with them for showing up late.

Miles calls for another twenty-two seconds, but Webster and Petteway don't hear the "Go" and get a late start. They don't reach the baseline in time. Miles calls for another sprint by holding up two fingers. He walks to Petteway and looks up to him. "You okay with that?"

"Yeah, I'm fine," he says, but he's tired, his face frantic as he bares his teeth.

Miles says he's done coaching the red-jerseyed players. They're on their own to figure things out. Harriman claps and shouts: "Yeah, gray. That's right, gray."

Then something happens, and it feels big to everybody.

A referee whistles Petteway for an illegal screen, and Petteway complains. Miles stops everything.

The two of them go at each other, Petteway's emotions pouring out about the call, about having to run, about play after play falling apart. He's talking back to his coach, taking him on, falling apart. Miles knows this is just competitiveness, not meanness. But he needs some self-correction fast.

Shields holds Petteway in a bear hug and walks him backward, talking him down.

"He don't need a hug. Let's run," Harriman says with a devilish grin.

"On the line," Miles says calmly.

Red runs an eleven-second sprint down and back. Petteway finishes first by four lengths. He watches Miles.

"Terran's out," Miles says, and ignores his best player, the scorer who has willed Nebraska to the wins over Minnesota and Indiana. The player who is climbing the individual scoring-leader list in the Big Ten. Just like he did to team leaders Scott Koenen at Southwest Minnesota State and Ben Woodside at North Dakota State early in his career.

The gray team scores on red, and Petteway sprints to the far end of the court to do burpees on the sidelines, including full push-ups, and leaps into the air. Nobody ordered him to do them. Miles walks that way and huddles with him, talking softly. After two minutes of this, Petteway starts nodding.

While this drama plays out, gray scores again. Then Tim Wagner, a freshman walk-on who has been hurt all year, snaps one of Tim Wilson's strength rubber bands around his ankles. Everyone and everything is snapping now. Managers crack up at the symbolism, but muffle their laughs with their hands.

Red gets a stop when Miles looks up from Petteway.

"Get a drink," he yells. "Both teams, get a drink."

Petteway walks over to the referees and apologizes to each one and shakes their hands. He doesn't drink.

After some better possessions for the red team and some end-of-game scrimmages, Miles stops practice early, making Owens's all-day practice prediction wrong.

"How was today?" Miles asks his team as it gathers around him at center court. "I'm just telling you, we practiced poorly going into Creighton, and we played like it. Now, Michigan is the hottest team in the country. . . . You have to finish ahead of Northwestern and Purdue if we want to get postseason."

Then he gives up on doing a reprise of the Big Ten positioning speech. He smiles instead. The Super Bowl is the next day. The Seattle Seahawks versus the Denver Broncos.

"Okay, Broncos over here, losers over there," Miles says. He's loyal to the Colorado team. He tells Jayden Olson to take a picture so players can't lie about whom they pick.

"Yeah, Richard Sherman," Petteway yells, referring to the Seahawks' outspoken, heavy-hitting cornerback.

"Let's go," Miles says, then he steals Petteway's line and changes it. "One, two, three . . ." Then he follows that with an insult.

The team instead yells "TEAM" and cracks up.

Petteway starts doing more burpees, and Miles says, "Come on, Terran. Let's go." He's served his punishment, and he's been forgiven. He has self-corrected. Petteway takes his jersey off and smiles.

24

Terran Petteway's Seahawks blew out Miles's Broncos, 43–8. Two nights later tenth-ranked Michigan blew out Nebraska.

The coaches sometimes talk about a college basketball maxim that works like this: twice a year your team will inexplicably dominate two opponents, and twice a year two opponents, for no discernible reason, will dominate you. Despite preparation, talent, aggressiveness, togetherness, toughness, or any other factor Tim Miles believes gives his team an edge, some days Michigan will just hit nine three-pointers in the first half and not stop missing for forty minutes. The Huskers trailed 16–12 before Michigan ran off twelve straight points for a 28–12 lead, and then the Wolverines stretched that to 43–15, and the Huskers felt as helpless as they were against Creighton.

"Even if we played great, we would have been down fifteen in the first half," Miles would say later. "Indiana tricked us [in the first half]. Michigan ambushed us."

Petteway finished with five points, three rebounds, and four turnovers. Miles emptied his bench in the second half, as did Michigan coach John Beilein. With the 79–50 loss, the Huskers were now 3-6, in the bottom half of the Big Ten, and Michigan led the league at 9-1.

Three nights later the Huskers were in Evanston, Illinois, to play Northwestern. They hadn't won a game in an opponent's gym all year, and in the first half that looked to continue. Meanwhile, Northwestern was shocking the conference with consecutive road wins at Indiana, Wisconsin, and Minnesota to build a 5-5 conference record. If the Huskers fell another game behind the Wildcats, the NCAA Tournament would probably be out of reach.

February 8 was way too early to be playing a must-win game. The Huskers came out tentative, like in the Indiana game, scoring sixteen first-half points to trail by six. Then Walter Pitchford started the second half with three three-pointers in the first 5:40 to give the Huskers a 28–27 lead. And with both Pitchford and Petteway scoring consistently, David Rivers and Benny Parker created havoc on the defensive end. Rivers blocked a shot that Parker turned into a conversion layup at the other end for an eight-point lead with six minutes left.

Northwestern made a run in the final minutes. Petteway missed a layup, and Wildcats coach Chris Collins called a timeout with 1:10 left and the score 49–46 Nebraska. Petteway came out of the break smiling and relaxed. He then hit a three-pointer with 23 seconds left to seal the win, and the Huskers won a Big Ten road game, 60–51.

Though Petteway was the Nebraska Corn Board Flex Fuel Player of the Game and Pitchford was the State Farm Player of the Game, Miles wanted to talk about Parker's defense and transition buckets on the radio postgame show. Parker and Rivers had combined to play 37 minutes, Rivers making things tough in the lane and Parker doing the same throughout the rest of the court.

The Huskers had survived the toughest part of their schedule. They had four wins in the conference, which was one less than they had all of last season, and they still had eight games to play, including five at home.

"Let's win all eight of them and not have to worry," Miles told fans on the Husker Sports Network.

Walking into practice two days later, Miles asks Leslee Smith about his thigh bruise. Without waiting for an answer, he breaks into an Eddie Murphy line from the 1982 film *Trading Places*. In the scene con man Billy Ray Valentine (Murphy) tries to brag his way out of a pummeling in his group cell by telling a story of beating up ten policemen. When a cell mate asks him why he doesn't have a mark on him, Murphy shouts: "'Cause I'm a karate man, all right? Karate men bruise on the inside. They don't show their weaknesses."

Most of Miles's cultural references come from the 1980s. He grew up listening to Bryan Adams and Huey Lewis, Run DMC and LL Cool J. Watching comedy specials by Murphy and Sam Kinison. Memorizing dialogue from Murphy movies *48 Hours* and *Beverly Hills Cop*, and even buying the soundtracks on cassette tapes.

So, most of his team has no idea what he's talking about when he says to Walt Pitchford: "Kung Fu masters bruise on the inside."

He butchers the line, but the delivery is dead on Murphy. But Eddie Murphy, to these players, is the donkey from *Shrek*, the bumbling father in *Daddy Day Care*.

His kids are helping him with this cultural reference problem, introducing him to Katy Perry, Beyoncé, and other music that isn't on his classic-rock or '80s satellite radio channels.

The line bombs, but still Miles is in a good mood. While watching the Northwestern film, he sees scout point guard Trevor Menke hand a towel to a starter coming out of the game.

"I see we have Operation Dumbass in full motion," Miles says.

The team cracks up. The coaches have been regularly pushing two mantras:

1. Watch your nonverbal language.

2. Figure out your roles.

For the second mantra, Menke's role is to run opponents' offenses in practice. To be a pest every day when guarding point guards Tai Webster and Benny Parker, who have more strength and speed. To be supportive on the bench as both a force of positivity and a seventh coach who can offer reminders from the elaborate game plans. As for the first, Menke offers a simple gift that helps players conceal the worst of their nonverbal language. When Miles or Craig Smith or Chris Harriman pull a player out of the game, half the time the player is pretty upset about getting his second first-half foul or back-to-back turnovers or whatever it took to get him yanked. Miles, actually, isn't a believer in pulling players for physical mistakes because the learning process is more important than the win, in theory, but repeated mental mistakes or lack of effort will get anybody jerked. Regardless of why he comes out, Menke will be there, offering a folded towel for the player to stuff into his face to cover up an angry look or any words that could be lip-read on the Big Ten Network or ESPN.

Operation Dumbass.

Film and practices are loose Monday and Tuesday with Illinois coming to town Wednesday. Miles wants to beat Illinois, which swept the Huskers in his first season and beat up Nebraska on the boards and in the lane. At home the Huskers gave up nineteen offensive rebounds to the Illini. He won't let his players forget that. He doesn't want any team bullying his team, especially not at home.

"Nobody's coming in here and winning," he says in Monday's film session. "We let one team get lucky enough to beat us here. I don't want anybody beating us here. This is the first season in a six-hundred-million-dollar project, and I want to set the tone for years to come."

His wife dropped the kids off at Monday's practice, and the Husker fund-raisers brought some high-paying boosters, too, as a gift for their gifts. They sit in the front row at Pinnacle Bank Arena, watching Miles play the roles of coach, teacher, father, comedian, and marketer. He rips reserve Mike Peltz for hitting an outside shot—apparently that's easy in practice, huh? He warns nine-year-old son Gabe to get off the far basket because they're going full court. He lets Craig Smith run through Illini sets while he talks to each booster, explaining what's happening on the court, what's important at this point in the season. Being better players each day, better teammates, protecting the lane.

"Tai, good job," he yells after his point guard gets a steal. Miles snaps his fingers. "You're all there. When we practice like this, it's great."

By the end Miles plays one-on-one with his son, Gabe, who scores at will. When he has the ball, Miles does impressions of his own players, who are watching as they shoot buckets on the other end.

"I got the Nate Hawkins move."

"Here's Shavon."

Hawkins stops shooting to watch, then yells, "He's got no left hand, Gabe."

After Gabe wins Miles shakes hands and takes photos on an iPad with boosters, and players do the same while Hawkins rebounds three-pointers Gabe launches from his hip.

That night, on his radio show, Miles tells stories about his philosophy on time-outs right before the half, David Rivers possibly goaltending his big block versus Northwestern, Benny Parker being an auto-reverse guy (whatever that means), Michigan State coach Tom Izzo's amazing in-bound plays, demanding video clips from Greg Eaton, getting PowerPoints from Teddy Owens, Walt Pitchford somehow being a perimeter player all his life at six-foot-ten, football coach Bo Pelini offering driving directions (whatever that means), recruiting North Dakota to New Jersey to Wichita in eight days while trying to win games in the Big Ten, and Terran Petteway shooting 57 percent with less than five seconds left on the shot clock. Last, he explains to host Greg Sharpe why he tosses his jacket to the bench early in games.

"I'm the hardest-working coach in college basketball," he says, grinning at the host. "I'm James Brown, man."

By the end he describes Illinois's season of extremes. The Illini come to Pinnacle Bank Arena in forty-eight hours, having won their first two Big Ten games, losing the next eight, benching two upperclassmen for freshmen, and beating Penn State on the road, where they looked more like the twenty-third-ranked team they were in December.

"I look at these teams," he sums up. "We could beat them. They could beat us."

Tuesday, the mood holds. He confronts operations guy Teddy Owens for talking Gabe into eating five pieces of Juicy Fruit and drinking a cold glass of water.

"Do you know how much that hurts?" Miles asks as the players warm up with slow lunges from one end of the court to another. "Do you know how much that hurts? I told him, 'Teddy Owens is the worst person to take advice from.'"

Owens smiles big.

"Not the worst, Coach," he says. "There's got to be some who are worse."

Then he advises Miles to drink local honey each day to fight off viruses. He read that somewhere, and he's trying it out. He hasn't gotten allergies yet since moving from Oklahoma.

"You really are the worst person in the world," Miles says, then coaches his team. This is some mood.

In practice Trevor Menke does his job by getting after Tai Webster and Benny Parker. He takes a shot to the head and sits out one play before digging in again. And his scout-team buddy, center Kye Kurkowski, battles with Walt Pitchford for rebounds. This is what all the coaches want from the scout team, and Miles, rather than jumping his red-team guys, compliments Menke and Kurkowski, which means something to them, because they don't get it much. They're from small Nebraska towns where they were starters, leading scorers, town heroes. Now, they're juniors without scholarships who have to follow all the rules, do all the work, endure all the stress, and they will combine to play twenty minutes this season and score five garbage-time points.

"Nice job, Kye," Miles says. "Way to work the offensive glass. . . . Walt, he's kicking your ass. Get him off."

Wednesday night in his first pregame talk, he reminds his players Illinois won a game in the NCAA Tournament last year, which Nebraska has never done, and were ranked six weeks ago. Then he talks about the Huskers.

"We are one loss from being eleventh [in the Big Ten], and we're one win from being sixth. What do you want your destiny to be? What direction do you want to go in this program? And we control our destiny. Five of our last games at home. Everyone in between is like us. It's an even game. But what's going to set us apart? What's going to make us a special team? Right now, we have a chance to be a special team. How do we make a run that nobody across the country expects us to make? One is, we're coming together at the perfect time. I think Us Always actually matters to this team. I think we're not playing frustrated. At Northwestern we stayed with it, stayed with it, and good things happened. Our bench matters. This guy picks us up, and this guy picks us up. Benny gets us nine points in transition. Dave gets a big blocked shot at the end. . . . We find guys that want to contribute all the way through."

He compliments Tai Webster and Leslee Smith for having good practices all week. Then he turns to defense, guaranteeing them that if they win in the lane, especially on defense, they will win this game. He talks about Super Bowl hero Richard Sherman of the Seattle Seahawks. Miles loves football metaphors for defensive mentality in basketball. He wants his guards to sit down in their stances at the elbows of the lane—the ends of the free-throw line—and raid anyone who tries to drive through there. Take the ball away like a great defensive back.

"You know Richard Sherman, right?" he says to Terran Petteway, who loves the cornerback.

Miles's friend Gus Bradley coached the Seahawks' defense for three years and told Miles that Sherman was an animal in practice on every play and was in the film room more than anyone. He tells them all of this.

"He plays every practice play like it's his last," Miles says, getting worked up now. "He says, 'I'm kicking your ass every play.' And if he gets beat, he says, 'All right, I'm going to kick your ass on this play.' And he never stops. He's unbelievable. He's fearless. But he's not even the most athletic guy on their team. But he works harder, he's a great teammate, he believes in himself and never stops. If we're those kinds of guys, we're in good shape tonight."

He sends the team back out to the court and returns to the coaches' locker room to work on last-minute additions to his game cards. That's where his mother's doubt takes over.

"I hope I'm wrong, but I don't have a good feeling about tonight," he says to nobody in particular. "I just, I don't know."

After his second speech, mainly about starting a legacy of never losing at Pinnacle Bank Arena, he's running late out to the court. He missed his goal of leaving 3:27 before tipoff. At 2:38 he says, "In the party of life, I'm always late."

In the first half Illinois owns the paint, leading 12–8 in points in the lane, but Ray Gallegos scores a fast-break layup at the buzzer to give the Huskers a 31–30 lead on the scoreboard, the crowd exploding for the first time since starting lineups were announced. Webster and Smith have disproved the theory that you play how you practice, and they've spent nearly all of the first half on the bench. But in the halftime locker room, Miles is clinical, not angry. He reviews the stat sheet, focusing on defensive rebounding. He reviews personnel and spends the bulk of his time talking plays he'll call in the second half.

With Terran Petteway in foul trouble, he calls a ton of plays for Shavon Shields, and the sophomore continually drives the right side of the lane to get fouled. By game's end he makes eight of his twelve shots from the floor and hits all fifteen of his free throws, the most free-throw-line perfection for a Husker in thirty-two years. He finishes with thirty-three points, including twelve Husker points in a row in the second half, for a career high, and the Huskers win, 67–58, to move to 5-6 in the Big Ten and 13-10 overall.

Miles doesn't even mention Shields's name, though, in the postgame locker room.

"Benny Parker's defense on the ball was the difference in the game," he tells the team. "You did a helluva job, Benny."

The team cheers wildly for Parker, especially Shields. Miles had been at his most animated on the bench with 5:51 left in the game when Parker pulled a Richard Sherman impression, eating up Illinois guard Rayvonte Rice, who couldn't drive as the shot clock descended to zero. Rice forced an air-ball three-pointer. Miles pumped his fist five times, and the crowd reacted to that as much as the defense. Parker finished the game with four steals in 24 minutes of playing time.

"I won't say another nice thing about you for a week, okay?" Miles says, smiling. Then he stops smiling and locks eyes with each player.

"What do we want to be?" he asks. "What are we here for? To make the run we want to make, we have to beat Michigan State [in four days]. Last year we played them tough, but let's send a message to the Big Ten what Nebraska basketball is about. We can't keep going on the road to Michigan and Ohio State and getting whomped. So what mentality is it going to take? What changes do we have to make so that we're in a better mind frame so we go out and have a chance to win that game? It's one thing to hang around Purdue, Penn State, and win at Northwestern. But what are we gonna to do against the elite, against a team that people are talking about for the Final Four?

"This is fun and all right. But, you know, I'm getting to the point where I expect this. So now it's on to the next. I want to make a big-time run. . . . We've got something special going on in this building, in this town, and in this program, so let's get our mind in the right frame when we practice Friday."

Miles is so locked into this message that he forgets the post-game prayer. After his players do their team chant, he pulls Tai Webster aside to buck him up and tell him he needs him.

They've won four out of five Big Ten games since the Penn State loss and the decision to trim the roster. They haven't done anything yet to make Miles think they can beat what he calls a "blueblood" Big Ten team on the road. Especially a blueblood coached by one of his mentors, Tom Izzo, at Michigan State. But he'll try to figure something out. What are the other choices?

25

When Tim Miles was a kid, his father took him pheasant hunting with a .410 single-shot shotgun. That was the way to hunt, an act of patience with pressure to perform if a bird revealed itself. In two fall seasons Miles remembers getting off six to eight shots. One day he finally hit a bird, and it was a hen.

"You're killing us, kid," Tip said to him. "It's a drought. We need to protect the hens."

"But I got it," his son said. "I got a bird."

Miles spent most of his free time indoors, especially in summer. Especially at a Doland pool hall that was constantly changing owners and names. Miles and his nonfarming friends would eat burgers and fries and play pool. The hall had a traditional eight-ball table and a snooker table. The boys would have to stand by to let the adults play over the lunch hour, but the table was theirs the rest of the time. One day when Tim was fourteen, Tip walked over from the house to catch them playing eight ball.

"What are you doing?" he said, and then he pulled him over to the bar.

"If you ever see this kid in here playing eight ball," he said to the bartender while pointing at Tim, "you call me, and I'll drag him by his ears out of here."

Then he sent Tim home, where he had two channels to watch that came through the rooftop antenna, and his buddies played eight ball without him.

To Tip Miles snooker was how you learned to play pool. The pockets were smaller and the game more strategic. Tim had to play defensively and wait for his chance to go on a run at just the right moment. He had to have more precision in his shots because mistakes cost him dearly, and his opponent would make runs.

Like basketball.

"My dad always wanted this preciseness, which was funny about my dad because he only sometimes acted like that in his personal life," Miles says now. "But when it came to sports and stuff like that, he was that way."

Twenty years later, while coaching at North Dakota State, one of his assistants started getting on him for comparing basketball to warfare. The assistant was Saul Phillips, who said, "No, basketball is like chess."

Miles agreed. Basketball isn't warfare, though he still uses his foxhole terminology. Basketball isn't checkers, where you just attack and jump people. It's chess. It's snooker. It's waiting still in the trees with that .410 single-shot.

"You wait and you wait and you wait, and I think that that meant something," Miles says during dinner the night before the Michigan State game. "I really do. Those are two things about patience that really helped me. I was nothing great as a pool player, but I wasn't afraid of anybody in snooker."

For the same reasons, he isn't afraid of Michigan State, either. This is operations guy Jayden Olson's schedule for the Michigan State weekend trip:

Saturday, February 15th 2014

12:00 pm	Leave Hendricks Training Complex
12:30 pm CST	Flight leaves for Lansing MI
3:15 pm EST	Flight Arrives in Lansing MI
4:00 pm	Check-in at Hotel
5:30 pm	Team Meal
9:00 pm	Light Snack/Supper and Film in Hotel
10:00 pm	Lights Out

Sunday, February 16th 2014

9:30 am	Wake Up
9:40 am	Breakfast in Hotel
10:00 am	Film and Walk Thru in Hotel
11:00 am	PreGame Meal in Hotel
1:15 pm	Leave Hotel for Arena
3:00 pm	beat Michigan State!
6:30 pm EST	Leave Lansing MI
7:30 pm CST	Arrive in Lincoln

Ten days earlier the University of Michigan had dazed the Huskers with nine three-pointers in the first half, and Nebraska was never really in the game. For Miles, the main problem with that performance—and with similar losses at Creighton in December and Ohio State in January—was how his team reacted. Crazy gym. Opponents hitting deep threes. Close calls going the wrong way. No breaks. Whatever the problem, the team couldn't mentally recover. And Sunday afternoon at Michigan State's Breslin Student Event Center, against the ninth-ranked team in the country, Miles predicted all that stuff would happen to them again. How would they react this time? That's what he asked his players at the team hotel the night before the game.

"The biggest thing for us winning is: (a) We're on the attack. (b) We got something to prove. Ohio State ran us off the floor. Creighton ran us off the floor. Michigan ran us off the floor. We have to prove we can compete with these dudes. Lastly, it's about frustration. We let frustration set in all three games, and that's why we lost. We kept our heads against Northwestern, and we won the game."

After Michigan beat the Huskers 79–50, Miles met individually with players. Terran Petteway surprised his coach. Petteway was his leading scorer, his main gazelle in an up-and-down game, the guy who could most rile up the crowd with ferocious dunks. He asked his coach to rein in the team.

"Coach, man, we have no idea how to win on the road," Petteway said. "We just go like it's an AAU game."

Most of the roster played summer AAU basketball as kids, up-and-down games that focused on one-on-one isolation scoring and constant fast breaks. In other words, they lost their heads offensively. Game plans were mentally ripped up, and bad shots came in bunches.

"So if I pull in the reins . . ."

Petteway cut him off: "Yeah. If you want to control tempo, control it all you want. Don't worry about it."

Petteway's words were significant for Miles because the message of holding back the horses was coming from their captain and leading scorer, not middle-aged coaches. So Miles went to his point guard Tai Webster to see what he thought. Petteway might have gotten to Webster first, because here's what he said:

"I think it would help if you scripted our plays. Like if you just gave us the next three plays, that would make me feel a lot better."

Miles started planning the first three or four plays at the opening of games, like an NFL coach. He'd script multiple plays out of time-outs. He'd give signals throughout the second half of games. He cut them loose to run some motion offense at home, but on the road he tightened things up. And it had worked at Northwestern. Just like it worked at earlier stops in his career.

In the hotel film session the night before Michigan State, Miles runs through every play he might call and some he's starting to work into the system. They watch yesterday's practice, call after call, play after play. Chin. Fifty. Fifty Punch. Fifty Heart. Phoenix. Horns. Virginia. Low X. Utah. He asks Webster why a play didn't work and is satisfied with the answer. He needs his struggling freshman point guard to understand not just what it's called but why. That's what he had at North Dakota State with Ben Woodside, who would dribble through a wall for his team but also recognized what would work when, and why. A coach on the floor.

For the last five games, Webster had averaged 3.4 points and 1.6 assists. He grew up in New Zealand, playing against older players and leaning backward to get his shot over them. But mostly, he just drove to the hoop. At the start of this season, he did that often, scoring or getting fouled against smaller teams. Now, Big Ten guards pressured him, and he'd become tentative. Maybe play scripts from Miles would give him less to think about. Just run the play. Keep it simple. Especially in an atmosphere like the Breslin Center and against veteran guard Keith Appling, who would be back from an injury for this game.

Miles releases the players, who will get a snack later tonight. The coaches will go out together, but Miles usually dines alone to clear his head. In fact, he rarely hangs out with players or coaches on the road. He uses the time to focus and catch up on recruiting and film and to be creative with the offense.

At this point in the year, he's staying up until four thirty most nights and heading to the office at about nine. He's lost 24 pounds since the start of the season, when he was 170. He usually loses only 8 to 12 pounds. He doesn't think the added weight loss is due to stress. He says he got over wins and losses years ago.

"When you get to 550 or 600 games, that goes away," he says.

He thinks he's losing weight because he cut back on food and drink after a full physical at the Mayo Clinic in Rochester, Minnesota.

He still finds time to run. He tells his team about once every two weeks his belief in getting your body going in the morning with a workout of some kind, which will make you productive all day. When he punishes his guys with thirty seconds on the treadmill at ten miles per hour, he tells them he does twenty minutes at that pace, so don't cheat him.

He bought Kari a $150 plant for Valentine's Day and ate dinner with her before this trip, but before the holiday he can't remember the last time they had a family dinner. That's why he likes to bring the kids to games early, when they can hang out with the other coaches' kids. Craig Smith and Kenya Hunter have children of similar ages as Gabe and Ava, and Chris Harriman's kids are a little younger. They sprint around the locker rooms, the court, and the back halls of the arena. A few of them, including Gabe, sweep the floor during time-outs and after players scramble for loose balls.

The road, though, is his time. If his family travels for a road game, usually for a postseason tournament, he gets his own room away from them and especially away from his extended family. That's how he has to do it, he says. That's how he can win. And Kari wants to win, too.

He eats a deep-dish sausage and pepperoni pizza and drinks a couple of beers at Peppino's across from the team hotel. He reflects on how much he didn't like coaching this team until it started to come together five games ago.

He's thinking about Michigan State and how he just has to grind out a game. Control the tempo. Make it slower than the Spartans want to play. He's convinced his players in practice and meetings that it will work, which started with convincing Petteway to slow down. He's thinking if the game is tight late, they'll believe in him, that he was right all along. That's how they played Michigan State last year, and it worked for thirty-eight minutes before they lost 66–56. So he knows the guys who played last year believe in it. Benny Parker and David Rivers, who somehow shot eight for eight in the game for a career-high eighteen points. Miles shakes his head. Maybe it will come down to Walt Pitchford, who will be playing in front of his parents, who live in Michigan. He doesn't know.

Petteway is the key, he says. If he's willing to slow down and protect the lane, they'll have a shot. He'll do it, Miles thinks. After a recent win Petteway posted a message on Facebook, and Miles keeps a screenshot of it in his iPhone. The message: "This guy believed in me even after I turned him down for another school. I can't thank him enough."

Petteway, averaging eighteen points per game, was in the running for a Big Ten scoring title and maybe all-conference awards. Before he came to Nebraska and outworked everybody during his redshirt year with Pitchford and Biggs, he was best known as the Texas Tech guy who punched a University of Kansas player. He'd been miserable in Lubbock, especially after Bob Knight's son Pat got fired and Billy Gillespie took over. Petteway didn't fit in the plans, so he called Miles and Craig Smith. They welcomed him to Lincoln, where he would redshirt and learn the system with Pitchford and Biggs. Now, he'd be playing in one of the biggest games in the country on Sunday, and he didn't want an AAU shootout and another thirty-point loss on the road to a ranked team.

So Miles would spend most of the night watching defensive clips of Michigan State and building his script for Tai Webster to run. Sets of three plays here, four plays there. Different sets to switch things up on the Spartans and to give his point guard a settling feeling of knowing what's coming.

Before that long night of homework, and before he pays his check at Peppino's, Miles gets a text from Pitchford, pledging he'll stay off Twitter tonight—he had tweeted at two in the morning before the Ohio State blowout—and he'll be good from now on back home, too. No more partying. Miles texts him back: "I don't want you to blow an opportunity, or your potential."

Then Miles's iPhone vibrates with a phone call from Kenya Hunter. The prep-school game he's been watching in New Jersey had to be called with nine minutes left because of an all-out brawl. Still, Hunter likes the guard they've been chasing. He likes other guys, too, despite the fight. They feel like what Craig Smith calls "Miles guys," tough kids who would fit into the system.

"Remember this, Kenya," Miles says above the sound of Michiganders talking and drinking and under college basketball games on dozens of TVs, "recruiting is all about your depth chart. If you need a guard, get four. If we can get four guys to visit, we're going to get somebody."

They discuss each player Hunter likes. Then Miles asks if Hunter has his travel lined up to ensure he's in East Lansing by morning.

"You've got to be here," Miles says. "I have a good feeling about this one."

26

The Huskers spend game-day morning in the Beaumont Room on the mezzanine level of the East Lansing Marriott. Breakfast, film, walk-through, lunch: a theme repeated out of the calmness of Tim Miles and the fire of assistant coach Chris Harriman. Avoid frustration.

Like Michigan, Michigan State starts two players—sophomore guard Gary Harris and senior Adreian Payne—who will go in the top-twenty picks in the NBA draft in a few months and more who will probably play in the NBA later. Harris will make crazy shots with hands in his face, even if you do everything right. "Just keep playing," Harriman says while the team watches video of each player. "They're gonna make a tough shot. They're gonna make a contested three. Keep your poise. Keep running our stuff. Stay together."

Michigan State coach Tom Izzo has worked with athletic brass to give 70 percent of the lowest sections of the Breslin Center to students, who call this area the Izzone, rather than reserving premium seating for rich alumni and donors. In return for this gift, the students have organized themselves into one of the most creative fan bases in college basketball, researching opponents and finding ways to affect game outcomes. In the past five years the Spartans have won seventy-two of seventy-nine games at home coming into Sunday's 3:00 p.m. matchup with Nebraska. And they're 284-38 at home during the past ten years. "Have poise and composure, fellas," says Harriman, who has much for them to understand. "Understand it's gonna be loud. Understand it's gonna be a big-time environment. Don't get flustered."

On the road Nebraska had been blown off the court by ranked teams. Michigan State wants to do the same. In doing his homework for the game, Miles has read stories in the media about the Spartans' goal of making the first four minutes of the game a mess for opponents, taking advantage of its crowd's early energy. "They just want to punk you," Miles interjects from a table in the back of the room. "They want to take away everything you can do. No catch is easy. Everything is hard on the ball. Everything is coming at you downhill. So you're in a war, right? So you better be ready to go at the tip because their whole thing is they're not going to let you run any offense. They're going to be physical with everything. We're gonna deny Terran all over the floor. So you have to be ready. Early on, they just take teams right out of what they're doing. They jump on teams right away."

Just as Terran Petteway had admitted after the blowout at Michigan last month, the team panicked and started trying to make hero plays on offense and defense, trashing the scout work done by the assistant coaches and ignoring the in-game planning from Miles. They didn't have enough trust in each other or the plan to withstand the pressure. Since then the Huskers had played well, mostly at home, and had sneaked a win at Northwestern. But facts were facts: they were 2-9 (1-5 in the Big Ten) on the road, with one of those wins coming on a neutral floor. To fight these facts, these trends, the daunting Michigan State roster, the Breslin Center atmosphere, Harriman tells them they first have to always transition their brains quickly from offense to defense, because the Spartans try to score in the first six seconds of the shot clock, catching teams off guard. Second, all five guys have to rebound. Secure the ball. Don't rush out on the break. Control the tempo. To that end Miles will script multiple plays, at the request of Petteway and point guard Tai Webster. "Our first four plays are: 1. Blast vertical for T," Miles says from the back, counting the plays on the fingers of his left hand. "2. Open for Shavon. 3. Trojan. 4. I'll tell you what the fourth one is when I think of it. Any questions on those?"

Then he wants to know if anyone is having trouble understanding what he has to do today.

"Coach Harry is exactly right on the keys," Miles stands up and says. "We do this, we're gonna be in great shape and have a chance to win at the end of the game. We got something to prove. I want you to show the Big Ten and the United States that we're a team capable of making the NCAA Tournament and winning when we get there. And I don't mean tomorrow or next year or whatever. But if we play with frustration, it ain't gonna happen."

Student manager Brad Shaw moves the projector and screen off to a side wall, and players begin moving tables out of the way for the walk-through. Shaw gives the scout team jerseys with Michigan State players' numbers pre-Velcroed on back. He tosses a basketball to Webster. They move to a cleared corner of the room, where Shaw has taped down a 75 percent scale of a lane and three-point line. The scout team runs Michigan State's sets while the starting rotation defends them. Then they switch into the sets the Huskers will run. Miles sits at a table with his hand under his chin and index finger over his lips, the gesture his son has perfected when he does impressions of his dad on the bench. Though his left knee vibrates to a song only he hears, Miles says little, knowing the game plan is clear to them. The question is whether they'll shake the Etch-a-Sketch four hours from now if they get down by ten or fifteen early.

He releases the players early, and they head to their rooms for a quick break before the 11:00 a.m. lunch. The coaches stay, though, wanting to hang out together, ask each other if they're forgetting anything. But they haven't. They've even spent time on the opening tip, when Michigan State runs a play for a dunk to explode the Breslin. Instead of rehashing strategy, they gather at a table to eat while Miles tapes his pregame show with broadcaster Kent Pavelka in the opposite corner of the room.

Between bites of Marriott-prepared rosemary chicken and red potatoes, Harriman talks about his awe for MSU's Tom Izzo and how tough he makes his players. He tells a story from a year ago of recruiting at a high-profile high school that is essentially a basketball factory. He'd finished talking to his recruit, who was a middle-of-the-road player. On the other side of a thin wall of drywall, he could hear Izzo talking with the team's prize recruit, who had offers from all the powerhouses.

"Izzo gave a long speech," Harriman says. "He said, 'We don't have a great arena. We don't have good facilities.' He talks about how this is bad, that is bad. 'We're not Duke. We're not Florida. We're not Kentucky. But every kid in the last fifteen years has made it to a Final Four.' That was a pretty interesting way to pitch a kid."

Video coordinator Greg Eaton jumps in to talk about the 2009 NCAA Tourney, when he was working as an undergraduate student manager—essentially a Woody or Brad Shaw—for Louisville coach Rick Pitino. In the Elite Eight, Izzo and Pitino faced each other. Both had streaks going where every one of their seniors had made Final Fours throughout the coaches' stints at the schools, but they both needed the win to keep it going. Izzo's team won 64–52 in Indianapolis in the regional to preserve the streak at fourteen years and made the championship game that year. This season his Spartans are 10-2 (21-4 overall), tied with rival Michigan at the top of the Big Ten and ranked ninth in the nation, but his streak of getting players into the Final Four is in peril again in his nineteenth season. Seniors Adreian Payne, Keith Appling, and Dan Chapman haven't made a Final Four. He isn't going to look past Nebraska. He wants every win he can get to put his seniors in position to get a No. 1 or No. 2 seed in the NCAA Tournament, a stratosphere Nebraska has never seen.

Across the room Pavelka has lived all those years of disappointment. The upset loss to No. 14 seed Xavier when the Huskers had achieved a No. 3 seed under Danny Nee in 1991, the same year Nee's teenage son and his friend Ryan Hanigan watched the Huskers upset Jud Heathcote's Spartans at the Devaney Center. The way the 1996 team had literally walked out of practice, just walked out on Nee, despite a ton of talent, and lost nine straight Big 12 games. That was twenty-two and seventeen seasons ago. In the back corner of the Beaumont room, Pavelka asks Miles his final question: "What's it going to take to steal a win here?" Miles is as honest with his fans as he is with his team.

"We have been underestimated our whole lives here. That's nothing new," he says. "My job is to put us in position to win. Chris Harriman has done an incredible job preparing the guys for what Michigan State is going to do to us. Now, it's the old Mike Tyson. What happens when you get on the floor and get punched in the mouth? How are you going to react? Because you can be as prepared as you want to be, but until you get in that arena, those kids are the guys who have to do it. How are you going to react when you get a lead? Do you lighten up and start beating your chest and lose your focus and concentration? Or do you get frustrated if you get behind or calls don't go your way? Or if the shots don't go in? There's a lot of ways to get frustrated. You have to have a mentality of 'We're prepared for this. We know what to do. Let's go compete.'"

With headphones plugged into his iPhone, Miles heads to the hotel treadmills for a workout.

...

Two sides of the Breslin Center are lined with students when Nebraska's bus descends a ramp beneath the main floor of the building. Once security checks names to faces, the players drop their stuff in a tight visitors' locker room and start shooting on the court. In a fifteen-by-ten-foot side room to the locker area, coaches hang their suits and argue over which university in the Big Ten has the best atmosphere. They eventually agree it's Michigan State, slightly ahead of Indiana and a few others, then head out to the court to keep players calm, to keep the stretch-and-shoot routine as normal as any game or any practice. Local reporters corner Miles, wanting to know how the team is winning games and what he thinks the Huskers' chances are. He smiles big and does his undersell routine. His team doesn't have much of a chance, but it's not here to lose. As soon as he can get away, he retreats to the locker room to write a review of the keys to the game on the board and crystallize his pregame speeches in his brain.

An hour before the game, Spartan students line the court, where they're greeted with a fan guide—a tool Husker student groups have replicated at the urging of the Athletic Department. The eleven-by-seventeen-inch paper on every seat offers stats at the top that show Michigan State has an advantage in every category, offensively and defensively. What it doesn't mention is the disparity in assists: MSU is 6th in the nation and Nebraska is 336th, or 13th from the bottom of the NCAA.

On the bottom of the sheet, student leaders have come up with clear instructions for messing with Husker players' heads. In the first half, when Nebraska's shot clock gets down to ten, students are to start counting down from seven. In the second half, they should do the opposite, counting down from ten when the shot clock reads seven.

In a category labeled "Free Throw Distractions," students are offered colors that will be shown on signs across from the visitors' bench that instruct which song or chant to launch, anything from "The Muffin Man" or "Itsy Bitsy Spider" to unexpected silence followed by shouting. At the bottom a student leader predicts Dan Chapman, a senior who rarely plays, "has a career night and drops 34 points and 13 assists."

The eight thousand fans who regularly fill up student sections cheer their team through warm-ups, and the MSU players oblige by putting on a dunk show on their half of the court. Guard Gary Harris takes three attempts to slam an alley-oop to himself. At the baseline a developmentally disabled fan pseudodirects the pep band, and between songs he sends bounce passes to guard Russell Byrd, who hits repeated three-pointers.

Players slap hands with students in the front rows. The Spartans are relaxed.

The Huskers clap as they return to the locker room to sit in gray folding chairs, simulating their seating arrangement for games at home.

Miles goes through his script of plays again. He reviews the matchups, including David Rivers guarding Adreian Payne. This is a big spot for Rivers, his first start since finding the doghouse early in the season. Miles is ready to play big and shut down the lane, as he'd discussed with assistants since the Cincinnati loss in December, when the Bearcats were so dominant in the lane with their size. He then urges them to overcommunicate to make up for the noise in the building. They've practiced this week with loud hip-hop playing, but nothing can replicate Breslin's student section. So talk to each other.

Then Miles reminds them of the moment: "The keys are pretty simple, guys. Togetherness is greater than frustration."

On the marker board, in green, he hasn't written "togetherness." He hasn't written "toughness." He's written something that looks like "tougherness." Players laugh more than they would usually at this. Miles laughs, too.

"This team is really coming together," he says. "Stronger and stronger all the time. We're going to need everybody. . . . They're ready, all right? We've seen it on tape. And our attitude has to be the same. If it's Us Always, we're in great shape. If we live it, we're in great shape. All right, let's go have a good warm-up. Hustle in. Let's go."

They surround their coach and do their "team" chant on three.

"I'm jacked up," Miles says to his coaches as players file back out to the floor. "Tougherness."

The coaches laugh. In their locker cell Miles complains about his wool socks and finds cotton backups that feel better, but he's still talking about his marker-board gaffe.

"We're tougherness," he says and looks over at equipment manager Pat Norris. "Put it on a shirt. 'Tougherness.'"

Miles tells a North Dakota State story while putting on his brown suit. In a pregame speech he told his Bison team it was time to hit the gas. The next day his equipment manager had "Hit the Gas" shirts ready to go for the entire team. Assistant coach Craig Smith smiles at the memory as he puts on his green tie, intentionally picked because it's Michigan State's main color. Their thinking is, "You have to go right at them." So Miles and Smith started choosing ties based on opponent colors in Colorado and went on a run, but they stopped when boosters complained, which still makes them grin.

With eight minutes left before tip-off, the players return, and Miles asks them if they've heard of Pat Riley, the Miami Heat general manager and former coach of Magic Johnson's Showtime Lakers, Patrick Ewing's hard-nosed New York Knicks, and Shaquille O'Neal's Heat championship team.

"How many world championships does he got under his belt?" he asks them. "A couple? Maybe like eight or ten or something like that."

Riley won titles as a college player, NBA player, NBA assistant, head coach, and general manager. Miles is a fan of his books, particularly *The Winner Within: A Life Plan for Team Players,* or at least its first chapter, "The Innocent Climb." Riley writes a story his father told him. Miles has stolen that story for this moment. The kid down the street was bullying Riley, who didn't know if he should tell someone, take it, or fight back.

"But his dad tells Pat, 'You know, every now and then, somewhere, someplace, sometime, you're gonna have to plant your feet, stand firm, and make a point about who you are and, really, what you believe in. And when that time comes, you simply have to do it.'"

Miles pauses to meet the eyes of each player, even the scout team in the back row. So far, in this cramped beige locker room, he's cracked up his team by mixing two words into one, and now he's silenced them with a quote from Pat Riley's dad.

"It's time for us to plant our feet against these top teams," he continues. "Time for us to plant our feet and send a message about who we are. Win, lose, I don't care. I want you guys to compete your butts off. I want togetherness over frustration. I want Us Always. I want team. And I want every guy on the attack no matter what. If we can do those things, we'll be in great shape. Show me what you got. Plant your feet. Stand for what you believe in. And if it's true, and Us Always, we're gonna be in great shape. We're gonna make the run we want to make, and we're gonna end up where we want to end up. But it starts today. Let's do it. Take a knee."

After the silent prayer, the players chant as Miles screams "Let's go, Big Red." If the room had no exit, the Huskers would have busted through the walls to reach the Breslin court, where 14,797 fans (48 over capacity), the ninth-ranked team in the country, and arguably the nation's best college basketball coach are waiting for them.

27

Sunday, February 16, 2014, is a big basketball day nationwide, with tonight's NBA All-Star Game in New Orleans. In Nebraska the attention is on neither that game nor the Husker game at Michigan State. Eighteenth-ranked Creighton is hosting No. 6 Villanova, which wants revenge for the thrashing it took from the Bluejays at home three weeks earlier. None of the Nebraska media is in East Lansing for what Miles considers the biggest game of the year for finding out if his team is ready to matter on the national scene. Not one.

Beat writers Lee Barfknecht from the *Omaha World-Herald* and Brian Rosenthal from the *Lincoln Journal Star* will watch on TV, take notes, and listen to the postgame press conference online. Editors didn't think the travel expenses were worth covering the blowout in person. If something unexpected happens, the writers will try to get hold of the coach via media-relations guy Shamus McKnight.

At the Breslin Center the public address (PA) announcer tells the crowd that Wisconsin just beat Michigan in Ann Arbor, which means a win today will put the Spartans alone atop the Big Ten. As fans go berserk Miles meets Izzo at the scorer's table to catch up. They can barely hear each other, so Miles hollers into Izzo's ear that he's a god in East Lansing. Look at this place.

When Miles relays this to his coaches later, he does a spot-on impression of Izzo's scratchy answer, "Yeah, but I lose two and I'm nothing. Everybody's talking about it."

Miles loves Izzo's humility and how after all his success—a national title, all the Final Four appearances—he still has that drive and that fear of losing. Miles's path has been different, jumping from school to school and state to state up the ladder as a head coach, while Izzo never left Michigan, coaching at a high school before becoming an assistant at Northern Michigan, then becoming Jud Heathcote's assistant at Michigan State. In 1995, while Miles was getting his first head-coaching job at nowheresville Mayville, North Dakota, Izzo got his first team by taking over a successful Big Ten program from a legend and then becoming one. To emphasize the point MSU students behind the bench start chanting "Look at the banners," so Miles obliges and turns to them, puts his hands around his mouth to create a megaphone, and yells, "I know. I saw them last year." They laugh.

All that said, Miles would love to beat Izzo today.

The student crowd continues to dominate the pregame, drowning out the PA announcer during lineups by calling out MSU players' names themselves. Then they jump up and down in semi-unison to Kool and the Gang's "Jungle Boogie" while awaiting the tip. Then they blow into paper bags to await MSU's first basket.

Petteway pulls the Nebraska starters into a circular hug near midcourt, and once the game starts Walt Pitchford hits his game-opening three-pointer and gets a block at the other end.

The next possession the students start counting down the clock early, as instructed, and David Rivers, the new starter, falls for it. But he drains his three-pointer, the only one he will hit all season, with a defender's hand in his face, and the crowd falls silent, especially when he gets a block on the other end.

The students pop their paper bags in what sounds like instantaneous gunfire when Gary Harris hits a jumper, but Nebraska extends the lead to 13–4 by the first television time-out. The Huskers weather the first 4 minutes. But they don't score for 7:26 of clock time, until Leslee Smith puts back a Shavon Shields miss to break the drought. The defense, meanwhile, has been good, especially off the bench. Smith takes a charge. Ray Gallegos blocks a Matt Costello three-pointer from behind. Benny Parker hassles MSU point guard Keith Appling for steals.

Still, Michigan has too much offensive talent. Harris makes back-door dunks, and Payne, all 245 pounds of him, powers to the rim for post moves. At the midpoint of the half, Payne draws a foul, and both Miles and Chris Harriman demand a charge.

After Appling scores a layup for a 17–15 lead, Rivers gets hammered trying to put back an offensive rebound. The junior from Arkansas, with big eyes and dreadlocks, steps to the line. The crowd starts slowly and loudly chanting "Whoo-pi, Gold-berg." Rivers, stoic, misses the first, which cranks up the volume. But he hits the second. A year earlier he had faced similar chants in a game at the University of Texas–El Paso, where the crowd chanted "Britt-ney, Gri-ner," referring to the six-foot-eight center for the Baylor University women's team. Harriman remembered Rivers hadn't handled it well.

Nineteen seconds later Rivers gets fouled again and hits both shots with the Whoopi chants raining down on him. With seven minutes to go in the half, the Huskers are up 18–17 on the road against the Big Ten leaders.

Then something happens that always seems to happen to the Huskers. *Omaha World-Herald* sports columnist Dirk Chatelain, at home watching the game on the Big Ten Network while he waits to head to the Villanova-Creighton game, swears the Huskers historically have found ways to lose big games like these, especially when they're on the cusp of doing something big, something dramatic. Something always goes wrong. A bad break. Something.

Benny Parker and Ray Gallegos force a bad pass from Gary Harris back to the point that misses Appling by at least ten feet. The ball sneaks over the half-court line and bounces lackadaisically toward the Michigan State basket, where Appling meanders after it, checking behind him for Huskers trying to chase it down. With nobody coming Appling picks up the ball, and all ten players expect a whistle for over and back. But no whistle comes. Appling looks down court and realizes it's still the Spartans' basketball, so he gets the team into offense, and Costello hits a three for a 20–18 lead. The Husker bench leaps out of seats, and Miles screams for a time-out to go after the officials. Kenya Hunter has to restrain him, with some help from Harriman.

Meanwhile, the Husker players are incredulous, and Craig Smith gathers them on the court amid the chaos of the crowd jumping on Miles, who is still jumping on the officials for the obvious noncall. Smith looks over at Terran Petteway, knowing his reaction to this play could determine how everyone reacts in this pivotal moment. Will he freak out? Will they freak out? Will the game plan get chucked? But what Smith sees makes him smile, because that's what Petteway's doing. He's grinning big, showing his teeth in laughter rather than baring them in anger. The whole team joins him, laughing at the ridiculousness of the call, and somewhat at the antics of their coach, who clearly has their backs.

In that smile Craig Smith not only thinks the Huskers have a chance today against a ninth-ranked team on the road, but also thinks this team has a chance to be good. A real chance.

By the end of the half, the Huskers maintain a six-point lead after Pitchford hits a three-pointer at the end of the shot clock, ignoring the crowd's premature countdown, to go up 31–25.

As the players squeeze into the locker room, Miles joins in the minicelebration.

"That's fun, red," he yells. "That's fun. Let's keep it up. Do it all day. All day, all night. Let's go."

Then he joins his coaches in their adjacent room to game-plan the second half. Players mumble about matchups that are working. They're talking about plays they think will work against the Spartans' aggressive defense, just as coaches are doing. Then Miles comes back out, followed by his coaches.

"You wanna know what I don't believe?" he asks, not waiting for a response. "You ever heard, 'Okay, now they're going to make a run'? I don't believe in that. Honest to God. I've never believed it in my life. I believe the team that's the more aggressive team wins. And that if we come out the first five minutes and absolutely punch these guys in the mouth, that there won't be a run. There won't be a 'They're a great team. They're too good not to make a run.' You hear announcers say this. I don't believe it. . . . The team that plays with guts, the team that plays hard, the team that controls tempo and absolutely takes it at them controls the game. And that's what I expect us to do. We have to play through a little bit of tired. We have to play through any frustration. Don't get frustrated."

He compliments everyone, even Tai Webster, who struggled in the first half, and Ray Gallegos, who missed three straight threes.

"Ray, you've had great looks. Keep shooting them—that's gonna go in," he predicts. "Odds are in your favor. You're gonna get about three in the second half."

He tells them this is the best of what the Big Ten is all about, a tough, grind-it-out kind of game like this, and "you've got to love it."

The stats tell Miles they've gone zero for four on getting loose balls, but they have eight offensive rebounds, so effort isn't the problem. Keep blocking out, he tells them, and get those loose balls in the second half. Offensively, you've survived our drought and kept playing. Keep doing that.

He tells them to sit in their seats for a minute alone to focus, and the coaches retreat to give them space. The players are supposed to be quiet, to visualize the second half or mentally review their responsibilities, but Petteway can't keep quiet.

"Don't get too high, yo," he tells the team. "We've still got twenty minutes, man."

Miles comes back exactly two minutes after he left them, and he's not as manic now. He revisits the quote from Pat Riley's father: "Every now and then, somewhere, someplace, sometime, you're gonna have to plant your feet. Stand firm and make a point about who you are and what you believe in. When that time comes, you simply have to do it. Let's not do it halfway."

He pauses significantly. Looks around the room.

"Team on three."

Petteway: "One. Two. Three."

Team: "Team."

"Twenty more minutes, boys," Kenya Hunter says.

On the way back to the court, Shamus McKnight takes Miles's Twitter dictation: "It was a good half and we have to keep battling in the second half. Nothing was easy, and I expect that to continue."

To start the second half Pitchford drives right through Payne. Both six-foot-ten players tumble to the floor, Pitchford pushes off Payne to leverage himself back up, and the crowd lets him have it. Pitchford responds on the next possession by faking a three to get Payne in the air and steps in to hit a two-point jumper for a 36–25 lead.

The Husker lead is 38–30 at the first TV time-out of the second half. Miles blasts Petteway for taking a quick three-pointer on a one-on-two fast break, exactly the kind of AAU-style play Petteway had asked his coach to stop. Petteway nods but doesn't drop his head. He scores down the middle of the lane on the next possession off a Miles play call.

Michigan State answers, but Parker and Rivers, both buried on the bench just five games ago, combine to force a steal, and the Huskers lead 40–34 at the second TV time-out. Rivers then gets his fourth foul and faces more "Whoo-pi, Gold-berg" chants as he goes to the bench.

Still at home, inviting driving and parking delays, Chatelain can't leave his house for the Creighton game in Omaha. He's glued to his TV.

With ten minutes left, Miles sits on the bench, looking through his folded game cards rather than the action, trying to think three and four plays ahead, while MSU cuts the lead to five. And with 4:42 to go, Parker bites on a Harris fake, so Petteway comes over to help and fouls on a three-point shot. Petteway goes to the floor and shakes his arm, angry with himself. The crowd screams in approval, and Spartan guard Kenny Kaminski bangs on the floor to rile them more. Harris hits all three free throws, then Kaminski passes to Payne for a jumper, and Nebraska's lead is down to 51–49. At the last TV time-out, the Huskers know the ball is going to Payne inside, so Pitchford plays him from behind, not giving ground, and Rivers comes over to double-team him, as they'd discussed in the huddle. But Payne kicks the ball out, and eventually Costello gets a wide-open three-pointer and misses it. Pitchford pulls down the board, and Payne fouls him with less than three minutes left. The two coaches are battling possession for possession.

Petteway hits a three after turning down a ball screen and walking right into the defense to rise above it. Harris hits two free throws, and the Spartans, trailing 54–51, resort to full-court pressure and fouling.

Petteway scores and hits his foul shots down the stretch as the crowd falls silent, the only noise in the gym coming from Husker-bench cheers, Miles's directives, and play-by-play man Kent Pavelka ramping up for one last big play. Pitchford dunks with 14.9 seconds left and screams at his bench players, who are on their feet.

The players and coaches shake hands with the Spartans, and Miles high-fives his assistants. The 60–51 win is the Huskers' first over a Top 10 team on the road since 1997. The Huskers are now 6-6 in the Big Ten, already winning nearly half of the thirteen games statistics guru Ken Pomeroy swore they would lose. Before Miles can get to his team in the locker room, Pomeroy has already sent out a tweet: "I'll never forgive @CoachMiles for breaking my computer."

28

Back in the coaches' room, Jayden Olson says they now have to win the next game, a payback at home against Penn State, who beat the Huskers a month ago, the lowest point of the season. Harriman turns on Olson and says: "Hey, I gotta enjoy this one for a couple of minutes. That was fun, man."

While waiting for Miles to do quick interviews, the assistants marvel at Petteway's boldness down the stretch in the face of that crowd. Pitchford hitting key shots. When Miles comes in, they join him in the players' locker room. Screaming and dancing.

"Hey, I'm proud of you," Miles says when they calm down and sit. "We did it the right way. But let's just keep—hey, how fun is this?"

They explode again.

"We can't let up," Petteway says.

"Complacency is the next part, right?" Miles says. "Hey, we owe Penn State. Do we, or do we not? We owe them, so let's go get them, all right? Take a knee, take a knee, take a knee."

The prayer lasts only a few seconds before they count and chant. In the coaches' room, Miles asks the assistants to predict how many texts they've received from around the country. All of them are on their phones. Apparently, Tom Izzo has called Nebraska a bunch of "junkyard dogs" in the postgame press conference. Harriman searches for the full quote. In a few seconds, he reads it aloud:

"Nebraska, they were junkyard dogs. They remind me of some of our old teams. They took it at us. They talked it. They walked it. They played it. I thought they were tough. I thought they played well defensively. I think they made some incredible shots. I think Tim [Miles] is one of the great new coaches in this league, and he did a hell of a job. To be honest with you, we got what we deserved."

Harriman looks around the room, which falls silent for the first time all day.

Later, Izzo would get beat up online from Husker fans for the comment, as if he were demeaning them. The next day he would call Miles to apologize, and Miles would say, "Are you kidding me? It meant a lot to us."

After Harriman reads the quote, Miles looks over at his bald Australian assistant, who is still struck silent by Izzo's statement.

"Good job, Harry," he says. "You know what? I mean, seriously, you were as on as I've ever seen you on a scout. You set the tone early, I thought."

"Thanks, Coach."

Then Miles tells the coaches that they have to be hard on the team between now and Penn State to not let them get complacent.

"You gotta be careful," he says. "You want them to enjoy it, but you can't get too high. You just gotta get back to the process. Get back in the process."

Craig Smith smiles at that. His running argument with Miles over the years is that the process is more important than the winning, and at times Miles even buys into it a little. Other times, not so much.

"It's about changing of stimulus," Miles says. "There comes a point in time in every season when you just have to all of a sudden change it, or they'll zombie out on you."

Then Miles complains about Petteway's late three-pointer with a hand in his face. But he admits his captain usually makes impossible shots, especially in the last five seconds of the shot clock, no matter what numbers the crowd counts out.

"So what are you going to do?" he says and shakes his head.

Harriman pipes up: "I was about to kill him for shooting that three. . . . The Dagger. That's his [new] nickname. Dude hits more late-clock, feet-kicking-in-the-air, leaning-back shots. Oh, man."

Then Dagger pokes his head in the door to see Miles staring at the game's stat sheet.

"No turnovers, Coach," Petteway yells and grins. "That's the big number."

Miles keeps shaking his head, and every coach laughs.

"Hey, five in the whole game," Miles says. Then he tells Petteway not to get too cocky because Penn State's D. J. Newbill is coming to town.

"He's got your number," Miles says.

"Psshshshst," Petteway says and heads out to meet with Shamus McKnight, who has MSU media bugging him for an interview.

Smith can't stop talking about Petteway's calm during the time-out after the blown over-and-back call in the first half. He's always looking for defining moments that might show where the team is headed.

Harriman gets a text from Mike Dunlap, the former Charlotte Bobcats coach who is now at Loyola Marymount: nobody respected Nebraska basketball, he texted, but this game changes all that.

Harriman continues to rave about the bigger lineup and the impact Rivers had on defense.

"We're getting closer," Miles says while changing back into sweats. "We gotta avoid the noise all week, boys. Avoid the noise."

In the arena Walter Pitchford stands with his mother and father, who are saying "the sky is the limit" for this team. Petteway does interviews with Michigan State media, saying, "Earlier in the year, we probably would have broke down and gave up a bigger run, but really we stayed together and played as a team. . . . It just shows that, you know, we're changing the program with Coach Miles and the guys we have on our staff. We're changing the program of Nebraska basketball, and there's a lot more. This is the beginning for us."

Miles's phone is up to 181 text messages. On Twitter, #Huskers, #GoBigRed, #Nebrasketball, and #TimMiles are all trending.

"That's bigger than the win," Miles says. He holds a serious face for a moment, then grins.

Nebraska is the talk of the town, state, and country, even as Creighton beats up on Villanova in what was supposed to be the bigger game.

The coaches' boss, Marc Boehm, calls, and they put him on speakerphone. He hasn't been coming to road games because he's busy, but the real reason, coaches joke, is he worries he's bad luck, and he takes superstitions seriously, so they're only half-joking. In the tinny phone speaker, Boehm congratulates them and says to make sure broadcaster Pavelka doesn't get too excited, like he sounded on the radio. He congratulates them two more times.

"Hey," Miles yells into the cell phone, "it was easy. Just don't tell anybody that. Thanks, though. We appreciate it. Just gotta keep winning. You know how it is. Gotta make a run on this thing."

Then Miles says he has to text his wife. He walks out to a nearly empty Breslin Center floor, texts Kari, and calls his mother from the front row, his feet on the court.

"Hi, Mom, how are you?"

. . .

"Yeah, it was cool. It was good."

. . .

"Yeah, I'm proud of 'em."

. . .

"Thank you. Well, we just gotta keep it going. You know, every night it's the same deal, so we just gotta figure out how to win. Penn State and Purdue beat us both last time, so we can't get swept by either of those two and expect to make the NCAA. Gotta find a way to win."

. . .

He tells her he's coming up to Sioux Falls to get them for the Penn State game.

. . .

"All right. Thanks, Mom. Love you."

. . .

"Okay. 'Bye."

He makes another call to a coaching friend and goes into what he's really thinking: "I told my wife, 'I'm a millionaire, we have the best facilities in the country, and I'm miserable. I feel like I have to start all over.'"

He goes on to talk about everything that happened since the Penn State loss three and a half weeks ago.

"And pretty soon it's pretty fun, you know?" he says, and takes a deep breath. After the calls he heads back to the coaches' locker room, where assistants are picking up their duffels. Benny Parker goes by the door on his way to the bus for the flight home. Last spring Miles tried to encourage Parker to transfer to a smaller school to get more playing time. The Big Ten was full of too many good, big guards, and he'd always have trouble on this level. Miles would even help him find a school that was a good fit. But Parker refused. He wanted to win with these guys, his friends. And today, he played twenty-two minutes, causing chaos for M S U's offense.

Miles stops Parker to repeat what he'd been saying all day: "Hey, Benny. There comes a point in everybody's lives where they have to plant their feet."

Parker smiles and heads to the bus.

Five
Tougherness

29

Jeff Kolpack covered University of Mary athletics in the late 1980s and remembers Tim Miles as some sort of a benchwarmer or student manager with the Marauders.

He was shocked when the little guy from South Dakota was rumored to have a shot at replacing Greg McDermott as the North Dakota State coach in 2001. Was that the same guy? Then he checked Miles's résumé of transforming Mayville State's and Southwest Minnesota State's programs. By then at the Fargo Forum, the biggest media outlet in North Dakota, Kolpack had covered the Bison's national dominance in football for a few years and had enjoyed covering Greg McDermott's one year at NDSU in 2000–2001, even if the women's team still outdrew the men consistently. He also covered North Dakota State's controversial and deliberate move to Division I, which cost the Athletic Department and its donors tons of money, relationships with its rival North Dakota Fighting Sioux, and any shot at the postseason during a five-year transition period.

But Kolpack was instantly impressed with Miles, who talked straight, once even telling Kolpack in a Bison Sports Arena hallway that he was certain he was getting fired after the 2-6 start to his third season. He liked how Miles energized the fan base, handing out tickets in dorms and saying all the right things publicly, assuring boosters the wins would come, no matter what he admitted to reporters in hallways. After the move to Division I—mainly a football decision in Fargo—Miles motivated his team, without a conference, by making up a fictitious league. Kolpack laughs when he thinks of it a decade later. Miles called it the UBL, the United Basketball League, which included schools such as the New Jersey Institute of Technology Highlanders and the Indiana University–Purdue University Fort Wayne Mastodons. He'd keep standings, acting as commissioner, searching for any way to motivate his players to win games that didn't seem to matter much because he had no standings or postseason goals for them to meet.

"He just made the whole thing up," Kolpack says.

He was Jackie Moon, Will Ferrell's lead character in the 2008 movie *Semi-Pro*. Moon would implore his Flint Topics to wins in the American Basketball Association by giving them a reason to finish fourth in the league. Miles convinced his team to go on a run, finishing the 2004–5 season 16-12 after a 4-9 start. Miles also embraced any idea associate media-relations director Ryan Perreault put in front of him to fill seats.

Miles's most brilliant move, according to Kolpack, was recruiting a full class of players and convincing them to redshirt that same year so they would have a shot at the NCAA Tournament their senior years, when the Bison would be eligible. Those freshmen beat up on starters in practice while they waited their turn to wear the green and yellow.

The key to that recruiting class was Ben Woodside, a point guard from southern Minnesota who didn't get a scholarship offer from the Gophers. Woodside set high school records in points, assists, and steals at Albert Lea, the smallest city in America at the intersection of two interstate highways. When Tim Miles stepped into the Woodside living room, he set his car keys on a coffee table.

"I'm giving you the keys to this basketball program," Miles said. "And I want you to be the driver."

Sold. Eighteen months later, in January 2006, he was a five-foot-eleven freshman leading the Bison into the Kohl Center at 11:00 a.m. on a Saturday to play the fifteenth-ranked Wisconsin Badgers, coached by Bo Ryan.

Kolpack and colleague Mike McFeely flew to Wisconsin in the Fargo Forum's private jet while the team drove eight hours to Madison. Athletic director Gene Taylor wanted the whole team— redshirts, student managers, all staff—to know and to feel a raucous Division I basketball environment and that NDSU didn't just have to be a football school if they did things the right way. Ryan had coached up small programs—Wisconsin-Platteville and Wisconsin-Milwaukee, and even junior high and high school teams before that—just like Miles.

The Badgers pounced on North Dakota State, 8–2, before Woodside hit a two-point jumper. Wisconsin nailed a three-pointer to go up 11–4, and Woodside hit a no-hesitation three to cut the lead to 11–7. As Woodside ran back on defense, he looked over at his coach, who was screaming at him: "Nonstop. All day, Woodside. All day."

Wisconsin would score five more points the entire half. Woodside and power forward Andrew Smith had outscored Wisconsin 17–16 themselves, and the Bison led 30–16.

Early in the second half, Miles looked up at the scoreboard, and then over at the clock, which read 11:59 a.m.

"I was thinking to myself, 'It's been a helluva morning,'" he remembers now. "We're up sixteen on the No. 15 team in the country on the road."

Through the rest of the game, Miles kept screaming, "All day, Woodside" or "All day, Smith," urging them to keep shooting, keep attacking. Wisconsin was never in sync, but at the end of the game fouls started piling up for the Bison. Smith fouled out, Woodside had four, and the Badgers cut the lead to 57–53 with 57 seconds remaining.

"Fellas, today is our day," Miles kept saying at time-outs and during free throws. "Today is our day."

Woodside hit all eight of his free throws down the stretch, including four in the last minute, and stole the ball on the Badgers' last possession for a 62–55 win in a Big Ten building over a ranked team. He'd taken the keys and driven the car right over a ranked team on its home floor. Assistant coach Saul Phillips, a former Ryan operations guy, was in tears. So was Taylor, the athletic director.

Wisconsin had shot 22 percent from the floor, with main

scorer Alando Tucker, who would play in the NBA, missing his first twelve shots and finishing two for eighteen.

Ryan was stunned and spent nearly an hour with his team before meeting with the media. "It's very difficult to ever try to analyze this without paralyzing yourself."

Miles met the media right away and was pragmatic: "It's going to help recruiting, obviously. It might hurt scheduling."

The move to Division I had been difficult, and the win provided some closure. On top of that, NDSU president Joseph Chapman claimed the win couldn't have come at a better time, when the Athletic Department was trying to raise money for improvements to the arena.

As soon as Miles finished interviewing and joined the Bison in the visitors' locker room, the players gave him his first ice-bucket shower at NDSU.

"He came in yelling, and we just dumped it on him," Woodside said.

On the bus for the five-hundred-mile trip home, the players were hyper and hungry by the time they hit Minneapolis. When they walked into a sports bar/restaurant, Minnesota fans, always ready to celebrate Wisconsin losses, adopted the team with big roars for the Bison.

"It was the best day of everybody's life," said guard Mike Nelson, a Wisconsin Mr. Basketball winner who wasn't recruited by Ryan.

"That's when ESPN met Tim Miles," Kolpack says.

Perreault handled a barrage of national media requests, from ESPN's Andy Katz, ESPN morning show *Cold Pizza*, Minneapolis's KFAN, Tim Brando on Sirius radio, bloggers. Miles calls the game his JFK moment. To this day, he still has coaches and fans tell him where they were when they heard about the upset. He still has a *Newsweek* that he had with him on the trip. He'd been getting so many calls and requests that he wrote names and phone numbers and interview times all over the magazine in pink Uni-Ball pen.

"It elevated our status like you wouldn't believe," Miles says. He'd planted his two feet in Madison, and in Fargo, and bigger schools noticed, including Nebraska assistant athletic director Marc Boehm in Lincoln.

In 2012 Miles attended his first Big Ten coaches' meeting. Bo Ryan came over to him with his staff and grinned, saying, "You're buying us dinner. The only reason you're in this room is because you beat us six years ago."

Hours after Nebraska upset Michigan State, Creighton dropped 101 points on No. 6 Villanova to win by twenty-one and solidify itself as the best team in the Big East in its first year in the conference and as a serious contender for a national title. None of that mattered much inside Nebraska's borders, as Lee Barfknecht's long-distance Huskers column—on the hope and buzz the Huskers were creating in the fan base—nearly doubled the hits of the Creighton game story on the *Omaha World-Herald*'s website.

He'd covered the Huskers since the mid-1970s, and he likened this game to breakthrough road games from at least a generation earlier. The game in '86, when Moe Iba's Nebraska team beat Norm Stewart's Missouri team, 75–66, at the old Hearnes Center, a week after all-time leading scorer Dave Hoppen injured himself for the season and his college career. The game in '91, when Danny Nee's team beat thirteenth-ranked Oklahoma, 111–99, one of the few times ever Sooners coach Billy Tubbs was so flustered that he called a time-out at home.

After the Michigan State win, sports radio hosts were claiming Nebraska, of all places, had become a basketball state, not a football one. That topic was a talker.

After watching the final two minutes of the game on a television deep inside Creighton's CenturyLink Center, *World-Herald* columnist Dirk Chatelain wrote, "Suddenly it's not so crazy to envision an NCAA tournament with Creighton and Nebraska. The Huskers haven't qualified in 16 years. The two haven't made

it together in 23 years. . . . For Nebraska, the fun starts with a
head coach who's part Urkel, part Butkus. Tim Miles acts like
your next door neighbor, posing with fans after big wins, dancing with his team in the locker room, dropping one-liners on
social media." Then he beats Michigan State.

Like that win at Wisconsin for the Bison, Miles and his team
were the darlings of the national media, too. Both Creighton
and Nebraska were the top stories on ESPN's college basketball
home page Sunday night. Hours after the game, the Huskers
were still trending on Twitter, along with the movie *12 Years a
Slave* and *Prince William*. ESPN reporter Myron Medcalf tweeted:
"Tim Miles just dropped the mic on Big Ten Coach of the Year."
ESPN's John Gasaway wrote that the bigger lineup would make
the Huskers tough to beat. The key wasn't the offense, he claimed,
but the defense and rebounding. And playing David Rivers and
Benny Parker.

USA *Today*'s Nicole Auerbach used her "Coaches' Corner" column to write about Miles's team being good and lucky in the
turnaround. She even wrote about the coach's heads-up pennies
on the floor of his locker before games.

Both Gasaway and Auerbach predicted the Huskers might
make the tournament. They were 6-6 in the Big Ten and could
finish with a winning record in the conference, which would get
them on the bubble for the tourney, or past it and into March
Madness.

The season had been over a month earlier. For perspective,
assistant coach Craig Smith was still stuck on the Terran Petteway moment after the blown over-and-back call in the first half.

"Terran, even six weeks ago, would have freaked about that
call," Smith said after the game. "Then the other guys would
have followed up. But when he came in [to the time-out] smiling, it was like, 'We're gonna go get them.' . . . Confidence is an
amazing thing."

He said Petteway's changed mentality was infecting the team.
He could see a new mean streak in Rivers and Parker. And all

of that started with Miles. Smith said the win and the possible aftershocks were a little reminiscent not just of the North Dakota State win at Wisconsin in 2006, but also a win at Colorado State during their last year in Fort Collins.

In the spring of 2012 the Rams had key Mountain West Conference games at Texas Christian and Boise State. They lost a nail-biter to Texas Christian University, and their GATA guy and leader, Pierce Hornung, played through what Smith swears was an undiagnosed concussion at Boise State, where they were awful in the first half.

"Miles just ripped them at halftime," Smith says.

They ground back into the game, and Wes Eikmeier, the Fremont, Nebraska, kid who'd transferred from Greg McDermott's Iowa State team, hit a couple of shots in a row down the stretch. Then he got leveled at the top of the key with no foul call. Smith and Miles were livid, but the Rams fought back to lead by one with six seconds left. Boise State called a time-out to set up a play for Derrick Marks, a left-hand driver. CSU coaches reminded their team of this, but Marks drove left anyway and hit a buzzer beater for a 70–69 win to drop Miles's team to 4-5 in the Mountain West and 15-9 overall, on the outside looking in at the tournament. That felt like rock bottom for the coaches, just like the Penn State loss for the Huskers in January.

A week later the Rams were hosting coach Steve Alford's New Mexico team, which led the conference and was ranked eighteenth nationally. But Colorado State was undefeated at home, and after getting beaten up inside, Miles switched to a small lineup. Inexplicably, Alford went small, too, losing his advantage in the paint, and the Rams won running away, 71–63.

"It still bothers Alford," Smith says. "When we see him, he still tells us, 'We messed up that game so bad. We were beating you before we went small.' But after we beat New Mexico, it gave our guys a lot of confidence."

The Rams won key games late in the season, including beating the University of Nevada–Las Vegas (UNLV) after trailing by twenty-one. They made the tournament and lost in the first round to Murray State.

For Smith, the Michigan State win felt like the New Mexico win, like something that could carry them places.

At the season's low point, the Penn State loss, Miles hit the airwaves up in the Twin Cities. He did it again at this high point. Host Paul Allen nicknames his 9:00 a.m. to 12:00 p.m. show "The Love Covenant," and Miles was a regular. Sunday, Allen had watched the Gophers sneak a win at Northwestern, but he wanted to talk to Nebraska's coach about the MSU game Monday morning:

Allen: "Time to celebrate a victory by an old friend of ours. Nebraska beat Michigan State on the road, and the coach of the Nebraska Cornhuskers is former North Dakota State University basketball coach Tim Miles. What's going on there, Tim Miles? . . . Feeling pretty good about yourself these days, aren't you, Mr. Miles?"

"I am bruised," Miles said. "My chest is bruised from beating it so badly. I have to watch out."

Allen fawned over Miles, the win, Terran Petteway, and the coach's poise on the sidelines—had he not seen Miles chase the officials after the over-and-back no-call? Miles gave Allen his chess metaphor of basketball coaching, that you have to be thinking about the next move rather than getting caught up in moments.

"So you've gone from some rube coach in Fargo at North Dakota State University, trying to get Ben Woodside into the NCAA Tournament. . . . You've gone from that to chess master."

Miles reminded Allen that he'd been a rube—Allen's word for a sports simpleton—at many stops, starting with Mayville.

Miles told him he'd been asked if beating Michigan State was his best win in his nineteen years of coaching. And he said it was pretty good, but beating Wisconsin that day was hard to top, and he reminded Allen that that win earned him his first appearance on KFAN in Minneapolis. Then he told a story.

He had a headache when he finally got home from East Lansing on Sunday night, but he was watching highlights from the game with his son, Gabe.

"Dad, that was a big win. I only cried twice during the whole game."

"Why were you crying?"

"Remember the time you were yelling at the refs because the ball went in the backcourt?"

"Yeah."

"I thought you were gonna be like the Iowa coach and get kicked out of the game."

Gabe was referring to Fran McCaffery getting booted from a game at Wisconsin six weeks earlier.

Then Miles told Allen about having to dump a player and how the team subsequently came together. He talked about Petteway's leadership, how it was starting to remind him of Woodside at NDSU. How he was so fearless. And he told Allen, and thousands of listeners, about the practice where he accused Petteway of caring only about his stats.

"Nobody's ever cared more," Miles said. "The only time he's given me any lip is when I told him he didn't care about the team. I was just trying to poke him a little bit."

At the end of the interview, Allen and Miles agreed that his next appearance on the show would be in a month, on the Monday of the championship game at the Final Four, when he would be preparing Petteway and the rest of his team for the title game.

30

Tuesday is Change the Stimulus Day. They beat Michigan State on Sunday. Had a day off Monday. Everyone is telling them how great they are. And Miles thinks they need to rediscover their edge. So before talking about how to get revenge on Penn State in the film session, Miles is in speech mode. But first, captain

Shavon Shields rides Miles a bit for being two minutes late to his seat.

"I had to get my clipboard," Miles says, and then he tells his favorite story about Jerry Tarkanian, the legendary UNLV Runnin' Rebels coach, famous for biting folded towels and winning the 1990 national championship. Miles says Tarkanian once warned his team the next player late for the bus would get left behind, and that player was Larry Johnson, his best player, a future No. 1 pick in the NBA. Tark asked his coaches, "Where's Larry?" But nobody knew. So Tarkanian shouted that he left his clipboard in his office and ran to get a second clipboard, giving Johnson time to beat the coach back to the bus.

"So, dumbasses," Miles concludes, "I'm always the last one on the bus. And don't give me any crap for being late."

And why is he always a few minutes late?

"I'm gonna meander down. And if anybody asks I just say, 'Oh, yeah, well, I forgot my clipboard. I had to make sure I had my clipboard.' But I'm not a three-clipboard guy."

Now that he's got their attention, he launches into his philosophy of humility. The theme is this quote: "Humility is not thinking less of yourself. It's thinking of yourself less." Some folks attribute the aphorism to author C. S. Lewis, of *The Chronicles of Narnia* fame. Others claim the words, those exact words, come from best-selling author and evangelical megachurch pastor Rick Warren. Miles attributes it to nobody. He just explains that he wants them to believe they can beat Michigan States and Ohio States, that they can outplay Michigan's Nik Stauskas and Penn State's D. J. Newbill. He just wants them to think about themselves less, and think about the team more, which is exactly what they've been doing for the past few weeks. He sees it when forward David Rivers plays with the starters but also works with the scout team. Anything to make the Huskers better. He sees it when backup to the backup guard Trevor Menke is buried in social science education homework, but makes the team a priority anyway to prepare the scout team and to whisper reminders in starter Tai Webster's ear fifteen times a practice or game.

"Okay, maybe just five," Miles admits.

He makes Craig Smith talk about his epiphany during the over-and-back call and the time-out.

"When I came back to the huddle, I remember Shavon and Terran specifically," Miles says. "Shavon kind of telling me to 'shut up' or whatever, or maybe it was Terran telling me to 'shut up,' and the other guy saying, 'We got you, Coach. We got you, Coach.' And I really felt that. And I'm like, 'I believe them. I think they got my back on this. I think they're going to go out and outplay these guys, and we're gonna win.'"

They were more together than Michigan State, he says. Izzo was frustrated with his players because they were playing like they were frustrated. By the Huskers. By bad breaks. By each other.

"We're more together," he says. Then he talks about how important communication is in basketball. And about avoiding the noise from family, friends, and fans. But then he throws his own noise at them. Praising them for their defense and how they've become the top-ranked defensive rebounding team in the Big Ten, somehow, "with you slugs."

Then he sets them up for the next two games. Penn State and Purdue beat them earlier in the season when the Huskers weren't together. Now, they're coming to Pinnacle Bank Arena. Though both teams are near the bottom of the Big Ten, he talks about their big wins. And tells his players they can't revel in their prosperity. They have to walk and talk with humility to prepare for payback. Penn State comes to town two nights from now.

"So we're up against it," he says.

He talks in metaphors and parables that include tigers and soldiers, homeless guys and millionaires. He talks about their chances of getting to the NCAA Tournament. He bucks up Tai Webster for playing better defense and promises to work with him on his jumper after practice today. He talks about his son, admitting he cried during the game, and that his wife told him they looked like a championship team. Then he brings them back to the "think of yourself less" quote and reminds them that they can go on a run now.

"So, we're gonna watch clips," he finishes. "We're gonna knock it out. We're gonna [practice] with seventy-five minutes on the clock and get you out of here. So get your work done today."

Before the Penn State game, equipment manager Pat Norris handed out charcoal "Tougherness" warm-up shirts. He'd been impressed with how the captains had been texting the team about what to wear for games, and on road trips, so they were coordinated and looked like a team at airports, hotels, restaurants, and arenas. Norris didn't hesitate in getting the new shirts made quickly because, he said, Miles makes him feel important. Once, Norris had hidden in the shadows at a booster event at the Lincoln Country Club during Miles's first year, even when the coaching staff was being introduced. Miles found him afterward, cussing him out for not going up on the stage.

"Do it next time," he said and nodded at Norris, adding some stronger words for added encouragement.

In eight years at Nebraska, he'd never been told anything like that.

"He makes me feel like things wouldn't run without me," he said.

Miles loved the "Tougherness" shirts, especially because they were born out of his idiocy. He'd spent the previous night at home watching video of his team melting down at Penn State last month. Gabe asked him why he'd want to do that.

"I want to be hungry," he told his nine-year-old.

In the coaches' locker before the game, assistant Kenya Hunter admitted to Craig Smith and Chris Harriman, "It's hard not to think about the future, isn't it? It's tough to take one day at a time."

They nodded.

In pregame speeches Miles told them to keep those feet planted and that they owed these guys, which was why he watched that 58–54 Penn State loss last night. "I want [to think of that] loss like an open wound," he said. "Today, I want to be a hungry dog. Penn State, you're not going to sweep us. We owe you one, Penn State."

Walter Pitchford made his obligatory game-opening jumper eighteen seconds into the game, and the Huskers built the lead to 39–27 at halftime, mainly because the Huskers harassed Penn State into shooting 26 percent from the field. The Huskers also were twenty-one for twenty-three at the free-throw line in a whistle-filled game, and twenty-seven of their thirty-nine points came "at the rim," in Miles speak.

"All night long. All night long," Harriman screamed at the players as they headed to the locker room.

In the second half Petteway kept driving, kept fouling, and kept scoring as the Huskers built a twenty-six-point lead. They won, 80–67, after the Husker bench gave up late points. In the locker room Miles didn't allow the letdown to bring him down.

"In the end I have to give credit where credit is due," he said once the players sat down. "When we were 0-4 in the league [in January], we had a staff meeting, and everything was wrong. We were bitching about all you guys. One guy stood up and said, 'We're gonna win twelve out of the next fourteen.' That's Jayden Olson."

Since then they'd won seven of nine.

"Purdue's next, and Illinois gets to sit and wait for us at home," Miles warned. "I'm proud of you, but I tell you what, we got a lot more winning to do to get where we want to go. At the end of the day, man, this is the time of your life. Give it everything you got. Lay low. Stay away from girls. Hit the books. Get some sleep. We're looking at five or six weeks where we can do what no Nebraska team has done."

Then he went home and watched a replay of the game. Then he kept watching it. And he watched more with assistants in the morning. Every time, almost every play, even every moment between plays, his mood darkened.

31

Coach woke up the next day, Friday, convinced his team couldn't pay back Purdue Sunday if they played like they did in the 80–67 win over Penn State. More important, they couldn't win big games or make any kind of tournament run if they didn't play every game, every minute, the way they did at Michigan State. They couldn't afford to take steps backward.

For perspective, a thirteen-point Big Ten win against anyone was a good thing for the program and the fan base. That a thirteen-point win could make the coaching staff borderline berserk might be proof that Nebraska basketball was coming of age. Miles met with his coaches, who all agreed with what Miles had seen on tape. Heavy doses of selfishness and complacency. No togetherness or toughness, much less tougherness.

He put video coordinator Greg Eaton to work to build a film package called "Us, Not Us." The film session would be vitriolic. That was the plan. Then Terran Petteway texted Coach minutes before film: his car broke down two miles away on East Campus. Then the other captain, Shavon Shields, texted Coach to say he'd be late. He trusted both captains, but he couldn't just let it go. He'd punished others for such mistakes.

"So what should I do?" he texted back to Shields.

In the end they agreed on minor punishments that took into account that they had communicated well.

"The other option was they could grab a toothbrush and clean my [office] toilet."

By the time everybody finds his spot in the Hendricks film room, Miles is ready to scorch everyone. Eaton shows fifteen clips of the team in "Not Us" mode. Not helping each other up after taking charges or diving after balls. Griping on their way to the bench after fouls or being pulled. Lazy screens by players who weren't getting shots.

Petteway gets blasted for letting bad calls affect his attitude.

Ray Gallegos for playing without passion, for being "a zombie all night."

Walter Pitchford for not making plays for teammates on offense, for his effort depending on whether he's hitting his threes.

Leslee Smith for climbing into a cocoon of self-awareness after turnovers.

"Why wouldn't he hustle back?" Miles yells at him. "That's just not us. That you would play like that, that's just not us."

Then Eaton shows five plays that look like the Michigan State tougherness, and most of them include little Benny Parker getting in the face of Penn State guards, who are bigger, stronger, and more statistically valuable than him. Guys who want to run him over and post him up, but he won't let them. He's down low on defense, working so hard the rest of the players on the floor—even the bench and the fans—feed off his channeled anger.

"Just look at Benny," Miles says in awe. Three months ago he wasn't sure he could even play Benny Parker. Now he's pleading with his starters to emulate Parker.

"In the end, how come there's five Us clips and fifteen Not Us clips last night?" he asks, pausing five seconds for them not to answer him. "You better figure it out. Why? Where does that get us? Losing one game at this point in the season is like losing three. You can't afford it."

Out in the gym each player has his own banner on the east wall. Miles tells them he could put one word on each of those banners, in fact maybe he'll do it in the spring, and he could put some cool word up there with the name and fancy PhotoShopped picture from the marketing people. *Tougherness.* GATA. Which word does each of them want by their names? Because that could go the other way, too. *Zombie? Emotional? Inconsistent?*

"Guys," he says, "this run means everything, but it doesn't

mean anything if we're going to deviate and become [what] we were in November and December."

He challenges Petteway to keep his cool, Pitchford to play consistently hard, Gallegos to show he wants to win, and Smith to get his confidence back.

"We're playing a team that just kicked our ass," he said, referring to the 70–64 loss in West Lafayette five weeks earlier. Now, Purdue is struggling despite its talent, but he warns that the Boilermakers don't respect Nebraska basketball, so they'd better do something about it, which means fix this Not Us problem. He tells them they made a liar out of him when he told a *USA Today* reporter, "We have a chip on our shoulder, and it's not a Dorito." But they played with Doritos on their shoulders last night.

"You know, when I get into trouble, it's because I'm a people pleaser," he finished. He explains that he texts and emails and signs things and runs errands and tries to do everything to please everybody. But sometimes he needs to focus on what matters in the moment.

"So it's important to me to be watching Purdue all morning. It's important to me to talk to Chris [Harriman, who is running the Purdue scout] and say, 'We have to have this ready, that ready, and that ready. We have to be rock solid on this scout, Chris. Because these [guys] are coming in here with nothing to lose.'

"Your behavior matters. Your attitude matters. I have no toleration for guys acting like babies. Dave [Rivers], I buried you. Why didn't I play you after I started you early in the year?"

"Rebounds," Rivers said.

"Rebounds. Did you bitch and moan about it? No, you came every day to practice, and when I finally decided it's time to get bigger, get Shavon back up to the wing, did you seize the opportunity? Yes. Have you stopped? No. You've been there every game."

He tells them he wants them all to be playing their hardest every night, like David Rivers, another guy he wasn't sure could play in the Big Ten. He tells them that even when his Colorado State team was going 0-16 and was outmatched in every game at every position, with just seven players on scholarship at season's end, they gave everything they had. Last year's team, led by Dylan Talley and Brandon Ubel, was just like that, challenging teams they shouldn't, winning games they shouldn't, game after game.

His Nebraska team has just won four straight games and is 7-6 in the toughest conference in the country. But now, in this context, they aren't even as good as last year's Huskers, 5-13 in the league, 15-18 overall, or his worst team in Fort Collins, 7-25 overall. And they believe him. He is selling them the edge he needs to sell to himself. Nebraska is the littlest dog in the fight, and they'd better remember that, and they'd better play like that, every game, every play.

"I love being in this league, and I want to kick this league's ass," he says. "I want to show this league that anybody from nowhere can kick your ass. I want to show you guys that Nebraska basketball can do the same thing to the country. But when you act like that [last night], we're screwed. . . . We won last night, but we lost last night. So you think it's one of two things, either they're babies and immature or the pressure is getting to them. This is not pressure, my friends. This is not pressure. This is the time of your life. We're either gonna make it, or we're not. For Ray [Gallegos] and Mike [Peltz, both seniors], I hope we make it. I want them to go around for the rest of their lives and say, 'We started a legacy. I had something to do with it.'"

He figures they have about twenty practices and games left in the season. Can they just give everything they have for twenty days?

Purdue didn't have a chance.

After the coach's rant Harriman told the team that nothing he'd tell them in the scouting report or on the court would matter if they weren't buying what Coach Miles was preaching. Later, he'd say he wasn't sure Miles planned to lay the paint that thick, but once he got going, there was no stopping him. The session reminded him of the late Rick Majerus and his accountability, his refusal to allow "slippage," as he called it.

The Huskers beat up the Boilermakers on both ends of the court to win, 78–57. By the end of the night, Petteway had twenty-nine points and Shields eighteen. The defense held seven-foot NBA prospect A. J. Hammonds to six points and five rebounds and suffocated Purdue to 30 percent shooting, 22 percent in the first half.

After the game Shields was laughing and grinning, and the biggest worry on his mind was that he had four assignments due at midnight.

"Let's have a homework party," somebody told him.

Miles gave them the next day off if they promised to be humble in their preparations for Illinois. He explained to his coaches they'd been connected to them for seven straight days, and they didn't need to see the coaches for an eighth. On top of that, they had become a good defensive team, and good defensive teams play well when they're fresh.

The coaches nodded their heads, knowing they'd get a break from their players, too, who showed in the last three games—and in the last eight days—that they could go either way. Beat Michigan State on the road, then play sloppily at home. Come together during stressful moments on the bench, then show terrible body language at time-outs. Have captains show up late to film, then practice like Navy SEALS.

Everybody could use a day.

32

When the RPI rankings came out Monday, Nebraska was 48th, and ranked 49th by Ken Pomeroy. Still behind Iowa and Minnesota, but exactly where the coach wanted his team. By winning eight of ten games, the Huskers had moved from last in the Big Ten to within a half game of fourth, behind Wisconsin, the two

Michigans, and Ohio State. ESPN "bracketologist" Joe Lunardi had the Huskers among the eight teams on the outside looking in at the NCAA Tournament.

They were right there.

As ESPN's John Gasaway had pointed out, since moving forward David Rivers into the starting lineup, the Huskers had gotten bigger and longer and had made packing the lane a priority, which the coaches called "elbows and blocks." They forced opponents to take tougher shots, and miss most of them, shooting about 30 percent each night. Somehow, without a true center, the Huskers also led the Big Ten in defensive rebounding. Effective defensive field goal percentage and defensive boards. Those categories were where teams find toughness and wins.

Of course, despite all this good news, Miles had an even worse feeling about the Illinois road game than he'd had in the coaches' locker room minutes before beating the Illini at home two weeks ago. Illinois was a Big Ten freak show. John Groce's team earned a spot in every Top 25 poll at New Year's by going 13-2, then lost ten of eleven games. Groce inserted two freshmen into the starting lineup, and the team won at Minnesota by thirteen points. Then he had a week to watch Nebraska play three games and get his new lineup ready.

On game night the Huskers shot zero for eight from three-point range in the first half, and Terran Petteway, who was toying with leading the Big Ten in scoring, went to the locker room with two points on one for nine shooting. But out of the break, Miles ran a play for Petteway that resulted in free throws and another play where Petteway lobbed to Walter Pitchford for a dunk. The Huskers led 28–27 a minute into the second half. But Illinois freshman guard Kendrick Nunn hit a three-pointer off the backboard late in the shot clock to open up a six-point lead with eleven minutes left, and the Huskers never recovered, losing 62–49. They held Illinois to 30 percent shooting on its home floor, but just couldn't score. Rivers, Benny Parker, and Leslee Smith had come off the bench to shoot eleven for eleven, but the rest of the team went nine for thirty-four, including Petteway's five for eighteen.

As Tim Miles had told them, a loss at this point of the season, with RPIs and brackets in the balance, was like losing three games. But he returned to Lincoln in an even-keel mood. The loss was understandable considering the schedule, and they hadn't collapsed from togetherness or body-language standpoints. Some nights the ball just doesn't go in the basket. Petteway wouldn't have many shooting nights like that one. On top of that, assistant coach Chris Harriman's son, Avery, was doing so well in his fight against leukemia that he'd had his medicine port removed earlier in the day. Why mope or rant? At least that's what he told himself to keep from sinking too deeply. He'd told his players repeatedly during this run to deal with prosperity the same way they deal with adversity, and he'd have to show them that this week with Northwestern coming to town. Even keel.

The next day coaches were talking Big Ten standings. Three teams, including Nebraska, were in a race for fourth place, and five teams were virtually tied for seventh. Meanwhile, Wisconsin had won five in a row to separate itself from everyone else. Everything would come down to the last week of the regular season.

"It's big time," Craig Smith said.

Then the coaches gave Kenya Hunter a hard time about the pressure on him with the Northwestern scout. Hunter told them all to back off, using the earthiest language he could find. The coaches were feeling good going into film at Pinnacle Bank Arena the afternoon before the game. All business. No impassioned speeches. Just Northwestern breakdowns.

The Husker Athletic Department had designated the Saturday, March 1, matchup against Northwestern the annual legends game, when the program invites former Husker players home to be recognized, mostly organized by operations guy Teddy Owens. Among those who showed up were Dave Hoppen and Erick Strickland. While other Big Ten teams invited former NBA All-Stars back for these types of events, the Huskers brought back players remembered by few fans outside the state's borders. And they would be on hand for Nebraska's practice, which went smoothly.

The players shook hands with the alumni, who were all over captains Shavon Shields and Terran Petteway, telling them how proud they were, what it meant to them that the program was relevant again, before everyone but the players climbed upstairs in the arena for a reception.

Pregame speeches Saturday were short, the first lasting less than three minutes and the last less than one. After the team hit the floor, athletic director Shawn Eichorst poked his head into the coaches' locker room, where Miles was alone with his game cards, looking at plays he wanted to run at the end of the game for Shields if the game was tight.

"Anything going on today?" the AD asked.

Miles smiled. "No."

"Mind if I use your urinal?"

"Nope."

Eichorst then made fun of Miles's tie. With 3:27 left on the clock, Miles went out to a crazy-loud arena, and his Huskers gutted out an ugly 54–47 win when Shavon Shields scored the final eight points of the game, the last two on a dunk off a Petteway pass.

For the eighth straight game, the Huskers held opponents to less than 40 percent shooting, something the program hadn't done since 1982, when six-foot-eleven freshman center Dave Hoppen controlled the middle.

In the locker room Harriman walked in carrying six-year-old son Avery.

"Dad," Avery said, "I saw Shavon Shields dunk."

Shields walked over to the two of them, and Harriman put Avery down. Shields lowered himself to eye level.

"Tell Shavon what you saw," Harriman said.

"I saw you dunk."

Shields smiled.

"Tell him, 'It's about time,'" Harriman said.

"It's about time."

Shields smiled bigger and picked Avery up.

"I learned that from you in your basement," Shields said.

The Huskers were 9-7 in the conference and 17-11 overall.

"This is the way it's going to be the rest of the way," Miles told his team. "Nothing will be easy. Now, we get to go to Indiana, and we've got to be junkyard dogs."

33

The North Dakota State win over Wisconsin put Miles and his program on the map in NCAA Division I basketball. A year later his redshirted recruits were sophomores, and he'd named point guard Ben Woodside his captain. They beat Wisconsin–Green Bay 85–73 on a Saturday in November 2006, but Woodside turned an ankle.

Just five games in, the season had already been a crazy one. The Bison had played Minnesota tough at Williams Arena and lost by thirteen, then traveled to Lubbock to play Texas Tech in Bobby Knight's last full year as a college basketball coach. The Bison led twice in the second half but lost some close calls, and the Red Raiders won 85–81. Woodside never came out of the game.

Afterward, Knight asked one of his staffers to go to the North Dakota State locker room to ask the Bison to wait before leaving for the airport. Meanwhile, Knight didn't make his players available to the media, and he held a terse press conference himself. Despite closing to within three wins from tying North Carolina's Dean Smith as the all-time-winningest college basketball coach, he was angry, blasting a *Sports Illustrated* reporter in town doing a piece on Knight and his protégé Duke's Mike Krzyzewski. In the end he proclaimed this: "This was a game that the wrong team won. This isn't a game of brilliant decisions. This is a game of outplaying people, outhustling people, outworking people and that's what they did."

Knight eventually marched to the visitors' locker room and told the Bison players the same things, while standing beside Miles with his arm around the much smaller coach. Miles swears to this day Knight didn't know his name in that moment.

"Our kids battled until their last breath of life in that ballgame," Miles told a media thirsty for more quotes. "I thought they did a good job, but I don't like losing. It was a game I thought we could have won."

The Bison recovered to win two home games before traveling to Marquette the next weekend for the forty-fifth Pepsi Blue and Gold Classic—the kind of early-season tournament the host team is supposed to breeze through with two easy wins—and then Woodside's ankle had swelled to the size of his calf. Miles had a policy that players who didn't practice didn't play. So Woodside hobbled around the Bison Sports Arena all week. In the first round of the four-team tournament Friday evening, the Bison were a first-half mess against Princeton, which hit eight of ten three-pointers to lead by five at the half.

Miles had recruited a big-bodied Wahpeton, North Dakota, junior college transfer named Andre Smith, originally from St. Paul, who hadn't scored and had just one rebound in the first half. He was angry and volatile, just out of control. He'd also been recruited by Marquette coach Tom Crean, who passed on him in the eleventh hour to take a player he felt was a surer bet. At least that's how Miles figured he got Smith to come to Fargo. That, and Smith's girlfriend went to NDSU, which didn't hurt. Smith was yearning to play Marquette in Saturday's tournament title game, to get revenge on Crean, and his play was costing him the chance. Woodside had only two first-half points and was icing his ankle in the locker room.

"Dre," he said. "Relax. I gotcha."

At the start of the game, only about a thousand fans showed

up, but with Marquette playing the second game, the BMO Harris Bradley Center started to fill in the second half. With just a few minutes remaining, the Marquette student section started chanting "Let's go Bison." The players thought they'd won over the crowd by playing hard, like Rocky winning over the Russians from Ivan Drago. But Miles told them in a late-game time-out the fans just wanted to play North Dakota State in the final, which should be a joke of a game on paper. Plus, they'd love to beat the team that beat Wisconsin last year to claim state supremacy.

"So let's give these [guys] what they want," he said.

Woodside scored eighteen in that second half and played thirty-nine minutes on his messed-up ankle to lead the Bison to a 57–50 win to set up a Saturday matchup with Marquette, the No. 8 team in the country. Smith pulled down his tenth second-half rebound at the end of the game and hit free throws for his first points. He was ready to play Crean's team immediately after beating Princeton.

The Bison were wild in the locker room. In the chaos Smith asked his coach if he could say something.

"Boys, listen," he said, and at six-foot-seven and 230 pounds, he didn't have to ask again. "You know how much this game means to me. I hate Marquette more than anything. I want to show Marquette more than anybody how I can play. But I want us to win worse than I want me to play good. Tomorrow night, I gotcha. We're winning the game."

The next day Smith scored twenty-six, while Woodside limped around the court to get just six, refusing to ever come out of the game. The Bison beat a Top 10 team, 64–60, on its home floor without ever trailing. Woodside had played seventy-nine of eighty minutes on a sprained ankle, then joined his teammates in dousing Miles with a water cooler.

"We were lights out," Tim Miles says now. "We just lit them up."

Tim Miles told the story of that weekend to his Nebraska team before it dug into a scouting report on Tom Crean's Indiana team. The story's morals were clear, from picking up teammates, to gutting out wins when you're not at your best, to players self-correcting after screwing up. Miles loved those messages. Even more, he loved telling a story about beating a good Tom Crean team on the road. And now Miles's Huskers were traveling to play Crean's Indiana Hoosiers with an NCAA Tournament on the line, arguably Nebraska's most crucial game in the past sixteen years, though some would argue even longer.

In Tim Miles's first season at Nebraska, he brought a team into Assembly Hall in Bloomington with a 3-8 Big Ten record, 12-12 overall. That same day, February 13, 2013, Duke and North Carolina were playing the biggest game in the country. A parody account for Indiana center Cody Zeller, who had an older brother who played at North Carolina, tweeted this out: "Duke & UNC are playing tonight. Tyler says its the best rivalry in college bball, but I think IU & Nebraska will be just as historic someday . . ." Later, ESPN college basketball national writer Eamonn Brennan would write: "The point, of course, was to laugh at silly little historically inept Nebraska. The Cornhuskers would never amount to a basketball rival for anyone, let alone the blue-blooded Hoosiers."

The Indiana center had nothing to do with the tweet, but he had something to do with Miles's yearning to win at Indiana. Before that game Miles decided he needed to spend more time with his eight-year-old son, Gabe, so he took him along to Bloomington.

He sat his son behind the bench, and equipment manager Pat Norris promised to watch out for him. But an usher told Miles Gabe couldn't sit there because he didn't have a ticket. They had to put him on the end of the bench, right by Norris.

The first half was a grind, and the Huskers couldn't stop Zeller inside. Senior captain Brandon Ubel kept fouling him. At the free-throw line, Zeller missed a couple. Right before halftime he went to the line again, and by this time Gabe was entertaining himself on the bench. As Zeller shot his free throw, Gabe stuck his thumbs in his ears, stuck his fingers out, and wiggled them in the air while making a funny face. Zeller missed the free throw. From behind the baseline, a voice boomed out from the student section: "Shut the f*** up, kid."

Zeller hit the second free throw, and the Huskers were down seven at halftime. Miles, who hadn't heard the student, started walking behind his team and to the locker room. At the end of the bench, he saw Gabe standing and staring at him, about to bust into tears.

Then he busted into tears.

Norris stood right behind him and explained what happened.

"So here I am," Miles would say later. "I want to just blast the student section. I want to calm my team down, but I've got to take care of Gabe first."

He took Gabe to the coaches' locker room and soothed him. Then with the time he had left, he told his team to hang in there. Upon his return to the court, he grabbed an usher and, in a voice that would make Bobby Knight proud, yelled loud enough for the entire student section and most of Assembly Hall to hear: "If anything else is yelled at my son, I want that student kicked the hell out of here."

The students didn't say a word in response or to Gabe for the rest of the game.

Indiana blew out the Huskers, 76–49. The simple truth was that his team was outmanned. But none of that bothered him as much as what happened to his son.

At the end of the season, Gabe had Indiana going to the Final Four in his tournament brackets.

"I thought you hate Indiana?" Miles asked him when he looked over Gabe's picks.

"Yeah, but they're good."

. . .

In the film room Monday at Hendricks, Miles reminded his team how important this game was for positioning in the Big Ten Tournament and any postseason chances.

"This time of year," he said, "you have two options. You either have to win, or you can't lose. So we have to replicate that feeling we had at Michigan State. We have to be junkyard dogs. . . . But Indiana is a good matchup for us Wednesday. This will be a big RPI win for us."

The Illinois road loss had dropped Nebraska's RPI to 54, and ESPN's Lunardi had released a bracket forecast with the Huskers not even among the eight teams on the outside looking in at the tournament. He had Creighton as a No. 3 seed.

Miles went on to talk about the last regular-season game of the year, when they would host Wisconsin, which was No. 2 in the country in RPI.

"That will be our biggest win," he said.

Two wins this week could put the Huskers as high as a No. 4 seed in the Big Ten Tournament and almost assure the Huskers of an NCAA Tournament bid. Privately, coaches figured winning one of the last two would put them into the tournament, regardless of what happened in Indianapolis at the Big Ten Tourney.

In practice, Miles was in elementary school teacher mode, inserting new plays and checking for slippage. He blew up only once, questioning whether Tai Webster could even make the team next year after Webster turned the ball over repeatedly. David Rivers, though, saved the day by taking a knee in the groin from scout-team center Kye Kurkowski, which instantly changed Miles's mood.

"Get the ice cup," Miles shouted.

"Boy, he's got balls," said center Leslee Smith, who never says anything. Rivers got up and grinned at Smith and his coach, who cut off practice early to do his last Monday-night radio show of the season. First, he pulled Webster aside to buck him up. He'd need him this week.

34

Walking into Assembly Hall is like walking into the architecture of college basketball history. For opponents showing up to an afternoon practice, that history can be as heavy as the Old Testament.

The players walk by black-and-white poster-size photos of Walt Bellamy and the Van Arsdale brothers, Quinn Buckner and Isiah Thomas, Steve Alford and Keith Smart. They half expect Jimmy Chitwood from the movie *Hoosiers* to show up around the next dark hallway, running the picket fence.

Tim Miles was on summer break from college at the University of Mary the first time he entered the building. It was closed. He and teammate Mark Wagner pulled on a locked door until they got it to open. They stared at silhouettes of championship banners in the dark rafters. Then they drove to French Lick, hopped a fence, and played one-on-one on Larry Bird's personal basketball court.

The Husker players drop their duffels in the front rows and race each other to the court to start shooting. They can't get the balls out of Woody's bag fast enough. The floor-only lighting in Assembly Hall creates an illusion that the upper-level seats go on forever, into an infinite outer space, and coaches walk the stairs to check them out and take photos from every angle of the arena.

Radio play-by-play man Kent Pavelka takes a seat at the scorer's table. He remembers coming to Assembly Hall forty years ago, when coach Joe Cipriano scheduled Nebraska to play in the Hoosier Classic right before Christmas. Creighton and Southern Methodist (SMU) were the other sacrificial lambs in the tournament. Indiana coach Bobby Knight's team was loaded: Quinn Buckner, Scott May, Bobby Wilkerson, Tom Abernathy, Kent

Benson, and more. Cipriano found a way to beat SMU 69–67 in the first round, and the next night the Hoosiers hammered the Huskers, 97–60. The Huskers would finish the season just above .500. Knight wouldn't lose a game all season until Kentucky beat him 92–90 in the Elite Eight. The next season, 1975–76, his Hoosiers would go undefeated, the last time a team ran the table in college basketball.

Miles sits in the front row opposite the benches and runs through his practice schedule on a legal pad. He looks up into the rafters. "They've got to have a camera in here somewhere," he says.

Operations guy Teddy Owens agrees. In full paranoia mode he says when they practice in another team's gym, they assume every team has a camera on them. "Except Michigan," he says. "[John] Beilein isn't that guy."

Miles smiles without looking up at Owens. Then he thinks of something and starts searching his Twitter feed, where a fan has asked him to wish his son a happy birthday. Miles does. Then he looks for an early-September tweet from Hoosiers coach Tom Crean. It's a photo of a banner that lists all-time wins in the Big Ten Conference. Indiana is on top with 1,716 victories, 24 ahead of Illinois and 41 ahead of in-state rival Purdue. Nebraska and Penn State, the eleventh and twelfth teams to join the conference, aren't even on the banner. Above the picture Crean has typed: "Indiana is the Dominant Program in the History of the [Big Ten]," which doesn't exactly mean anything. At the time of the tweet, Penn State had won 108 conference games in twenty-one years in the Big Ten. Nebraska had won 9 in two years, the same number it had won so far this season. But Miles finds a way to turn the tweet into an insult, another way the bluebloods of the Big Ten don't respect Nebraska basketball, another reason to be the littlest dog in the fight. He'll have to work that into a team meeting at some point before the game. No, let's just use it now.

Miles walks to center court. The starting rotation has been shooting on one end, while the scout team perfects Indiana's offensive sets with Harriman on the other. The team now makes a circle around Miles, who shows them the tweet.

"See? No respect. You want to do something about that?"

Then he launches a full walk-through. The players defend Indiana's plays, with Trevor Menke playing Indiana point guard Yogi Ferrell and Sergej Vucetic playing freshman Noah Vonleh, who will be a Top 10 pick in the NBA draft in the summer. Harriman watches closely to make sure they're paying attention to Indiana's personnel—who drives right and should be forced left, who posts to his left shoulder and should be pressured to go the other way, who is shaky with the ball and should be raided by multiple defenders into a turnover.

Mostly, Miles keeps things light. He jumps Woody for not having a whiteboard ready at the exact moment Miles wanted to draw up a new play.

"Where the hell is the student manager?" he yells, not able to hold a stare, breaking up when Woody holds up the clock he's running at the scorer's table.

Then Walter Pitchford misses a fadeaway shot after not running hard on a cut.

"That might work at some prep school or some other place in Florida, but not good enough to play for us," he says and jerks Pitchford out of the full-court scrimmage.

Five minutes later David Rivers cuts hard and hits a fadeaway.

"Go to the basket," Miles says. "I just jumped Walt for that."

He turns to the sidelines. "See, Walt? I yelled at him for the same thing."

He brings Pitchford back into play, and the six-foot-ten forward buries two scout teamers on screens.

"Good job, Walt!"

Terran Petteway has been nursing a sore knee, being as quiet as possible about it, and when he misses a fast-break layup and comes up limping, Coach shuts him down. "You're done," Miles tells him.

"Aw, man," Petteway answers, shaking his head and heading for the front row of seats.

After running a few end-of-game plays for Shields and Pitchford, Miles closes the practice with slow claps. The team claps, too, and meets him in the middle of the court. He has nothing much to say, so he looks at freshman point guard Tai Webster, an eighteen-year-old from New Zealand who will try to lead a team to a win at Assembly Hall. This is the same kid who asked him what "the bubble" was the other day. Miles makes as serious a face as he can muster.

"Tai, get your shit together," Coach says.

Webster looks at him with his eyebrows scrunched down.

"No Facebooking girls tonight," Miles adds. "Let's beat these guys tomorrow night."

"Frickin' right," Harriman says, and they return to the hotel for dinner.

While players pack up and take their time getting to the bus, Miles checks scores on his phone. Creighton is getting upset by Georgetown, a team that's on the bubble with Nebraska. Nebraska could use a Georgetown loss, and, of course, Creighton won't come through for them.

"I guess we can't count on anyone else," he says. "We just got to win."

Harriman and Miles believe Indiana doesn't play defense well. They also think their own team doesn't run its offense hard enough. And thinks too much. That is the theme of the night film session in a basement meeting room at the Hilton Garden Inn, just off campus. Run your stuff "with pace," Miles says more than ten times. He wants guys to run to set hard screens. To set up defenders, then cut as hard as possible. Not walk around.

He asks senior guard Ray Gallegos if he thinks about every step he takes when he goes up and down stairs. That's what he looks like running the offense, like he's thinking about every step, which slows him down.

"Stop thinking. Run it with pace."

Harriman, in preparing the scout, also sees Indiana is susceptible to turnovers. If the Huskers attack the ball, even when sitting back in zone, they should get steals. He and Miles have picked the Hoosiers they want to attack every time they get the ball, including Ferrell, one of the leading scorers in the conference. They're asking something that's somewhat complicated of their team. Attack the ball, but stay back to pack the lane. Run offense hard, but keep the pace of the game slow. They don't get back on defense, so score in transition, but don't just try to outrun these guys. That's what they want. The players keep nodding. They beat Indiana at home, and if they keep their heads, they can beat them at Assembly Hall on Senior Night.

The team sticks around to eat hotel chicken with the assistants. But Miles needs time alone to think, to see if he's missed anything, to catch up on e-mails and texts and Twitter. At Lion's Pub two blocks from the hotel, he's thinking about recruiting, still working on getting a center for next year, hopefully a junior college monster. He's thinking about Gabe's basketball game a few nights ago. Miles showed up late, and Gabe saw him sit down with Mom. Gabe stood up on the bench and held three fingers up and pointed at the basket. Miles smiled.

"What's he talking about?" Kari asked.

"He's gonna shoot a three," Miles said. "He's calling it now."

Ten minutes later Gabe heaved it up from his hip and rattled it home. On his way back to play defense, he did the airplane, his arms tilting against the turbulence. Miles had never seen him so fired up. Then Gabe hit another one and airplaned again.

Dad had to fly out of town on a recruiting trip, to watch a point guard. Then to Iowa to see a forward the next night. All while trying to get his team into the NCAA Tournament. The future matters as much as the present, maybe more. Always recruiting. Always selling. Worry about Indiana while worrying about finding another point guard, a center. He has seven to ten recruits on his list, and his assistants have fifteen to twenty. He'll make at least three calls tonight to high school or junior college players, that's for sure. A call to his wife? Maybe.

Kari had made the deal with him way back at Southwest Minnesota State. Do what you have to do to get better players. Winning with a husband on the road was better than losing with a husband at home and getting fired. But as they've moved up every level of college basketball, recruiting has become a bigger battle for coaches and their families. With more resources—more money and travel and technology—recruiting never ends. Miles is impressed with himself a little, though. He can't remember the last time he took his wife out for dinner, but he got her a nice plant for Valentine's Day.

The truth is now that they're winning, now that they're on the bubble, Miles feels pressure to be doing more than ever.

"You just can't enjoy it," he says between bites of a pub burger. "You don't want to enjoy it. I always think I should be watching more tape. And then I start watching, and I'm just bored. It's the same thing. So, I might just focus on the last five minutes of a game. You can learn way more about what they're truly like and what they're going to do."

Now he's thinking about each of his players and which buttons he has to push when the pressure builds through these last weeks. Jump on certain players, then build them back up, like with Webster and Pitchford this week. Ways to keep others interested and showing life. Distractions for the nervous ones who succumb to their fears by making them angry, usually at him. These Huskers haven't been in this position. Only the coaches really get it.

Webster, the point guard running the team, literally asked Miles the other day what the bubble was. He wasn't joking. Miles tried to explain the brackets to him, the idea that if you're somewhere among the last teams to get into the tournament, or the ones trying to be among those last teams, you're on the bubble. You have conference champions getting automatic berths, then you have sure bets, then bubble teams. Webster may have understood perfectly, but he wasn't letting on that this American basketball algebra was computing.

"Look," Miles finally said, "being on the bubble means your bubble could burst, all right?"

Miles grins. Then he thinks about the big picture. Where they were in January, at 0-4 in the conference. He really believed they were dead on arrival. He'd said it out loud to his coaches in meetings, which made the possibility more real. The season was over. The players didn't believe in what the coaches were doing. They didn't believe in each other. DOA.

He looks at the same players now. They're rebounding. They're packing the lane, contesting every shot inside. Playing together occasionally. And Petteway's making every big shot when his team looks vulnerable. And they're having fun.

Still, it makes no sense that they've gone 9-3 in the conference since that rough start. Losing only one game at home all year, on a missed tip at the buzzer, and winning three of their last four on the road. He shakes his head.

"We're awful," he says. "We're not even close to where I know we can get. So that's encouraging. We're awful. And that's encouraging."

35

For Tim Miles, locker-room pep talks come from anywhere: a recent book, an old mentor, or maybe a movie that shows up on cable for the 587th time. Most often, though, they are mined from the top of Miles's head or from a conversation he's had with his assistant coach handling the scouting report.

Miles scouted opponents for Northern State's Bob Olson in the early 1990s as a graduate assistant. Olson won 305 games in fourteen years, the last 100 with players Miles had recruited from across the Great Plains. Olson would always come to Miles a few days before games with the same question:

"Can we beat them?"

"No," Miles always said. Then he'd tell Olson exactly how they would win. And usually they did, qualifying for NAIA national championship games in two of Miles's last three years as an assistant.

Now, he always spends significant time with his scout coach, which rotates among assistants, as chosen by Craig Smith.

Like most coaches, he has pet favorites he can lean on when lightning refuses to strike. His go-to speech is "The Toughest Team Wins." The earthier version of that speech is "Church Bells," as in "You're going to have to have balls as big as church bells tonight," Smith remembers.

In December 2010 at the Cancun Governor's Cup tournament, Miles's Colorado State coaching staff limited its sightseeing to local bars, where late in the night assistant Niko Medved coined the phrase "las balls grande," a poorly translated form of the "church bells" theme. That's what they would need to win the tournament, he said, "las balls grande." The Rams then beat Appalachian State by three, Ole Miss by seven, and Southern Miss by five to win the tournament. The coaches repeated the phrase the rest of the season, going as far as to look up "las bolas grandes" for accuracy before reverting back to Medved's version out of superstition.

Tonight, and most nights before road games, Miles prefers solace. Yeah, you're only in Hawaii once, but you also only have a chance to sweep Indiana a few times in a lifetime when both teams' seasons are on the line. So he prefers distance from the team and the coaches. Time to focus and maybe wind down with some channel surfing. Time for lightning.

He's searching for a theme for tomorrow night, even though he already knows his theme for Sunday's home finale against Wisconsin. Miles once hired former Husker volleyball coach Terry Pettit as a consultant to help him turn around the Colorado State program. Miles had an apprehensive team. And Miles was apprehensive himself about the team and its chances in an upcoming game. Pettit looked him in the eyes and said, "What if I told you I already knew the outcome of the game? Would you be curious if we won or lost?" Pettit paused, ramping up Miles's curiosity. Then he continued: "I know you'll win. Now, how does that make you feel? You'll win." To know that you'll win. That's a powerful thing. It erased all fear. That's what his team would need before playing the Badgers, a potential No. 1 seed, while the Huskers played for their first NCAA Tournament berth in sixteen years.

He goes up to his room.

By morning, the theme is intact, inspired by a Stephen King character named Andy Dufresne, who climbed through a sewer to glory as the protagonist of an Academy Award–winning film.

Players and coaches eat a $10.95 buffet breakfast at the Hilton. The morning's news: Terran Petteway's knee has no swelling. He's ready to go.

After eating they meet downstairs for one last film session. Miles walks in last, when he's sure everyone's there, and hands the day's sports section to assistant coach Chris Harriman.

The Huskers are picked to lose by six points. He wants them to think nobody's giving them a chance, the opposite of what he'll want them to think later in the week against Wisconsin.

Before diving into Hoosier clips on the big screen, Miles reminds them Indiana is holding Senior Night ceremonies after the game.

"Let's mess up Senior Night," he says. "It's a big night. Don't give them anything. Nothing easy."

After Harriman finishes his reminders on each player, on each offensive set, Miles has a last word before the team heads back to Assembly Hall for some shooting practice and final walk-throughs.

"I'm so ready," Miles says. "I would play this at noon. Let's go, baby."

At the shootaround senior Ray Gallegos starts nailing threes before anyone gets on the court. Later, Miles checks himself into the walk-through scrimmage, pretending to be Gallegos at the top of the key.

"Let's see it, Coach," Shields says, begging him to take a three-pointer.

He refuses. "I'm not taped up."

Later, he steps in for Benny Parker and gets down low, exaggerating Parker's size. Then he exaggerates Parker's defense, hip-checking assistant Craig Smith, who is defending on a screen. Then Miles grabs Smith and elbows him.

"That's an illegal screen, Coach," Shields yells. Petteway cracks up.

Afterward, Gallegos keeps shooting with Woody, the student manager, rebounding for him and firing Gallegos passes as quickly as he can.

"You look tired, old," Miles says to him from the scorer's table, where he's fiddling with pink game cards.

Miles smiles, but Gallegos doesn't, and hasn't all practice. He led the Big Ten in three-point shooting last season, but now he's a bench player, averaging almost ten fewer minutes per game, rarely scoring in double figures. He's shot three for sixteen in his last three games and hasn't shot more than 50 percent since the December holiday tournament in Charleston. Miles has been riding him for playing without passion, but he's continued to run plays for him to get threes. Captain Shavon Shields walks back on the floor and sets screens for Gallegos to cut through, a more authentic simulation of the shots he'll take tonight. Woody hits the shooter with rifled chest passes and bounce passes. Gallegos swishes nearly every shot.

The team returns to the hotel for a 12:30 snack and a 3:00 p.m. team meal. It's Ash Wednesday, and Craig Smith limits himself to salad and baked potatoes. He keeps reloading them for the brain food he needs to prepare the scouting report for Sunday's home Wisconsin game, which will be the biggest game of the year, he figures, no matter what happens tonight in Bloomington.

At 5:00 p.m. Chris Harriman is one of the last to step on the bus for the final ride to Assembly Hall. He always feels calm from 4 hours to 2 hours before tip, but the last 120 minutes are a crescendo of anxiety. He wants to win his scout games.

On the bus he tells the other coaches about his St. Louis Billikens beating Dayton by twenty points two successive years to ruin the Flyers' Senior Nights during his basketball PhD under Rick Majerus. He starts nodding and rocking back and forth in his seat.

In the locker room Miles lays out his lucky charms. A rock from his wife. A heads-up penny. Except for video coordinator Greg Eaton, the coaches all accept and feed into Miles's superstitions, which go back to his grad-assistant days, when he'd call his grandmother to say rosaries for him over the phone minutes before big games. He'll almost forget to remove his underwear at the last minute tonight, too, which got him a win at home a few weeks ago.

In coaches' minds, anything could help. Video coordinator Greg Eaton, though, stays quiet during the superstitious talk. He's originally from Boston, and no superstitions worked for him and his Red Sox. When he gave up his last superstition of wearing the same clothes every day during the 2004 playoff run, the Red Sox won the World Series, ending the eighty-six-year curse of the Bambino.

With players out shooting, Miles moves to the team locker room to write his keys to the game in Michigan State green on the whiteboard:

- HC [half-court] game
- Play smart off[ense]
- Rebound. Win Paint
- Shock the world!
- Its our time!

He chooses to save the theme for the thirty-two-minute pre-game talk, and when the players return for it, they're silent in their beige folding chairs, staring at their shoes. The coaches come out of their smaller adjacent locker room. Miles follows and reads the keys to them. Then he launches the pep talk.

"Nobody expects us to win," he says. "I promise you."

He talks about planting two feet. Togetherness over frustration. He talks about being 0-4 in the Big Ten, 8-8 overall in January. Then he asks them if they've ever seen a movie called *The Shawshank Redemption*. Even Serbian center Sergej Vucetic knows the film.

"We've come a long way," Miles says, quietly now. "We've been through a lot of bullshit. How does Andy Dufresne break out of jail, Coach Smith?"

"Through the sewer," Smith says without looking up.

"He's an innocent man, and he breaks out of jail. He chisels for a year and a half until he gets a hole big enough. He has a picture of Marilyn Monroe over this thing, right?"

In the film, an adaptation of a Stephen King novella, Dufresne uses a Rita Hayworth poster to cover his escape hole. Then a Monroe poster. Then Raquel Welch. But nobody's fact-checking Miles because he's getting louder and more worked up.

"He hops out, and it takes him down to the sewer line. He crawls on his hands and knees. Through a river of shit. Andy Dufresne crawled through a river of shit. And he sucked it up, and he came out the other side and stood up."

Miles poses like Tim Robbins as Andy Dufresne in the film, forming himself into a cross as he's cleansed by the rain, lit by lightning strikes.

"We've been there," Miles says, still holding his arms out. "We've been crawling through that river of shit. How do we come out the other side? We come out together because we believe we can do it and because we'll do anything it takes."

He's to the end of his *Shawshank* story, but there's no stopping him. This is the longest pep talk of the year. Longer than the Michigan State "Plant Your Feet" speech he took from Pat Riley.

"Nobody thinks we can do it. My mom is saying two rosaries for me today. She's only said one the whole year, and now she thinks we need two because it's Indiana."

He reminds them he's beaten Tom Crean on the road in the North Dakota State–Marquette game. He knows how to do it. He knows they can do it.

"It doesn't matter what it says on their jerseys. It doesn't matter how many people are pulling against us. It doesn't matter how loud it is or how loud the boos are. We're a better basketball team than these guys. I was thinking about it today. We're better than Ohio State. . . . I can't wait until Wisconsin, playing for a 1 seed. Let's go. I'll put us against anybody right now. Tonight's our night. It's our time. Let's make it work. We've swallowed enough shit. Let's do this right. Any questions?"

None.

"Let's go. Team on three."

Petteway: "One, two, three."

Team: "Team."

So that's the theme: "Andy Drufresne's sewer crawl." Exactly twenty-four hours earlier, Miles sat in a booth at a pub lamenting, "We're awful." Now, he's telling the team, the coaches, and himself, he'd take them against anybody.

Any questions?

36

Ten minutes before the game, coaches learn Indiana's freshman center, Noah Vonleh, won't play because of an injury. Smith resets the matchups, and Harriman tells Miles that Indiana plays straight-up defense in the first three minutes of every game.

"We'll just run our best plays early," he says, and chooses a quick three for Shavon Shields for the opening possession. If

Shields doesn't have the shot, he can hit Walter Pitchford on the wing, and nothing will stop him from shooting.

Security guards lead Miles to center court as the Indiana band plays Guns N' Roses' "Welcome to the Jungle." Crean greets him with a handshake.

Miles coaches his team through Indiana's scoreboard video montage and starting lineups over the public address system. He then jokes with his assistants.

After the tip Shields hits Pitchford, who hits the jumper. He then hits a three-pointer and two tip-in offensive rebounds, and Pitchford leads Indiana 9–3 at the first television time-out.

Later, the lead grows to 11 points when Terran Petteway blocks Indiana senior Will Sheehey at the rim and Benny Parker goes end to end for a layup, and Petteway hits a baseline jumper. But Rivers commits a foul to give up free throws, and then Petteway takes a quick three without swinging the basketball. Indiana hits a layup on the other end off the long rebound to cut the lead to 27–20.

Miles calls a thirty-second time-out. Petteway's head is down, his hands on his knees. But in the huddle, he nods his head, and Miles doesn't scream.

In the final minute of the half, Miles runs a play for Ray Gallegos to get a three-pointer at the top of the key. He hits it over Indiana's speedy point guard, Yogi Ferrell. It's his only make of the half, and the Huskers lead 34–26.

In the locker room Miles tells them he doesn't believe in clichés. At least not two of them. The team that wins the first five minutes of the second half wins the game?

"No. We're winning all twenty minutes."

The other team has a run in them?

"No. We'll eliminate that and play with the lead all night."

He was almost right.

In those first five minutes of the second half, Gallegos hits back-to-back threes to put the Huskers up 46–35, their largest lead of the night. But Indiana follows with a 17–6 run, mainly on four three-pointers of its own, the last one a wide-open shot by Sheehey after the Hoosiers steal another offensive board.

The game is tied 52–52, and Miles calls another time-out with exactly ten minutes left. His Huskers have to win one of the last two games of the season and not embarrass themselves in the Big Ten Tournament, and they'll have a shot at March Madness. They have to get this game.

He sets a play for Gallegos to get another three, but he air-balls the shot from the left corner. Harriman, though, convinces Miles to switch the Huskers into a zone defense, and Indiana can't get shots off.

Petteway blocks a shot.

Parker taps the ball away from Will Sheehey and then dives into the Husker bench. The officials give the ball to Nebraska, and Miles slaps Parker's hand.

They keep running plays for Shavon Shields, who either scores or gets fouled.

With 1:55 remaining, Pitchford hits a three off a throwback pass from Petteway to give the Huskers a 62–58 lead.

Indiana is still confused in its zone offense. The Hoosiers miss three layups and two wide-open threes down the stretch, while Parker and Petteway hit all six of their free throws in the final minute. The Huskers win 70–60 and never trail.

The gym, on Senior Night, is silent. Out of respect for their team, Hoosier fans remain in their seats, waiting for the Huskers to celebrate and shake hands in the lineup. Then they stick around for a somber postgame celebration for Sheehey and the other seniors.

In the visitors' locker room assistant coach Kenya Hunter jumps in the middle of the players to dance. He mimes sweeping the locker-room floor, sweeping both games from Indiana and essentially sweeping the Hoosiers out of the NCAA Tournament.

"Who's got the broom? Who's got the broom?" he yells, and the players roar.

Miles comes in next, and Pitchford yells, "Where's the broom? Where's the broom?"

So Kenya does the sweep dance for Miles, and players roar more loudly.

Then Miles reminds them of Wisconsin awaiting them in four days, hoping to cement a No. 1 seed in the NCAA Tournament.

"Listen, I'm proud of you," Miles says. "We have been through it. The *Shawshank*. We've done it for weeks on end. Now, let's make it pay dividends. Stay focused. We can all live our lives in the summer, beat our chests, the whole thing. But Sunday is going to be a special day for a lot of reasons. Let's get this done."

In the coaches' office, Miles takes a deep breath and looks at each of his staff members: the assistants and operations guys, his trainer, video coordinator, and equipment manager.

"There is nothing better than that," he says. "How about that sweep dance of Kenya's?"

Everyone loses it. Even Miles.

Six

Why Not Us?

37

John Hanigan watched the Huskers play from a hospital bed during two stays while a tumor grew in his lung. Before the Northwestern game, his sons met at Brewsky's bar in East Lincoln to talk about the turn Dad was making. Things didn't look good. How should they handle it?

Darin and Ryan then joined Dad in his hospital room for the Illinois road loss, smiling as he swore under his breath as the Huskers missed shot after shot and could never catch up. He worried about Wisconsin in the last game of the year.

"We'll never make the [NCAA] tournament," he told them.

Youngest son Ryan saw Bishop John C. Conley enter his Dad's room to bless his father and thank him for his financial advice for the entire Catholic Diocese of Lincoln.

Before the last week of the Huskers' regular season, though, John wanted to be home, so the family moved him Sunday, March 2. He was eating better, feeling better and more engaged in conversation. They'd bought a whiteboard for him, which fed into his ex-army respect for structure. They loaded it with his daily exercises and medications, appointments, and Husker basketball games. A lifelong friend came to the house to say John looked good and looked forward to the Huskers making the Big Dance. As the friend left John told him, "I'll be around to watch the tournament, and they'll go on a deep run."

Monday was even better. He got up to walk three times, ate three meals, and even snacked. More friends came over that night, telling stories and laughing.

Tuesday started well with breakfast and lunch. That night Ryan drove from Omaha to watch Creighton's twelve-point loss to Georgetown on TV with him. John ate less at dinner and didn't talk much. He was wiped out, dozing off in the second half. Ryan's father looked over at him and asked for the time.

"It's about eight, Dad," he said.

"Well, you better be getting to work," he said, and went back to sleep.

Wednesday was worse. John's brother-in-law, also the family physician, came over. Darin and his mother were also in the room.

"I am done," John said.

Darin hadn't heard anything like that from his dad before, but he could see the relief in his father's face. That was the afternoon before Nebraska's win at Indiana.

Thursday, he ate a banana. On the phone he told Ryan he was doing okay. He never said he was in any pain. Ever. But he was out of breath, and by this time he probably had a grapefruit-size tumor in his lung.

Tim Miles threw out the first pitch at the home opener Friday afternoon for Darin Erstad's baseball team, and players wanted to talk about the throw, especially senior Mike Peltz. The guard from the Nebraska panhandle hadn't played much during the Big Ten season. Privately, he told Miles not to feel a need to play him Sunday against No. 9 Wisconsin on Senior Night, his last home game. Winning was more important. He had another idea he wanted to keep between himself and Coach until game time, and the team could learn about that later. But publicly, he wanted to see his coach squirm.

"Coach Miles, I heard you one-hopped it to the plate," Peltz said as Greg Eaton set up the film from the Indiana game. "Is that what I heard?"

"It was a full house," Miles said. "The catcher says, 'It's an 0-2 count.' I say, 'I got you.' So I throw a little slider down and away and one-hop it to see if he'll swing, right? To strike him out."

His players aren't buying it. Neither are his coaches.

"Wasn't it your first pitch, Coach?" Assistant Craig Smith yelled from the back row.

"Was there a batter out there?" Chris Harriman asked.

"No. Okay, it wasn't my best day on the mound," Miles said. "Let's just put it this way . . ."

The players weren't having his excuses and started yelling at him. Terran Petteway almost fell out of his front-row chair. Shavon Shields stood and pointed at his coach. Accountability matters. So does transparency.

"He's making excuses," Kye Kurkowski said.

"All right," Miles said. "Everybody's got all the answers."

The Huskers were feeling good. When Miles walked into the office that morning, Smith told him to calm down. "Take a nap," he'd said. With the win at Indiana Wednesday night, ESPN bracketologist Joe Lunardi had moved them from not even among the next eight teams to reach the NCAA Tournament to a No. 11 seed. As of now, they were in. *Lincoln Journal Star* beat writer Brian Rosenthal reported Thursday that a Harriman conversation with a friend from St. Louis had spawned the phrase "No-Sit Sunday" for the season finale against No. 9 Wisconsin. The Athletic Department embraced the idea and started promoting it. Could the Huskers actually expect Nebraska fans, famous for sitting down at football games, to stand from tip to buzzer? The prospect of a crowd even louder than they were for the Michigan or Ohio State games had the players and coaches buzzing, especially Harriman. In fact, Harriman was so happy after winning his scout game over Indiana that he was looking for reasons to be upset. He found one in an Adidas marketing campaign called "Made in March," showing new NCAA Tournament alternate jerseys. Mainly on Twitter, the German company revealed samples from across the country. One for the Hoosiers. None for the Huskers, one of Adidas's biggest contracts.

Harriman was livid, and Miles told him to calm down, but the slight played to Miles's affinity for being the little dog in the fight, and he couldn't let it go himself. By Saturday he would trade e-mails with high-level national brass at Adidas.

"It's really a sweet-looking jersey," he wrote. "Could we get some of those for the tournament?"

He knew that would be logistically impossible, but he couldn't help himself.

"Sorry, coach," was the response. "Those decisions were made last summer. We're reevaluating how we do March Madness now."

Miles smiled as he told the story.

In Friday's film session, he also told the team about phone calls and texts he'd received, all describing how good they looked offensively. Running sets hard. Moving the ball. Setting hard screens. Then he reeled them back, asking if they were good enough yet.

"We gotta get better this time of year," he said. "We're so far from being where we can be. Every time I watch film, I'm like, 'That's awful. That's terrible. We're not even close.' We do enough to win, but are we fulfilling our potential?"

The team knew to say "No."

He kept going: "We got to get better. We can't be satisfied with pretty good on offense, pretty good on defense, sometimes in conversion. We gotta get better."

He told Walt Pitchford he may have gotten the first nine points at Indiana, but Wisconsin was going to smother him.

"You're an ass-kicker early, I tell you," he continued. "Good job. That was a great mentality. What I have found is that every time I cuss you like a sailor the night before a game, you just play lights out. So, brother, on Saturday morning at 10:00 a.m., you prepare yourself. You and I are going toe to toe."

The players laughed, but Pitchford didn't.

He complimented Ray Gallegos's shooting, Tai Webster's passing, Benny Parker's defense, Shavon Shields's ability to score in multiple ways.

At the end he wanted to know what the team thought.

"What did you see that we can get better on? Shavon?"

"Defensively we're doing pretty good, but we probably could have beat them by more."

"What'd you think, T?"

"Little things on defense," Petteway said, "taking myself out of plays. Little stuff like that."

"Ray, what'd you think?"

Gallegos rarely answered a question in film or practice, and when he did Miles always made him repeat it so others could hear. He didn't have to repeat his answer this time. "Transition defense," said Gallegos, who'd shown up early to hit three hundred three-pointers with Harriman rebounding.

"Yeah," Miles said.

Miles and Craig Smith told the team that Wisconsin was a whole different animal than Indiana. While preparing the scouting report, Smith feared the Badgers could swamp the Huskers early and blow them out, like what happened at Michigan and Ohio State. But neither coach said this out loud to the players. Not in so many words.

"Let's get to work," Smith said, launching into his scout.

38

When Southwest Minnesota State athletic director Butch Raymond hired Miles for his second job, he told the thirty-year-old coach he had to fix a couple things with the way he went about his job.

"You're too easy to prepare for," Raymond said.

Miles loved to play a motion offense and man defense. Motion appealed to his idea of how the game should be played, allowing smart players to be creative within the flow of the offense. Man defense was a pride thing. Get down low, outwork people, and beat them straight up. But Miles started getting more creative about calling set plays, or sets, and mixing in zone. Then Miles began to explore a balance between being average at many things or great at a few things. In the end he chose to make his team great at everything. When he prepares to beat a team, like Wisconsin, he's exploring his team's repertoire for sets that will work against the Badgers' weaknesses. The defense, he mostly leaves to Smith.

As for stopping the other team? That scouting system has evolved since Miles and Smith first looked at videotape in those first years at Mayville State, where mice didn't even try to hide in the corners of their offices. Things had changed, including technology, resources, terminology, and strategy. In the Big Ten scouting can be nightmarish because of the variables. Unlike the steady weekend games in the now-defunct North Central Conference, where North Dakota State played before going Division I, the days you play change every week in the Big Ten. You may play Illinois twice in two weeks, and not play Purdue for two months. You play four teams only once each season, such as Wisconsin Sunday.

Smith rotates his scouting-report duties among the assistants, working new guy Kenya Hunter into the Husker Way and giving Harriman teams he scouted last year. It's a puzzle. But nothing like the old days, when he did every scout at Mayville and NDSU. Every one.

"And I loved it," says Smith, whom Miles calls Mr. Superlative.

Like most coaches across the country, they learn all opponents' offensive and defensive tendencies, maybe steal most of their verbal and nonverbal play calls. The Huskers, though, put an extra focus on personnel. They want to know who and where to attack and know what to take away. Miles and Smith had that going at Colorado State, where their players thrived off taking away each opponent's strengths, exploiting their weaknesses. That's how they beat the more talented teams and reached the NCAA Tournament their final year there.

When Smith handles the scouting report, he'll get up at a quarter or half past six each morning to chart plays. Then he'll eat and play with his kids until they go to school. Back to work at home, where he can focus. He wants to know how many times each player shoots a jumper off the dribble to his left. How many times he'll drive right. And how many times he's successful at each offensive play. Same for team defense. You name it. After eight to ten games, he has a pretty good idea, and themes develop. By eleven he's eating at the training table and meeting with Miles to agree on the three or four themes and the practice plan. Then prep the film session. No assistant gets much sleep when they have the next scout.

For the Wisconsin game, Smith and Miles started their discussions on the plane home from Indiana. With the Badgers Smith is convinced they need to rethink everything because Wisconsin can shoot the ball, unlike many of the teams they've been holding to 30 percent from the floor. They're Michigan and can go on Wolverine-style runs. But what he's really obsessed with are their fouls and free throws. They don't foul. They make you foul. And then they beat you at the line. He has proof in numbers.

In the film session Smith tells the team about last night's Wisconsin game at Purdue. The Boilermakers outscored Wisconsin 40 to 16 in the lane, which should be a winning recipe. But the Badgers shot 31 free throws to Purdue's 14. Wisconsin 76, Purdue 70. Before that, they outshot Indiana 24–3 at the line, 36–20 over Minnesota, and 20–9 over Michigan State. All Wisconsin wins.

In league play the Badgers make 8.8 more free throws than opponents. That's like walking in the gym with a 9-point lead.

"That's the deal: it's all about fouls," Smith says. "We got to do a great job defending personnel for thirty to thirty-five seconds every possession. We got to lock in. They're going to run way more than they ever have and take quick threes. But if they don't get it or they don't get something at the rim, what are they going to do? They're going to pull it out and make your ass defend for thirty-five seconds. And most teams can't guard them for thirty-five seconds because eventually they get lost on some sort of screen, right? And they give up open shots or foul."

Miles reminds them they had a shot last year at home, losing 47–41 at the Devaney Center early in the Big Ten season. At the end of the year, though, Wisconsin drilled the Huskers, 77–46, in Madison.

"They could have named the score," he says.

Now, they're averaging 75 points per game, and only one team in the country fouls less than the Badgers.

"They're just a really good team," Miles says. "They're playing for a No. 1 seed. But we have our advantages, too. They don't have our athleticism, and we're a way better defensive team than they are."

Practice has shifted a bit this week. Every drill is geared toward the eight main guys in the rotation. Scout teamers are finding new ways to help—Sergej Vucetic using the padded bat to hit them on layup drills and Trevor Menke whispering in Webster's ear between plays, Nick Fuller and Kye Kurkowski double-teaming guards to simulate full-court pressure, Peltz repeatedly running over Webster and Benny Parker in his role as Wisconsin's Traevon Jackson, a strong, driving point guard.

Players are loud, talking on defense, talking on the sidelines when subbed out, led by Petteway, Shields, and Pitchford.

"We've got great energy today, don't we?" Smith asks Teddy Owens at the scorer's table while stuffing his mouth with Spearmint Extra gum.

Miles sprints from end to end. Teaching and joking.

"I'm the only one who's beat these [fellas]," he reminds them. "So you better listen up."

Then he shuts them down early. Good defensive teams need fresh legs.

That Friday morning hospice nurses showed up. John Hanigan did his tax returns with an associate from work and took care of his estate. In the afternoon he beat a longtime friend at cribbage. He struggled with the pegs, but not the math, and took a buck-ninety off his buddy.

Later in the afternoon Ryan came over after Darin had called to say things didn't look good. He'd been up all night with Dad, giving his mom the night off.

Ryan cried, ducked out the back door, and drove to Lincoln. Outside his parents' home, he met a hospice nurse leaving. She told him Dad had twenty-four to forty-eight hours left.

"Hi, Ryan," his father said when his son got to his bedside. "Is the Wisconsin game over?"

"That's Sunday, Dad."

The family had planned to honor a decades-long tradition of ordering a Valentino's Family Value Pack No. 1 with an extra pizza—one cream cheese and pepperoni, the other three-quarters hamburger and a quarter sausage with black olives—and watching Husker basketball together Sunday night.

Later in the afternoon John asked Ryan twice more if they'd beaten Wisconsin.

"Yeah, Dad," Ryan finally said at eleven o'clock Friday night. "We beat them."

He wanted his father to relax, get some sleep.

When the boys' older sister, Jennifer, arrived after a flight from Los Angeles, John smiled and started taking his pain meds.

He had his family with him; the Huskers had beaten the Badgers. He was ready to go.

39

Saturday morning, the team watches Friday's practice on the big screen.

"Man, I'd play this game at 10:00 a.m., noon, whenever, and again at midnight," Miles says as they start watching. "They've won eight in a row. They're going to have no fear. But I tell you what, we're not a normal team. And we're going to beat them."

They watch the offense, especially a play Miles worked in yesterday, a holdover from the 2006 game when Woodside led North Dakota State over Wisconsin. He brags about it.

Then they watch Terran Petteway miss an awkward half-pull-up jump shot and half-layup from ten feet. Miles asks Petteway what he calls that. No answer. Miles says he's seen his twelve-year-old daughter make one of those in a game. If Petteway wants to see it done right, he should come along to St. Michael's School for his daughter's game at 5:00 tonight. There's no game tonight, but the point lands. In fact, Miles is in such a good mood that he can't muster anger. So he sticks with sarcasm throughout the session as he does both play-by-play and color commentary on the practice, and it's the kind of show that would get solid ratings on the Big Ten Network.

Shavon Shields misses a wide-open three: "It's okay. We'll get a shooter over there next time."

Tai Webster can't get the offense started against the scout team: "Tai can't quite handle [Trevor] Menke here, but that's okay. It'll be much easier against Wisconsin, I'm sure. Good job, Menk."

Webster runs the offense through to get a layup a few possessions later: "So why was it better that time? Well, one, we subbed out Dave [Rivers]. Two, we got a pin down. Just kidding, Dave."

Miles starts getting too many laughs, so he turns serious.

"In ten days, I want to be ranked in the Top 25," he stands and says. "Don't tell anybody that, but that's my goal. If we do everything right, we'll be ranked in ten days."

That would be after the Big Ten Tournament. After Selection Sunday, when the Huskers will know if they're in the NCAA Tournament for the first time since 1998. Today, they are ranked 41st in the daily RPI, not too far behind Iowa (33) and Ohio State (28). Sunday's game could change all that. In the Big Ten standings, the three teams were in a virtual tie for fourth. The Huskers could win tiebreakers if they won, which would give them a bye in the first round of the conference tournament, while the other two would have to play the first round. All kinds of incentives to win.

"We're going to have a great game plan," Miles says, reminding them for about the tenth time that he's beaten the Badgers and they haven't. Trust him. "We're going to guard them better than anybody in the league."

He hands the session off to Smith to talk defense. Reminders. Reminders. Reminders. Players nod.

"It's all about poise and toughness and staying together," Smith says.

On the floor afterward Miles challenges point guard Tai Webster, who keeps messing up in half-court defense. Traevon Jackson will eat him up Sunday if he can't guard scout teamers running Wisconsin's offense.

On the next play Webster hardly moves before Miles blows the whistle. His coach questions the point guard's heart.

"Play or sub out," he screams.

Terran Petteway grabs Webster's jersey from behind, not allowing him a choice. Then Petteway helps him out on the next possession when Webster gets screened off the ball, and Webster recovers.

"Great job, Tai," Miles yells even more loudly. Honestly, he's happier about Petteway's reaction than Webster's. He's so happy he takes a break on the bench. What has him grinning the most today is Rivers, who said he'd like to come off the bench to let Ray Gallegos start his last game at home.

"Good," Miles told him. "Because that's what I'm going to do."

The other senior, Peltz, told him a second time not to play him "just to play him" on Senior Night.

"I want to win," Peltz said.

That is fine with Miles, who isn't a huge Senior Night–ceremony guy. He'd recorded a video for the seniors so he wouldn't have to say anything live Sunday. Let them be the show. And frankly, he'd just rather take the seniors out for dinner after they graduate.

Peltz has outworked everyone in the weight room, and his bench press is the best on the team. He'd barely subbed out Friday as the scout-team point guard, but he finally had to come out Saturday.

"Look at him," Miles says to Teddy Owens and a few student managers. Peltz has opened a seldom-used corner door and stands in the frame, letting cool outside air wash over him while he hunches over.

"He's sick or something," Miles says, "but he won't say anything. He'll be right back in."

And he is. The Huskers are tougher than they were in January. They are more together. They are ready for Wisconsin.

Before practice ends, ESPN's Andy Katz takes to Twitter, responding to a Badger fan's Tweet by saying Nebraska-Wisconsin would be the best game in the country Sunday.

Darin Hanigan gave away Dad's tickets to Sunday's game. On Saturday Monsignor Liam M. Barr, a family friend for forty-seven years, had come over from St. Joe's Church. He said some final blessings for John, and then Ryan's mom started reciting the rosary. The family gathered around John, saying it together. Dad had always been an impatient man, Ryan says, and later the siblings would joke about how he'd had to wait for them to finish the rosary. He didn't quite make it.

"To Mom's credit," Ryan said, "she kept going to the end."

The next night the family would sit down together to eat Valentino's and watch the Huskers and Wisconsin. That was Dad's plan.

Tim Miles shows up late for the 10:30 a.m. film session and shoot-around at Pinnacle Bank Arena Sunday. The game's not until 7:00 p.m., but assistant Craig Smith is itching to run through the keys to the game and all his reminders.

"Come on, Miles," he says to himself in the film classroom, but the other coaches and staff hear him. Like Miles, he'd just rather play the Badgers now. No more waiting.

Miles sticks his head in the door: "How we doing?"

He hands video coordinator Greg Eaton a hard drive of clips he wants to show from yesterday's practice. No speech today. He gives them basic reminders and then turns the floor over to Smith, who spends thirty-five minutes on the last page of the stapled scouting report on Wisconsin and showing their plays. He and Miles have made a change: they're going to double-team Traevon Jackson every time a teammate screens for him. They want to harass him inside the three-point line and take the ball out of his hands.

"We have to play defense for thirty-five seconds a [possession] for forty minutes," Smith says, then works his way to the keys to winning: "Get into the ball. Get them off their spots. And let's make history. We opened up this arena the right way four months ago, and let's finish this thing off the right way tonight."

Harriman can't help himself. He tells a story. A staff member heard a Wisconsin player offer a backhanded compliment about the Hendricks Training Complex last night. "These facilities are crazy," Harriman quotes him as saying. "And they're not even any good over here." Then Harriman makes sure his point is clear: "That kid has zero respect for you." As if they need more reasons to play well.

Miles jokes with Benny Parker during the ensuing walk-throughs on the PBA floor. Ray Gallegos and Walt Pitchford shoot threes. Miles is all encouragement and pulls players to the side to talk to them quietly, alone. After Terran Petteway misses a jumper during the final offensive drill, Miles smiles at him. "Don't practice missing." Then he ends the workout. No speeches.

Hours before the game the Railyard District outside the arena is full of fans, including students lined up more than a block deep to race to lower-level spots in student sections. The atmosphere is what city planners prayed for when they took a chance on the $378 million public works project in the Haymarket west of downtown, $186 million of it on the arena.

Pinnacle Bank Arena would barely break even its first year, and revenue from Husker men's and women's basketball would be more meager than the city's projections. UNL, though, did fine with its share of the deal. The women's team averaged 6,161 fans in eighteen home games to finish eleventh in the nation in attendance. The men sold out every game at the ticket office and averaged 15,419 people in their seats for sixteen home games. Nearly a quarter-million people filled seats to see Tim Miles's Huskers, good for thirteenth in the country—behind twelve teams with bigger arenas, including Creighton.

Tonight, they'd pull in a record 15,998, but none of them would be in their seats. And some of them paid dearly to be there. Online, seats in the lower section were going for up to $300 the last days before the game. Outside the arena scalpers were asking up to $250 after buying them days earlier for $100.

"This is the best game that I've ever worked," one scalper says. "And I've been working football games [here] for ten years."

The line outside the arena keeps growing, but students are smiling in seventy-three-degree weather, a high that is up sixty-eight degrees from the previous Sunday. Harriman brings them pizza.

Miles drives to the arena with his family in his black Escalade. Ava and Gabe make him play two songs through his iPhone. One is "Dark Horse" by Katy Perry and Juicy J. Gabe says the team is a dark horse. So "Dark Horse." The other is "Timber" by Pitbull and Ke$ha, including the line "The bigger they are, the harder they fall." Ava says they have to listen to that again because "We're taking down a giant." Actually, she'd first told him that before the Indiana game, too, and Miles mouthed the last line of the song right before he left the coaches' locker for tip-off at Assembly Hall: "It's going down."

Before he shows up, the coaches wait on their stools in front of their lockers.

"You know why we're winning this game?" Harriman says, but not like a question. Nobody answers him. "Because Miles will coach with complete composure."

They nod.

In a side room Miles muscles through a Big Ten Network interview, telling viewers Wisconsin is too good. The Badgers have been in this position before, year after year, and are probably bored. His Huskers have no idea what to do, but he isn't going to worry. But if they turn the ball over or take bad shots, "then I'll probably start coaching."

The Miles undersell-overdeliver.

Later, back in the coaches' locker room, talk focuses on positioning for the Big Ten Tournament next week. Iowa beat Michigan earlier in the day. And Ohio State is in a battle with Michigan State, the game on a TV in the training room. If the Buckeyes win, the Huskers will have to win for a first-round bye in the tournament. Whatever happens, the Huskers will probably play Ohio State in the quarterfinals. But Miles has his mind on bigger tournaments.

"Well," he says, "we gotta beat these guys or Ohio State on a neutral court [probably in the second round of the Big Ten Tournament], right?"

They all nod. That would get them into the NCAA Tournament, they're pretty sure. One more big win, and the selection committee would have to send them.

Athletic director Shawn Eichorst comes in to wish them luck. He's just gotten back from the Big Ten wrestling tournament in Madison via two commercial flights.

"Why aren't you on a little plane?" Miles asks, referring to a charter.

"That's not my style," Eichorst says.

"That's 'not your style.' Well, if you need some help on travels, let me know where you need to be. We want to get you there on time," Miles says.

"I'm here. I'm here to help you recognize the seniors and go get this one done, all right?" he says before leaving. "Have fun. Good to see you guys."

The coaches thank him. He's a hands-off AD who hasn't said no to them very often. They work more directly with Marc Boehm, who supervises both basketball programs. But they haven't seen him. Boehm's so nervous he can hardly talk, and he doesn't want to bring them bad luck.

Coaches learn Michigan State missed a shot at the buzzer. Ohio State wins. The Huskers must win to get the No. 4 seed in the conference tournament.

"That's okay," Miles assures them. "We don't want to back in. Here's the deal: I'd rather win this one and be at ease than worry for another week."

40

Miles is all business in the first pregame talk thirty-eight minutes before tip-off. He's giving a *Cliff's Notes* version of Craig Smith's scouting report. More than anything, he says, they have to trust Smith when he tells them to defend for all thirty-five seconds every possession: "You gotta love that. You gotta look forward to that every minute you're out there and just kick their butts. . . . Most importantly, focus and concentrate the whole time you're out there. Believe in us and love the process, and good things will happen. Let's do this."

Petteway: "Team on three: One. Two. Three."

Team: "Team."

Miles changes into his suit. White shirt and dark-red tie.

"You know," he tells his assistants, "I've been talking about Top 25 stuff just to get their minds off the tournament. . . . Try to raise the bar and give them something to think about that doesn't have much consequence to it. Today's game does, though."

He laughs. He removes his underwear in a bathroom stall. He borrows some of Kenya Hunter's shoe shine, the stuff he rips Hunter for by calling it "juco shine."

Normally, he'd be buried in his game cards, but he acts as if he remembers something and jogs out to the floor for Senior

Night. At center court he introduces Ray Gallegos and Mike Peltz. Gallegos thanks everybody. When Peltz gets the microphone, he takes out some notes he has saved on his phone.

"This is the beginning of a new era for Nebraska basketball. On another note: I don't like dancing, but it's time we put our shoes on and dance. One more thing: we all know the rules for tonight. There's no sitting or kneeling, but I need to make one exception real quick."

Then he proposes to his girlfriend. The team and most of the assistants stand shocked in front of the bench. The crowd goes nuts.

"Let's go, baby," Benny Parker yells on the way back to the locker. "We're not losing tonight."

"That was pretty cool," says Smith, who had forgotten about the proposal until Peltz came to him minutes beforehand to say he was nervous.

"That's normal," Smith said to him. "It's a big game. You're going to have butterflies and stuff."

"No, Coach," Peltz said. "I'm getting engaged in eight minutes. Any words of wisdom?"

"It's too late," Miles says, interrupting Smith's retelling of the conversation in front of their lockers. That's what he would have said to Peltz.

Kenya Hunter looks at Miles: "Did you know he was doing that?"

"Yeah. You didn't?" Miles grins. Then he stands to give his last pregame pep talk of the regular season, and the assistants follow him into the classroom, where players are having trouble calming down, still smacking Peltz on the shoulder and back. But Miles has nothing to say to them. No planting two feet. No *Shawshank* rivers of sewage. No church bells.

Before game time, #Peltz is trending nationally on Twitter. Soon, #Nebrasketball and Nebraska would be trending worldwide.

Nebraska hit its first four shots, including the obligatory Walt Pitchford three-pointer to take a 10–3 lead and force Bo Ryan to take a time-out. Husker fans hadn't taken a seat yet, including eighty-nine-year-old Dick Knudsen, who sat across from the Husker bench. He wouldn't sit down all night.

Wisconsin ties the game at 15–15 five minutes later, but Shavon Shields and Walt Pitchford both dunk.

Wisconsin keeps scoring, usually in transition, unlike the thirty-five-second possessions coaches had feared. The teams trade buckets the rest of the half before Wisconsin center Frank Kaminsky tips in a rebound with thirteen seconds left for a 35–33 lead.

Shields has twelve points, all at the rim, but he's livid and yelling in the halftime locker room. Petteway tries to calm him and tells the team, "We have to rebound better." The Huskers had given up long rebounds on missed three-point shots by the Badgers, who made them pay, rebounding five of their nine missed shots overall. The Badgers were five for nine from the three-point line, shooting 54 percent from the floor, and had shot seven free throws to Nebraska's none. And the Huskers trail by only two.

Miles reminds them about the game plan. Guard hard all night. Offensively, they're fine. Then he gives his only pep talk of the day:

"Are they a mentally tough team?" he says. "Yeah. And right now in the first half, that's what they won. They had more composure than we did. We had more emotion than they did, but we're behind. . . . We've got to maintain our composure and act like a team that knows exactly what they're doing at every moment you're out there. Don't let frustration settle in. . . . Let's go out and have fun."

On his way back to the court, Miles gives associate media-relations director Shamus McKnight his tweet: "We have to get defensive stops and get to their shooters. We gotta find a way to win!"

Outside the arena #Nebrasketball still trends worldwide. A UNL student posts: "I can hear the PBA driving past Lincoln . . . @Huskers #GBR #Huskers #Nebrasketball." Another fan: "Why am I standing? I'm at home. #NoSitSunday #Nebrasketball."

In Belgium where he plays pro ball, former Husker Brandon Ubel tweets: "Another 20 minutes . . . This is going to be a marathon! Loving it! #GBR." More tweets of support come from former Husker athletes, such as Will Compton in the NFL and Joba Chamberlain in Major League Baseball.

Wisconsin jumps ahead 40–33 and holds the lead until Benny Parker just snatches the ball away from Traevon Jackson, and Shields hits a jumper to give the Huskers a 47–46 lead with 13:36 remaining. Miles pulls out his go-to offensive sets that he convinced himself to hold back in the first half. He has to win the chess match, not just the toughness battle.

Off a TV time-out with 7:50 left, Ray Gallegos hits a three on an old-school play called by Miles for a 53–52 lead. Then Shields dunks, and Ryan has to call another time-out.

Nebraska will stretch the lead to 65–57 on a Pitchford three, his third of the night, and Wisconsin never closes the gap. The Huskers win 77–68 over Wisconsin, a team that will make the Final Four in a few weeks, by holding the Badgers to 34 percent shooting in the second half and owning both lanes.

Students storm the court, waving Miles signs and a John Travolta *Saturday Night Fever* meme poster that says "Let's Dance."

At that moment Dick Vitale, one of the loudest and most recognizable voices in college basketball, tweets out, "Incredible job in building Nebraska hoops by Tim Miles—hey that is a new bucket list 4 me in hoops—visit Lincoln . . ."

The fans start bouncing on the Pinnacle Bank court. They pick up the smallest player they can find, Benny Parker, and put him on their shoulders.

Radio play-by-play man Kent Pavelka can't contain himself: "Tim Miles has punched our ticket, Husker fans," he yells into his microphone. "It's time to twerk. Let's go dancing."

Yelling and dancing continue in the locker room. Coaches' kids high-five players. When Miles comes in, the team roars, then roars again for Shields after he's finished his interview.

"Guys, that's what college basketball feels like," Miles says. "You just beat a team that's probably, well, they're Top 10 in the country . . . but I'm just telling you: this was fun, and it's going to be over tomorrow. Just know that."

He reminds them of their goals. Where they want to go.

"This is just not it," he says. "We think about where we started, where we are now, and where we want to be. Do we want this to end?"

Two players holler, "Hell, no."

"All right," Miles says. "I didn't hear everybody hell-no-ing."

Everybody starts yelling the two words. Over and over.

He tells them their number-one goal is to win the Big Ten Tournament that starts Thursday in Indianapolis. They'll play the winner of Purdue–Ohio State in a 2:30 p.m. game.

"We'll be ready to roll," he says, and then he softens. "So just enjoy it. . . . We've put together a championship-style run, but this is not where we want to end. So we have to keep going to get where we want to go. And once we get to that tournament, then we go to the next tournament, and we're going there to win. And we all know this: Are we all hitting on all cylinders? Are we all playing at our best? No, we're not even close. And we're gonna get there. We're just gonna keep plugging away, until we get there."

Then he really softens.

"I love you guys," he finishes. "I really think we can do anything with this team."

He reminds them he put a sign on the practice gym wall that reads: "If you're not here to help us win the Big Ten championship, then you're in the wrong place."

"How many of you guys thought I was an idiot when we put that on the wall? Well, you just made a championship-style run, and we got a chance to win a championship next week. And every one of these teams coming in here knows that we're the real deal. So let's go keep doing it, keep earning respect, and keep beating people. But it's going to take our process, great defense, smart offense, and togetherness over frustration all the way. I call that 'tougherness.' . . . Let's go take a knee. All right, come on, let's go."

They pray.

They chant.

They all run to Peltz, making fun of him as much as congratulating him.

The Valentino's tasted great. Ryan Hanigan hadn't lied to his father. The Huskers did beat Wisconsin.

41

After the game Wisconsin senior Ben Brust came up to Tim Miles.

"Coach, that's the most fun I've ever had playing college basketball," he said. "And we lost. It was a good, hard-fought game. The crowd was unreal."

Brust didn't have to do that, especially after getting beaten in a game the Badgers needed, Miles told his team Monday. Both Brust and senior Josh Gasser complimented the facilities and Pinnacle Bank Arena. They were on the team two years ago when Wisconsin last came to Lincoln to play in the Devaney Center.

"They're just good dudes," Miles said, and he doesn't say that often about opponents.

Before that coaches had asked Mike Peltz if he had any buyer's remorse after his public proposal.

"Sucker," Miles said as he entered the room. "Do we have a date?"

"I'm leaving it up to her," Peltz said.

"She'll have it set up for Thursday," Miles said.

That's when Purdue, the bottom seed in the Big Ten Tournament, would play fifth seed Ohio State. Nebraska would fly to Indianapolis Thursday night after practice and play the winner of that game Friday afternoon. While watching film of the Wisconsin win, Miles praised Benny Parker for how he frustrated Traevon Jackson, but he rode others for getting frustrated. Walt Pitchford played well late by self-correcting, he said, but he needed to never get into that place where frustration takes over.

The Huskers ranked No. 35 in the RPI with the win, the fifth-highest team in the conference, behind Wisconsin (6), Michigan (12), Michigan State (21), and Ohio State (23). They slid ahead of Iowa and Minnesota. But coaching friends have told Miles a bad loss could still knock them out of the tournament. They won't know if they're in, for sure, until Sunday night's "Selection Show," aired on ESPN, which has turned the event into a live news event, like a professional draft. No relaxing until your team is called.

"That's just the way it is this time of year," Miles said. "All you can control is what you can control. Playing great. But we have to practice great to play great."

He wanted them to feel lucky to play Purdue or Ohio State, teams they split with during the year, all teams winning at home. Three years earlier, when he started winning at Colorado State in his third year, the Rams built a steamy rivalry with New Mexico, among the class of the Mountain West. In that 2010–11 season, Miles split the series with Steve Alford's Lobos, losing 68–61 on the road and winning 68–62 at home, when the Rams fans stormed the court. The teams were so close, a one-point difference in eighty minutes of basketball. Then they met in Las Vegas in the No. 4 versus No. 5 game, where the game was tied with 4:04 left before the Lobos finished with a 10–4 run to earn a 67–61 win.

Nebraska's relationship with Ohio State had followed the same path this season, except the Buckeyes had blown out the Huskers before the home-game court storm. Miles wanted the rubber match Thursday. Not so much to excise New Mexico demons, but to ensure the Huskers couldn't lose to a lower-ranked team like Purdue, hurting their chances for the Big Dance.

While they watched Pitchford clean up rebounds on the big screen, Miles reminded his players Ohio State had the most wins in the Big Ten Tournament's sixteen-year history, had made the championship game in eight of them, and had won it four times, including last year, when the Buckeyes swamped the Huskers 71–50 in the quarterfinals and Aaron Craft took home the tournament MVP award.

"I mean, how fun was it playing at the end of that game?" he said, looking to Ray Gallegos, then to Benny Parker and David Rivers, who all played garbage minutes in that game. "There were twelve hundred people there giggling and laughing when we were out there. Honestly? Remember that. That was a blast. Where we were. Where we are now. Where we want to be."

That was the end of the season last year. He didn't want to end up there again. He didn't want to end up hosting a National Invitational Tournament game Tuesday and losing. He didn't want to finish the season Monday in a first-round NCAA Tournament game. He wanted to at least get to the second weekend of the tournament, with a chance to play in the Final Four.

The coaches' eyes got big in the back row, and they leaned forward. Was he allowing them to think past this game or this tournament? Or was he just distracting them again from the pressure of the moment, like he did with the Top 25 talk?

"Look," he said. "Our mind-set has been good, but it's not going to be any good if you've found a finish line. To me, the finish line is somewhere deep in the NCAA Tournament."

Then he returned to the Wisconsin film: "You guys, you beat a really good team last night. They don't beat themselves."

His worry, though, was whether his team will beat itself and how he can prepare them mentally to avoid that.

That same day Michigan's John Beilein was named Big Ten Coach of the Year by the media, but the coaches give their award to Miles. Beilein says publicly the award belongs to Miles, who worked a $50,000 bonus into his Nebraska contract in case that happened. He'll make another $150,000 if his Huskers make the NCAA Tournament.

That night his wife asked him, "What does the Coach of the Year want for dinner?"

Within minutes they were pounding a Tombstone frozen pizza.

By Wednesday his team is committing so many turnovers in practice, especially against the press, that he moves his starting point guard, Tai Webster, to the scout team.

"Tai, that kind of weak cut won't work over here," Miles says, referring to this continent, far from club basketball in New Zealand. "So do you want to play eight minutes or twenty?"

Terran Petteway smacks Webster gently on the shoulder: "Let's go, Tai."

On the next play scout-team guard Trevor Menke, from Beatrice, Nebraska, steals the ball again as Webster fails to get open against the press. Miles pulls Webster, who walks to the far corner of the Hendricks gym to think before getting water.

"Menke's been balling," assistant coach Craig Smith says to Benny Parker and David Rivers. "Cutting hard, hitting threes. Lit up Benny last week. And now . . ."

"That was just one time," Parker says, smiling.

Last week Menke impersonated Josh Gasser in practice for the scout team. This week he is Ohio State's Aaron Craft, and his scout team keeps messing up Nebraska's press breaker. Turnover after turnover. Miles calmly walks over to talk to Webster and Shavon Shields at the half-court sideline about offensive Xs and Os. Yelling won't help him now. He starts a slow clap and pulls all of them to center court, where they're all clapping, but heads are down. They haven't practiced well.

"Look, early in the year, you guys thought it was difficult to win," Miles says. "But that's what it's about. It's about winning.

And you guys can win. You've come together. You're trying to be better teammates. You have a good work ethic, and you have talent. . . . So now let's get a good night's sleep, let's get better tomorrow, then let's beat Ohio State and win the season series."

Even though a charter plane is waiting, Miles stalls film and practice so the team can shoot and enjoy each other on the court while they watch the Big Ten Network on the big screen in the Hendricks practice gym. Purdue is taking Ohio State to the wire. No sense going into film until they know whom they'll play.

Ohio State gets a three-point lead in the last seconds, and a debate erupts among assistant coaches and players about whether to foul. Petteway wants to attack. Just play defense. Miles says he's seen both strategies work, and he's been burned by both. With a three-point lead, he likes to foul with less than five seconds left and the ball in the opponent's backcourt. Ohio State doesn't foul, and Purdue gets a shot to tie. Petteway jumps up and down, yelling, willing it in. Ohio State wins.

The mood changes immediately to a businesslike tone as they walk into the adjacent film classroom to watch yesterday's mess of a practice.

"Okay, we're going to see good pressure against Ohio State," Miles starts. "Don't use your dribble. Use your ball fakes. Pass to the first open man. If we don't turn it over, we'll win the game. And I'm not interested in playing our way out of the Big Ten Tournament and out of the NCAA Tournament. I'm interested in winning the tournament. We have to practice better than this today."

As they watch Miles gets angrier at yesterday's turnovers. Finally, he has Greg Eaton close his laptop and shut down the projector.

"That's enough."

Miles stands up to face them.

"Is that a good practice? Is that good enough? You guys are

at the end. That's what you look like, a team going through the motions. If that's all you care about, if that's all you have in the tank, let's not waste [my time]. Just send me out recruiting. I'll go get guys who actually care. Because you're not showing me one ounce of evidence that you guys know what you're doing out there. It's an embarrassment."

His point: Ohio State will be harder on you than I am. You'd better not melt, panic, get frustrated, shut down.

Then Kenya Hunter starts the Ohio State scouting report, but doesn't get far.

"All right, fellas," he says. "Ohio State—"

"We make it hard on you one little bit," Miles yells from his seat in the front center, "and you guys become babies and go through the motions."

Then he's quiet, hand over his mouth.

When Hunter is done, Miles is calmer.

"The only way they beat us is if we beat ourselves," he says. "If we turn it over, we're lazy, we don't concentrate—like practice yesterday—you beat yourself. That's the only way we lose the game. We got to play like we owe them something. Everybody in that gym voted us last. Don't ever forget that."

After a short walk-through of offensive sets and half-court defense, they pack their bags and jump on a charter bus that takes them through a gate to the tarmac at the Lincoln airport. After showing their IDs as they leave the bus, they load their duffels onto a cart and walk to a charter plane, where various Huskers Athletic Department officials await them in the front rows. Student managers have loaded each seat pocket with two Gatorades and oranges. The coaches filter to the plane last, most of them dropped off by wives and kids, some of whom will fly commercial to the game tomorrow. The team takes one manager on the road. The rest will drive for ten hours to Indianapolis as spectators on their own dime.

Miles, the last to board, will watch film and listen to music the whole trip. In Indianapolis a bus will pick them up right on the tarmac to take them to the Hilton, blocks from Bankers Life Fieldhouse, where they'll face Aaron Craft and Ohio State.

He'll send them to their rooms to relax and then separate himself from the players and coaches to walk downtown Indy and get food. The players will eat at the hotel.

Then they'll come together at 9:45 p.m. for one more talk before a big sleep. He'll remind them again that every coach at this tournament picked them last before the season, when he had to attend Big Ten Media Day and tell journalists he should have to answer only one question. But they're good now, and coaches have prepared them for everything. So they'd better be fearless. "That's what it's going to take to win this thing," he'll say in the final meeting of the night. "It's not going to be arms and legs. It's going to be mental toughness and intensity and concentration and togetherness and no frustration."

42

In January Tim Miles and Craig Smith were on a charter jet headed to Comanche, Oklahoma, to watch a high school recruit. At one point during the flight, Smith looked over at Miles and grinned, and Miles knew exactly what Smith was thinking. How had they come this far?

When Smith joined Miles right out of college to coach at Mayville State in 1996, they had birds flying inside the weight room and mice burrowing in their shared office. They'd have to bring in electric space heaters and wear gloves and hats while they made nighttime recruiting calls.

"It was so fun," Smith says.

His favorite memories are road games. They had no budget, so they rode buses with the women's team, two players to a seat. They'd argue over whether the women got the front of the bus this time, or if one team should take the left side and the other the right.

Miles and Smith would share a hotel room. They ate only Hardee's because the daily special was the cheapest meal available. Hot ham and cheeses for everybody on Monday trips and hamburgers on Thursdays. Two specials for everyone with a water, maybe cheese on the burgers if players asked politely and were winning.

"If they were lucky, they would get [a] lemon and maybe a toothpick," Smith says, almost giggling.

When they splurged on pizza, usually for the three-hundred-mile trip across Interstate 94 to Dickinson, North Dakota, three players shared a pie.

When they recruited Miles drove his own car, and five minutes into the trip he'd crank the FM stereo and claim he loved the song and leave it cranked for hours.

"That was his signal that he was sick of listening to me," Smith says, giggling again. Eventually, Miles would start hitting the seek button. The station would lock on 92.9, and he'd yell "Eagles" seconds later. He'd be up 1–0 before Smith knew they were playing a game. Next station, "Eminem," Smith would say, and they were tied. Then a country station would come up, and they'd look at each other, stumped. They'd waste an hour that way.

Miles bought his own meals, often Smith's, too, on those trips and never turned in receipts. He wanted to stretch the budget as far as he could. He was making less than thirty thousand dollars and raising a thousand dollars just to give Smith something to get groceries with while Smith's wife worked three jobs to pay rent.

On one recruiting trip during their North Dakota State stint, they took off for a nine-hour drive from Fargo for Sheridan, Wyoming, for a national junior college tournament. They got six and a half hours down I-94 to Miles City, Montana, where Miles had been denied a job "with my name all over it." Smith had forgotten to get a hotel room, and they hit four hotels before he found a Motel 6.

"Real old school," he says. "And Miles is not happy with me whatsoever. So, of course, I go at him."

In the room Smith told Miles he was getting soft as a head coach, moving to Division I. Smith was never allowed to book hotel rooms again.

In Sheridan they watched games for a few days, but still hadn't found a thick center they needed, so they kept trucking to another tournament in St. George, Utah. It was like a never-ending vacation, and Miles had become the dad, Smith the annoying son. Miles was telling Smith how to drive through the back roads of Wyoming. Eventually, Miles was done with his assistant coach. They got to Las Vegas, and Miles booked a flight home.

Smith grinned the whole way home, only after making a stop up in Washington State for more games, driving Miles's white Chrysler 300.

Some of Miles's assistants dreamed of becoming big-time Division I coaches, flying charters everywhere, with buses waiting on tarmacs. But Smith, even at meager Mayville State, couldn't imagine being happier. And though Miles could get crabby with him on the road, Smith knew Miles felt the same way.

They couldn't believe they got paid to coach basketball.

One time, for a break from the Mayville State offices before the season started in November 1996, Miles bought them tickets to Hootie and the Blowfish. Terrible seats in the new Fargodome, less than an hour south of Mayville State. Miles wanted to sneak down to the floor. Smith made it to the front, against the stage, but Miles got caught and couldn't talk his way through security.

"But that's my assistant coach up there," Miles yelled. "I don't even think he's really an assistant. He's like a volunteer. He doesn't get paid anything."

The security guard didn't care.

Smith grinned back at him.

Miles finally found a friend who got him up front with Smith, and the band played nine more songs. They couldn't imagine life getting any better. Front row to Hootie and the Blowfish in Fargo, North Dakota.

Now, they were taking charter flights to win the Big Ten Tournament. Staying in Hiltons. Eating whatever they wanted. Even at Colorado State, they took only one charter flight in five years, and that was to fly across the country to play Duke.

Now at Nebraska and on that recruiting flight to Oklahoma, Smith said to Miles, "Can you believe this?" They were coaches in the best conference in college basketball, "and can still just act like little kids and have fun."

In Oklahoma they watched their recruit, who would sign with the Huskers, and they were home by eleven so they could sleep in their own beds and wake to send their kids to school in the morning.

The night before the Ohio State game, Miles thinks it would be fun, and funny, to eat in a restaurant catering to Ohio State fans. He has watched conference tournament games across the country, many including bubble teams like his own. Every score could affect the Huskers' chances in the NCAA Tournament. His games and meal are interrupted every fifteen minutes or so by fans from Minnesota and Ohio State, wanting to congratulate Miles on the season. To tell him how much they like how hard the Huskers play. If their team isn't playing, they're cheering for the Huskers.

Miles asks each of them questions, trying to find out if they both know any of the same people. He asks what they think of Minnesota's chances. He talks up their favorite teams and leaves them feeling good.

A ten-year-old Ohio State fan says Terran Petteway is his favorite player.

"How many hours are you in a driveway or park shooting baskets?" Miles asks him.

"Six to eight hours every day."

"Basketball is a game of skill, and you just can't have enough skill. So play all the time. Even if Mom yells at you."

Miles loves the idea of winning over Ohio State fans the night before he plays them. Recruiting away their fans, their future players.

He takes a call from his wife, who wants to know exactly who she should be cheering for in these games.

He tells her to cheer for Northwestern, which is beating Iowa in the final minutes of its first-round game. That would knock back the Hawkeyes, who are rated lower than Nebraska in the RPI but beat them by ten in their only meeting of the year, part of that 0-4 start in the Big Ten.

Miles is so excited about the score he texts Northwestern coach Chris Collins to congratulate him before the game ends while watching him on the bench. What if he checks his phone? How great would that be?

Northwestern wins. Miles is pretty sure Nebraska will make the tournament no matter how they play against Ohio State. He's said as much in the media, to send a direct message to the committee. They're 10-2 since the Penn State loss and letting Deverell Biggs go. They're a different team than the one that started 1-5 in the Big Ten, 9-9 overall. Like ESPN's John Gasaway and statistician Ken Pomeroy have written and said, the Huskers got bigger and better defensively. They have had bad losses to lowly ranked teams early in the season: Alabama-Birmingham, Purdue, Penn State. But good wins lately against bluebloods: Ohio State, Michigan State, Indiana, Wisconsin.

And honestly, how could the selection committee leave out a team that finished fourth in the Big Ten, the best conference in college basketball?

Despite all those reasons, Miles still wants his team to feel like it has to beat Ohio State. That's why he jumped on them for practicing poorly.

"You constantly have to reset 'em," he says. "It's like a video game—things are going good, things are going bad, then they just quit playing. This is the generation we're dealing with. We're doing good now. So we can't go on cruise control. You gotta reset them."

Tonight, he'll spend time on his game cards, working the chess pieces, visualizing scenarios over and over in his head. He figures he'll let the team run offense in the first half, and then, when the teams switch ends and the Husker offense is right in front of him on the bench, he'll start running things. Save his best plays for the right moments. Especially his "50" sets, because everybody gets to touch the ball on those. Everybody's happy. He thinks about getting Walt Pitchford off to a good start.

"If he makes that first one, it's Katie-bar-the-door time," he says. "But if he misses . . ."

And that's the worry with his whole team. If they get in trouble, what will they do? Be the team at Michigan State that smiles at the bad call and muscles its way to a win? Or the team at Michigan or Ohio State or Illinois, the one that melts and shakes the Etch-a-Sketch, forgetting what got them into this position?

43

In the coaches' locker room, Miles again plays Pitbull's "Timber" and starts dancing like a kid from small-town South Dakota.

"I love it," assistant coach Chris Harriman says. "I love it."

Miles switches to "Dark Horse," and at exactly 3:27 before tip-off, he lip-sync's Katy Perry's last lyric: "There's no going back."

He'd told his players in the morning walk-through that ESPN's PickCenter picked them to lose by five points.

"To a team that finished behind you in the standings," he added. "They're still picking you last, boys."

Other than that line he's tried to keep them as loose as he is. After the morning walk-through, he argued with operations guy Teddy Owens over shaving-cream brands, accusing Owens of using too much Dove for Men. In the end he concluded operations guys were easy to replace. Owens agreed.

Miles is ready to play, and so is his team. He has no doubts.

Walt Pitchford misses his game-opening three-pointer, but buries one on the next possession for a 3–0 led. Soon, though, the Huskers trail 11–3, forcing Miles to call a thirty-second time-out, but then Terran Petteway gets a steal and hits Shavon Shields on a drive. He gets fouled and hits his free throws. Then Leslee Smith pokes the ball away in the lane, and Benny Parker flies in for a layup at the other end, where two Buckeyes get a piece of him, sending him into the standard that holds up the backboard. No call.

Shields gets fouled on the offensive rebound and gets a whistle and free throws.

But Miles is still livid with the no-call on Parker's fall. He has to be restrained from the officials by Shields and Kenya Hunter. Petteway and Smith carry Parker off the court. He hops directly to the training room.

Shields screams and then calls his team together to calm them before his free throws. Minutes later, Parker hops back out to the bench to watch Ohio State extend its lead to 20–12. A few minutes later he checks back in and gets a steal at the top of Kenya Hunter's packed-in zone defense. He starts a fast break that ends in Shields finding Ray Gallegos for a three to tie the game at 25–25. Gallegos hits another shot right before the half, and Craft misses. The Huskers lead 31–28 at the halftime buzzer.

"Good job, guys," Miles yells. "Way to come back."

He then retreats into the coaches' locker room to talk strategy with assistants. Petteway writes keys to the second half on the board. The team lists them for him, mirroring Hunter's morning reminders.

Petteway claps and says, "Stay with it. Stay with it. Us Always.

Nothing we can't do." He sits in his front-row seat, turns to Parker in the second row, and asks, "You good?"

Parker nods and doesn't speak. Petteway nods, too.

Then Miles returns to rile them up.

"Guys, look, in the other locker room, they think they're better than us. But I know we're better than they are. They took one of our guys out. Right? Then we took it to them for the last eight minutes. Send them the message that that's the way it's gonna be the rest of the night."

He's yelling now. They've survived a half with only three turnovers against Ohio State's pressure, but he knows the Buckeyes will turn up the full-court heat the rest of the game.

For the first 6:20 of the second half, the Huskers play their best basketball of the year, outscoring the Buckeyes seventeen to two to open an eighteen-point lead. Petteway scores nine of those points by continually driving to the hoop. Pitchford and David Rivers take down every defensive board. Parker scores twice and pushes the ball up court before Ohio State can set up pressure. He barrels in for a layup by going right through and over Buckeye forward Sam Thompson.

Last year's tournament MVP, Ohio State's Aaron Craft, is zero for five from the field. He has no points. The regular-season Big Ten scoring leader, Petteway, has sixteen. The Huskers are up eighteen points on Ohio State in the first round of the Big Ten Tournament with 13:40 to go. If they win this game, Miles could see them stealing a No. 9 seed in the NCAA Tournament. If they win tomorrow in the semifinals, they could be seeded even higher, with an even better first-round matchup and a real chance to win a game in the Big Dance, something the University of Nebraska has never done. Less than two years ago, in his first Nebraska press conference, Miles promised Husker fans they'd win a tournament game. Here they are. Already.

Then something breaks.

The Buckeyes hit a three and a two, and Nebraska fouls three times in one possession to slow the momentum. Officials call for a TV time-out. Assistant Chris Harriman would later say he'd never seen anything like it.

"It was complete panic," he would say. "Guys pointing fingers. And we were winning."

The Huskers miss free throws, and the Buckeyes start getting steals in the press. Within five minutes of play, the lead is cut to 56–47. That's when Petteway sees Walter Pitchford streaking to the hoop behind the Ohio State defense and lobs the ball for a wide-open alley-oop. Pitchford tries to reverse dunk as hard as he can, but misses.

At the other end LaQuinton Ross beats everybody down court for a layup and foul. He hits the free throw and cuts the lead to 53–50. The horn blows for a TV time-out, and Petteway is yelling, his hands over his head. He doesn't join the team in the huddle right away. Nobody's smiling, like they were at Michigan State.

The rest of the game is a grind. Pitchford hits a three-pointer with 4:19 left for a 61–56 lead, but the Huskers wouldn't make another basket. With the game tied at 63–63, Ross drives down the lane and a whistle blows. Miles wants a travel, but Petteway is called for his fifth foul. He's gone.

The Ohio State press forces more turnovers, and the Buckeyes seal a 71–67 win on free throws and an Aaron Craft layup. After the 17–2 Husker run, the Buckeyes outscored Nebraska 41–19 the rest of the way.

Miles doesn't blast the team. He tells them, "We imploded. We did this to ourselves." He asks them to look him in the eye, and only Shavon Shields, David Rivers, and a few others can follow that order. He's forced to do TV and radio and meet with dozens of print journalists. He supports his team. Says they have to learn from it.

He's livid about how officials allowed Ohio State to play so physically in its press, but doesn't let much of that leak into his comments. When he finally gets time to himself in the coaches' locker, about forty-five minutes after the end of the game, he takes a deep breath.

"Who do I want to strangle first? That's the game I play in my head," Miles says.

Like the game at Indiana, he still felt like they were going to win with two minutes left. A rebound here. A call there. He checks his phone.

"The one good thing about losing," he concludes, "is you only have twelve texts."

With that he goes to the bus. They race to the hotel, pack up, and take a quiet charter flight home. In the air associate athletic director Marc Boehm asks his men's basketball coach if he still wants to go through with a Selection Sunday watch party at the new arena.

"Of course," Miles says. "If we don't get in, the fans will just burn the place down."

Back in Lincoln Saturday's 11:00 a.m. film session lasts an hour and forty minutes.

"Any thoughts about last night?" Miles starts. "Ray? Shavon?"

His captain Shavon Shields speaks up: "I just think we can take it as a learning experience. We have to stay together and not get frustrated and things like that, and how good can we be? Like last night, things fell apart . . ."

"In a hurry," Miles adds.

"Yeah," Shields says. "When we stay together and we're Us Always, like we say we are, we're really good."

Textbook answers. Ones he's heard repeatedly from Miles during two seasons.

"Here's what confuses me," Miles says. "It doesn't take much to get us in a bad place."

Miles goes through his players one by one and lights into them, challenging them. He's talking to them individually and to the team at once. Each player is guilty of some sort of offense—allowing refs to get to them, bickering with teammates about not getting the ball, not running the offense with pace—but all players are a little bit guilty of all of them. Except for David Rivers and Benny Parker, who get praise for their consistent play. Parker has a sore ankle and a more painful wrist from his spill into the standard. Miles gets on Walter Pitchford, but then commends him for self-correcting like he did the previous week.

His longest assault is directed at his Big Ten scoring champ Terran Petteway for getting down on himself. The most intense anger goes to freshman point guard Tai Webster.

"I expect more out of this team," he says. "Do I think we're in the NCAA Tournament? Yeah. But I don't know. But I don't really care. Getting to the tournament isn't my goal. I want to make a deep run in the tournament."

They will watch the Selection Sunday show on the scoreboard at Pinnacle Bank Arena from the floor, while fans fill in the student section behind the benches. He tells them to enjoy the event because they deserve it.

"But when your head hits the pillow, it's over."

The coaches have tried to find answers to explain the loss. The best they can figure is players wanted the win so much that when things went wrong, even a little bit, they crushed themselves with self-imposed pressure. They've also decided they need to prepare players for not getting calls against higher-profile teams. As good as it will feel for the coaches, players, and fans if Nebraska makes its first NCAA Tournament in sixteen years, he can't have his players buckling beneath the pressure of that history.

"Pressure is self-applied," Miles yells at them now, pointing up at Chris Harriman. "Pressure doesn't exist. There is no pressure. You want pressure? Take your kid to the hospital and get a diagnosis of leukemia. The only way he's going to live is if he gets a bone-marrow transplant, and what are the odds? Fifty-fifty?"

"Not even," Harriman says.

"Not even," Miles repeats.

Miles will apologize to Harriman for using Avery to make his point, but Harriman will tell him not to worry. Harriman's inclination is to always be harder on players when their mental makeup isn't good. Especially when they have slippage. Especially this time of year. He understands Miles's point, and now the players understand it, too.

Miles launches into his speech about three kinds of players. He'll give this talk to coaches and other groups, and his veteran players know the spiel. Every program in the country has a roster filled with difference makers, winners, and losers. Difference makers have a long list of attributes that boils down to making everyone around them better, especially at crunch time, when they win you games. Winners do all the little things and understand their roles to help you win. Losers score twenty one night, then disappear. They work as hard as they have to work, then they fall apart when the team needs them most.

The message is for everyone, but Petteway is in a position where he could be any of the three, and maybe had been each of the three in the last three games—carrying his team through the pressure at Indiana, doing all the little things to win and support Shields's big game versus Wisconsin, and losing his composure against Ohio State.

Miles categorizes only one player for now; the rest will get theirs at the end of the season, when coaches will really know what this roster can do. The one player he calls out in this meeting is Benny Parker.

"Benny's a winner," Miles says, pointing at the five-foot-seven backup point guard he tried to talk into transferring away last summer. "Benny got told, 'Benny, I'm not sure.' Benny said, 'Coach, I'm gonna work harder. I can do it. I'm gonna prove it to you.' What does he do? He gets body-slammed by two guys last night into a standard and goes in the locker room, tapes up an ankle, tapes up a wrist, and comes out and plays twenty-two more minutes."

He cues Greg Eaton to start the tape. Miles goes through clips from the first half and the entire second half. He does play-by-play and color commentary. He calls out players for making mistakes and bucks up players making plays. He's looking for evidence of both. His tone is lighter, but no less honest.

During the Ohio State comeback, Miles dissects each play. His message is to just keep playing. Don't watch the scoreboard. Make the next best play.

"We only turned the ball over eleven times all game," he says. "But look at us. You'd think we'd turned it over twenty-two times."

"The same thing happened at Indiana," Harriman cuts in, "but the huddle was rock solid."

Miles tells them they're like a kid at Christmas who had six presents on his wish list and got five of them. All he can think about is the sixth.

He tells them they won't get benefit-of-the-doubt calls from the officials when he sees Ross travel down the middle on a no-call and Shields get whistled on a travel that could go either way.

Then he runs out of things to tell them.

"I think I've said anything I needed to say. Do you have anything to say? Ray? Terran?"

Terran Petteway: "I just want to apologize. Attitude-wise, I'm just embarrassed watching that."

"Do you know why?" Miles asks. "I do think you care about winning more than anything. You don't care about yourself. But do you know why you went there? Because I haven't seen you there in a long time. Like since your redshirt year. This team needs you."

Walter Pitchford apologizes.

And Shields restates the moral of the story: "We just got to learn from it. We know what frustration looks like and what it does to us."

Miles agrees, and he does what he always asks of his team—he finishes with a flourish. "We can go to the Sweet Sixteen," he says.

"Yes," Kenya Hunter yells. Hunter has coached in the NCAA Tournament nine times while at Xavier, North Carolina State, and Georgetown. Miles respects that kind of postseason experience and knowledge. He wants Hunter sharing that with players from here on out.

"We can go as far as you want to go. We can go on a run," Miles says. "Go out and get a good stretch, and we're going to shoot."

As soon as the last player leaves and the door slowly shuts, Miles turns to the coaches in the back of the room. "Was I unjust to anybody?"

They shake their heads. Miles starts blaming himself for sticking with their new press breaker too long. He could have made other adjustments. They shake their heads at this, too, though some agree that the press breaker needs work.

Then they argue about what's going to happen tomorrow on Selection Sunday. Miles thinks they'll be a No. 10 seed in the NCAA Tournament. Others think that's too high. Joe Lunardi, the ESPN bracket forecaster, has dropped them down to a play-in game on Tuesday. Should they prepare for that, each coach taking a team or two and getting to work? Maybe. The analysis of what the tournament might do gets so specific they're eventually discussing the ramifications of a Louisiana Tech–Tulsa Conference USA Tournament championship game. Hunter breaks up laughing at their own paranoia. So Miles reels them back to the present problem of their own team. He tells them they're in triage mode. They're like child psychologists, who take children into a sandbox to talk about getting beaten up, or abused, to get them in a comfort zone.

"Shooting is their sandbox," he says. "Just do some shooting drills with them and talk to them. This is their comfort zone."

Then they'll do a team free-throw drill to bring them together again.

After the shooting, players break up into groups of three and four at the four baskets. Miles will call out a player to start the drill. A shooter will take one shot at each basket clockwise around the gym until they hit six, then seven, then eight in a row. The team calls out the makes. After a miss they start over at zero. Two minutes to get to eight or they have to do twenty burpees, a punishment more about making them look silly than sweaty. The drill makes them work as a team and puts pressure on them as the number gets higher. When they fail, which they always do a few times, they have to react the right way to eventually succeed. Exactly what they need right now, Miles figures.

Parker winces when he catches a ball to shoot and then shoots with one hand and misses. Miles pulls him from the drill and puts him at center court, where he does one-handed pushups on his good wrist without being told. Harriman joins him, grinning. The coaches look at each other. The kid is a winner.

The first two tries, they get to six consecutive makes and even seven, with Parker counting them out for them. The third time they can't even get to six in a row. And redshirt Nick Fuller, one of the most pure shooters on the team, keeps missing.

"What am I going to do if I have to put you in there with an eighteen-point lead?" Miles says matter-of-factly. "I'm just saying."

On the fourth try Petteway, Trevor Menke, Ray Gallegos, and Shavon Shields race to the front of their groups to grab the ball. They get to only seven. Miles starts intensifying punishments. This time they run and do ten fingertip push-ups. Parker again does them one-handed.

On the fifth try they hit four in a row, miss one, hit six, miss another, then hit seven before Menke swishes the eighth, all in forty-two seconds.

Miles slow claps the team to center court and has them sit down to explain their roles in the Sunday Selection Show. CBS will air it after the last tournament championship games are done, including the Big Ten's Michigan State versus Michigan game back in Indianapolis. The Wolverines clipped Ohio State by three, but that won't be mentioned.

CBS will cut to arena cameras in case Nebraska's name gets called while the brackets are released.

"If we get selected, they'll show us, and if we don't get selected, they'll show us," Miles says. "I said it'll be great TV either way because if we don't get in, they'll burn that place down. . . . Either way, it'll be great for ratings."

They're worthy of the tournament, he tells them, but you never know.

"It's out of our control," he said. "Go in with a hopeful mind, but understand that if we're disappointed and we don't get what we want, we can't act like babies."

Left unsaid: like we did in Indianapolis.

He talks about the bubble math, listing losses that hurt them and wins that helped them. He talks RPI versus BPI (basketball power index), Lunardi rankings versus Ken Pomeroy rankings. Some players have had these discussions in their apartments for weeks. Others have worked hard to avoid all the bubble talk.

"I think we're in, but I could easily be wrong," Miles concludes. "I feel good about it, but I don't feel great."

The team starts debating what to wear. Eventually, they agree on their "The Husker Way" shirts and black sweats. Miles says he doesn't care what they wear as long as they shower and shave and clean up. He stares at Petteway as he finishes that line, and Petteway laughs.

44

Tim Miles has regrets. He's had to make tough decisions in his nineteen years of coaching, and sometimes he can't help but think about them. He's had to let go of players, like Deverell Biggs, whom he deeply wanted to help succeed. He wanted to bring Craig Smith with him to Southwest Minnesota State from Mayville, but couldn't win a fight with administrators. But the biggest decisions have come when he had to decide between his program and his future, or the future of his family.

In two years he pushed Mayville from a perennial 2-22 team to two-time conference champs and NAIA-II Tournament contenders. Going to Southwest Minnesota State in Marshall the spring of 1997 made sense. He claims to this day that he left Mayville so broke that he owed eighty-eight hundred dollars on two Visa cards at 19 percent interest. He took the SMSU Mustangs from a nine-year absence from postseason play to winning its first NCAA Division II Regional and making the Elite Eight in 2001. Fargo was a bigger program, bigger city, more money, a free Dodge Durango, and the kids were still young enough not to notice the change. Tim and Kari loved Fargo. They loved the Bison players and the Bison people, and they were beloved. Miles had taken the program from Division II anonymity to Division I national attention, despite the team's inability to play in the postseason, or even in a conference, because of the five-year waiting period after moving up to the big time. His redshirted recruits, as sophomores, had just won twenty games and had beaten Wisconsin and Marquette on the road in their first two years on the court. But when Colorado State called in the spring of 2007, offering more money, a better conference, and a chance to see if he could succeed outside the Midwest, he took a shot. That meant again leaving behind friends, his wife's friends, his kids' friends. Making his daughter switch schools.

Leaving also meant leaving those redshirted recruits and the potential of that roster. He'd built a ship in landlocked and football-only Fargo. If he stayed another two years, those recruits would be seniors and eligible for the NCAA Tournament. He could coach Ben Woodside, the kid who responded when Miles threw his keys down on the table. Woodside, Mike Nelson, Brett Winkelman, and the rest of those guys—who knows?—maybe they could make a Cinderella tournament run, the kind that ruined fans' brackets throughout the country. That would mean a great deal to him. To his family. To Fargo. To the Dakotas.

While Miles was losing twenty-plus games in Fort Collins for the second straight season in 2008–9, Woodside led the Bison into the NCAA Tournament under loyal Miles assistant Saul Phillips. Miles watched them win the Summit League title game over Oakland University with Craig Smith in then-UNLV coach Lon Kruger's office.

"You could see how proud he was of them," Smith says. "He had sold them on the vision." Then he sold his CSU team on winning a No. 8 versus No. 9 game in the Mountain West Tournament.

"It was like we won the Super Bowl," Smith says.

North Dakota State then drew Kansas in the first round, while Miles's CSU team was done. The Jayhawks were loaded with NBA talent—Cole Aldrich, Tyshawn Taylor, and the Morris twins—but Woodside played fearlessly, putting up thirty-seven points. The Bison closed to within two possessions of the defending champions with 1:11 left in the game when Woodside hit Winkelman for a three. Kansas won 84–74 and would eventually make the Sweet Sixteen.

"Saul was there the whole time we were there," Woodside says now, between seasons in Italy's pro league. "He coached us when we were the scout team as redshirts, battling all the older guys. For us, it wasn't much of a change. But I always wonder if Miles would have ever wanted to finish what we started."

Of course he did. But one of his biggest regrets came his last year at Colorado State, when he told his athletic director he didn't want to have a watch party during Selection Sunday in March 2012. The Rams had gone 20-11, 8-6 in the Mountain West, three years after losing forty-seven games in the first two. He had a team of what Smith calls "Miles guys," who soaked up scouting reports and refused to beat themselves, outworking and outsmarting better opponents to gut out four wins in the last five conference games, putting them in a position to make the NCAA Tournament, often with lineups of players six-foot-five and shorter. Despite everything else Colorado had to offer, fans started showing up to Moby Arena for those wins. He'd worked with Rams marketing guy Ben Chulick, now at Arizona, to build the Twitter following. He'd opened his practices and locker room for Mountain West Network cameras for three seasons of a reality TV show, like HBO's *Hard Knocks,* but with whistles when he cussed. Anything to fill that arena for his "Miles guys." Miles even brought his coaches to his daughter Ava's Catholic school to play "Are You Smarter than a Third-Grader?" to get those families to show up. Fans and recruits responded.

But on the edge of having the Rams in the tournament, Miles had doubt. Despite the twenty wins, a tough schedule, and a strong RPI, he wasn't sure Colorado State would get its name called during the Selection Show. So he declined to host an event. He declined transparency. The team watched privately, and they got in. That should have been a celebration his team shared with the fans.

Murray State blew the Rams out, 58–41, in the first round in March 2012, and Tom Osborne and Marc Boehm came calling during the Final Four with their new practice facility, a voter-approved arena project near completion, and a mess of Husker cash, both for his family and for the program. The next year, in March 2013, veteran coach Larry Eustachy held a public Selection Sunday party before taking Miles's Colorado State guys to the tournament, where CSU beat Missouri before losing in the second round to Louisville by ten at Lexington, Kentucky, essentially a home game for Rick Pitino's Cardinals, who would go on to win it all.

Now, after a brutal first two months and an inexplicable last six weeks, Miles felt good about Nebraska's chances to get into March Madness for the first time in sixteen years. He had seen media brackets with his Huskers as high as a No. 9 seed, but more often as a No. 11 seed, possibly having to survive a Tuesday play-in game to get in to the final sixty-four teams.

The selection committee picked thirty-two conference champions in automatic bids and then chose the next best thirty-six teams. He figured they had to be the fifth best team out of the Big Ten, the best conference in the country. How could they not get picked? But the unthinkable wasn't all that unthinkable. The committee could pick Iowa, which had beaten the Huskers, 67–57, on New Year's Eve, over them, despite the Hawkeyes' late-season troubles. Maybe committee members would want Minnesota Gophers first-year coach Richard Pitino, a coaching legend's son, in the tournament, or Southern Methodist coach Larry Brown, who won a title at Kansas in 1988. Those stories would translate to ratings for CBS. Nothing was a lock.

When associate AD Marc Boehm had asked Miles if he was sure he wanted the watch party, Miles wasn't sure they'd get in, but he was sure he wanted his coaches and players to get one more night with Nebraska fans, who had carried them to the best home record in the Big Ten at 8-1, 15-1 overall, the one loss at the buzzer to Michigan, a game that will always gnaw at him.

Boehm and his team went to work. They put chairs for the coaches and players at the sideline, in front of scarlet-and-cream leather couches filled with coaches' families. Behind them about twenty-five hundred fans spread out in the student section. Players were introduced over the PA system and came out to big applause. While the coaches waited for their names to come next, they kept debating their chances, running through every bubble team's résumés versus their own. Despite Nebraska dropping to 46 in the RPI, Joe Lunardi had them in the tournament this morning against Dayton, at Dayton, in a play-in game to get them to San Antonio in the second round.

"I've checked brackets once or twice, taken a nap," Miles swears. "I'm serious."

Miles gets the loudest standing ovation, just a little louder than the applause for captains Terran Petteway and Shavon Shields. Once seated they face twenty-seven photographers and videographers at center court, with print journalists lined on the far side. The pep band has already played the school fight song multiple times. Cheerleaders are doing their jobs. Miles takes the microphone and starts selling. Always selling.

"Are we having fun yet?" he yells. "In about five or ten minutes we're going to find out if all these young guys in front of us worked so hard to be where we want to be. At the beginning of the year, we had a love-hate relationship. They loved to make me hate them. And somehow it flipped."

The fans rise to their feet.

"We are blessed here at Nebraska," he continues. "We have unbelievable fans. So, thank you fans. . . . When I interviewed I remember saying, 'It's time for Husker basketball to do their part.' . . . But you can make a difference. This home-court advantage: 15-1 and we lost on a fluke deal, on a half-courter. Next year, we're gonna let nobody get lucky in here. . . . The good news is we're not done yet! Let's go, Big Red!"

He sits as the CBS Selection Sunday show starts on the scoreboard. The players crane their necks to watch and listen: "Dreams will be fulfilled in the next few weeks," sportscaster Adam Zucker says from New York. "Hearts will be broken as teams wait to hear their names."

The coaches sit with players. Miles keeps checking his phone as the first bracket is announced. Old Big 12 football rival Colorado gets in, and the crowd boos. Then fans boo Ohio State. Miles starts rocking forward and back.

In the second bracket Saul Phillips has gotten the NDSU Bison in again, the second time in five years. Miles claps along with the fans, who know their coach's history. Then Creighton gets awarded a No. 3 seed and a cushy matchup in San Antonio with Louisiana-Lafayette. Out of the pep band a trombonist screams "Go Ragin' Cajuns!" and the crowd applauds.

The next matchup in San Antonio is No. 11 Nebraska versus No. 6 Baylor. No play-in game. A shot at Creighton redemption if they win a tournament game, which Nebraska has never done.

Terran Petteway and Benny Parker jump up and slap hands more than a dozen times. Walt Pitchford hugs Miles before Kari can get to him. Shavon hugs everyone. Marc Boehm does, too.

"Dad," Avery Harriman screams to his dad, "you did it! We're going to Texas!"

The Husker football team's Tunnel Walk song, "Sirius" by the Alan Parsons Project, cranks on the sound system, and fans start hollering "Can you feel it?" Petteway bounces. Pitchford dances. Then everybody dances, sixteen years of frustration lifted.

"Look at 'em," Miles says, turning around to take in the fans, too. "Awesome. Just exactly as you'd hope."

In the next bracket Iowa must go to Dayton, Ohio, for the play-in game against Tennessee that Husker coaches feared. They all laugh in tension release. Nobody pays attention to the last bracket. Neither Minnesota nor Southern Methodist is called.

Miles takes the mic again.

"So, I still got goose bumps. Who's with me?" he yells. "This is what college basketball should be about for you guys."

Then he points to his players, who are back in their seats.

"This is what college basketball should be about for these guys."

He lets the fans applaud for a few seconds, much longer than he waits for his team to answer a question in film or pray before or after games.

"I think the state of Nebraska is gonna take over the River-walk," he yells. "I want you to be nice to those Creighton fans."

Fans laugh.

"Don't dump 'em in the river. Be nice. Be nice. They're good people. But let's hope for a second-round matchup with those guys. They would welcome that, and we would, too. This is gonna be a great moment in my life—in my family's lives. A lot of hard work by everybody goes into this. I appreciate you supporting us when we were crappy, when we couldn't get it together. Now, things are kind of getting on track. So once again, we want to tell you, this is not the finish line. We're still ready to give more. Let's get to San Antonio."

45

Tim Miles tweeted a selfie while talking to Jim Rome for thirteen minutes on the host's national radio show that week. Miles talked about every stop on the way to Nebraska and about how he doesn't want to be the flavor-of-the-month coach, or team, in the NCAA Tournament.

"You know, you've talked to a lot of guys like me," he said, "where you're hot one day and cooked the next. I don't want to be a flash in the pan at Nebraska. I want to be one of those guys where we're on the scene for a long time and you can expect Nebraska to be a team that you'll have to deal with on the national level."

Within eight days he also appeared on Fox Sports Radio, the *Dan Patrick Show,* and Minneapolis's KFAN. Monday before practice he talked to ESPN Radio's Scott Van Pelt and Ryen Russillo about #NoSitSunday against Wisconsin and the Ohio State meltdown. Could the loss help the Huskers going into the tournament?

"If you put the lesson you learned into the game plan, yes," he said. "But if it's a symptom that we're just a bunch of chokers, then no."

Later in film Monday, Miles was done talking about Ohio State. Like all sixty-eight coaches in the tournament, he was scrambling to scout and prepare for a good team in less than five days. He left assistant Chris Harriman and the scout team on the court during film to run through Baylor's offense and unique zone defense, something the Huskers hadn't much dealt with all year. Harriman planned to pull an all-nighter to dissect the Bears' schemes and personnel. Meanwhile, Craig Smith would prepare for Creighton and Kenya Hunter for Louisiana-Lafayette, in case they made history at Nebraska by winning their next game.

For now, Miles talked his top eight players through Baylor's 74–65 loss to Iowa State in the Big 12 Tournament championship. Baylor's season had mirrored the Huskers' turnaround. It started 2-8 in league play, but won seven of its last eight games in the regular season and three more in the tournament before the title-game loss.

"So, they're playing with an enormous amount of confidence," he said. "Obviously, playing in Texas, they're viewing this as a home game."

They watched clips from the first half and the entire second half. Miles told the team what he'd probably run against the zone, what they'd probably do to defend Baylor's height, which in basketball terminology is now called "length." He compared the team to Cincinnati—which smothered the Huskers in December with its size—but not as tough.

"I'm telling you, if you guard them, and be patient with offense—you know the recipe, all right? We'll beat them. But it comes with challenges. They're long, and we can lose our minds on this stuff. Any questions?"

They practiced for just an hour, giving coaches more time to watch video of Baylor, Creighton, and the Ragin' Cajuns. But that sixty minutes may have been the most physical practice of the year, because Harriman had instructed his scout team to play that way, even if it had to foul. Thirty minutes in Walter Pitchford got beaten for two rebounds by the newly engaged Mike Peltz.

"Baylor's going to be physical," Miles yelled. "So you got to have your mind straight."

Pitchford claimed he kept getting fouled, and Miles, rather than escalating the confrontation, calmly said, "This is just like Ohio State" and put his whistle in his mouth.

Shavon Shields intervened.

"You can't get frustrated, Walt. You can't," he said.

Pitchford then took a charge. Then he got a rebound.

"You got to get this next rebound, Walt," Miles said. "You got to get it."

Peltz muscled Pitchford to the ground, and seven-footer Sergej Vucetic bowled right through Pitchford, who bounced back up after the play with no complaints. Peltz slapped his hands in approval. Pitchford's teammates shouted for him.

"That's right, Walt," Petteway said when they calmed down.

Ten minutes later Petteway took issue with a shot-clock problem, of all things. Miles blew his whistle and called his red team together, but he stared down Petteway in the huddle.

"You can't be a ref, and a coach, and everything else," he said softly. "That's my fault [on the shot clock]. But you can't go to that place where you were last Friday. I need winners right now."

When Tim Miles and Craig Smith started their careers in Mayville, North Dakota, one of their biggest fans and critics was an older man named Leif Karlstad. He'd walk right up to the coaches and tell them what the Comets were doing wrong. The coaches didn't always agree with his analysis, but they agreed he was always honest.

Eight years later in the fall of 2004, Smith left Miles's North Dakota State staff to try to replicate Miles's success as head coach of the Comets. The team had won one game the previous year, and Smith's theme for the season was "One Win to In" the NAIA National Tournament. They did it, improving to seventeen wins and a national tournament berth. The town backed the team and filled the gym regularly, including Leif Karlstad.

On a Sunday Smith stopped by his office after church and before a send-off pep rally with the team and fans. As he walked out the door, he noticed the red light blinking on his phone.

He checked the message, which was sent at 2:36 a.m.

"Coach, I just want you to know how proud I am of you," Karlstad's voice said faintly. "And how proud I am of your team, and I just know how well you'll do at the national tournament and for years to come. I'm just the biggest Comet fan you'll ever find."

And he hung up. Here's the thing: Leif Karlstad had died at 3:30 that morning. Everybody in town knew. Smith was listening to the man's last words.

"It was amazing," Smith says ten years later.

It's just basketball.

"But it's life, too," he says.

In San Antonio Thursday, the day before the Baylor game, the Huskers will hear stories about what their run has meant to some Nebraska fans. How it means more than basketball.

In the morning film Chris Harriman and Miles tell the team

they have to be mentally tough. Iowa State started the Big 12 title game o for 13 from the field, but held things together to tie the game at halftime and rolled Baylor in the second half. They know Baylor is the favorite, a No. 6 seed for a reason, just as Nebraska is No. 11 for a reason. The players need to be able to handle things not going their way.

Sheriff's deputies on motorcycles escort the team to the AT&T Center, the home of the San Antonio Spurs, for media interviews and a mandatory open practice, which they finish with a half-court shooting contest. Miles misses his shots by five and seven feet. Redshirt Nick Fuller swishes two to edge Ray Gallegos, Walter Pitchford, and Chris Harriman for the win. Before leaving the arena Miles has won over CBS broadcasters Craig Sager, Marv Albert, and Steve Kerr, whom Miles tried to shame into the contest.

Then the motorcycle cops lead the team to the University of St. Mary's gym for a closed formal practice. On the bus Miles tells his story from 1996 about not getting a job at the University of Sioux Falls, a private Baptist college in South Dakota. A USF administrator told him he was the best coach among all the candidates, but he just wasn't sure Miles was "the right man to mold young Baptist men." So Miles stayed at his Mayville State job. The coach laughs now because he just got a text from a friend, who remembers how angry Miles was about not getting that Sioux Falls job in his home state and says he can take it out on Baylor, a school that molds young Baptist men.

Outside St. Mary's Miles takes a selfie with the deputies and runs into practice. Ray Gallegos hits seven of eight three-pointers from the baseline, where he should get shots against Baylor's zone. The team runs through plays Miles has constructed just for Baylor, one called "Waco," against no defense, then against the scout team in Baylor's zone. Then they defend the Bears' offensive packages.

At one point Pitchford yells after contact in the lane. Harriman rushes to him and puts a hand on his neck and whispers in his ear. Pitchford nods and walks away with no more flare-ups the rest of practice. Harriman's next task: find a birthday cake for his son.

Later, the bus heads from the Marriott hotel to a bar on San Antonio's Riverwalk for a Husker pep rally. Miles brings Alyce and Tip with him in the front seats, and they talk about the one-minute *Go Big Red* video Doland High School posted on You-Tube. The half-hour rally is a chanting and selfie fest. On the way in Miles sees nothing but red. He can't say no to anyone with an iPhone, even with his sports information director and assistant coaches prodding him to move along.

After seven selfies he sees someone in a blue Creighton Blue-jays shirt who couldn't be more out of place. That takes guts. Wearing the shirt is Ryan Hanigan, who's come down with friends, a week after his dad's funeral, to cheer on both Nebraska teams and to get away for a weekend.

"I have a story to tell you," Hanigan hollers into Miles's ear and above the noise.

But he can't get any more words out. Miles grabs his hand to shake and then pulls him in for a quick hug.

"Thanks," Miles says. "Thanks for coming."

They take a selfie, Miles's white Husker pullover next to Hanigan's Bluejays blue golf polo. Hanigan apologizes for getting choked up, and they agree to talk later, when this craziness is over.

After Miles selfies all the way to the microphone, the crowd has trouble quieting down for him to speak.

"If you get a chance, grab these players and tell them they can do it," he says. "I've been a head coach nineteen years in every conceivable place you've never heard of. I know winners when I see them."

He introduces his wife, his kids, his parents, his coaches. Then someone else.

"This is a special occasion," Miles says. "We got a young guy in the crowd. Coach Harriman's son, who had a bone-marrow transplant and is doing phenomenally well."

The crowd cheers more loudly than they had when the team showed up. Miles brings the microphone down to the seven-year-old's mouth.

"My name is Avery. Go Big Red."

"Today is . . . ?" Miles asks.

"March 20th."

"And?"

"It's my birthday."

Husker fans, many with drinks in hand, sing for him, then devolve into a "Go Big Red" chant.

"I just want to thank you guys for being the best fans in the world," Miles says when they calm down. "One more thing: tell those guys they can do it and this is just the beginning."

They chant: "You can do it."

For twenty more minutes, he takes selfies, one every ten seconds.

On the bus back to the Marriott, coaches track North Dakota State's game with Oklahoma. Saul Phillips is up eight on Lon Kruger's Sooners. Miles parks his parents in the lobby bar to eat dinner and watch the rest of the game. He jogs up the escalator to the second-floor meeting room for one more film session. But instead of showing more Baylor clips, or practice clips, or talking any strategy, Miles shows a photo of a family of Husker fans, one of whom had throat cancer.

"Guys, I want to tell you a few stories," he begins. "I just want you to understand the impact you're having on an entire state."

The team hears about the Stehr family, more specifically the man in the middle of the photo, who came to the Huskers' win over Minnesota. That's when the team was playing terribly, but David Stehr believed in them. And despite his throat cancer, he showed up, and he stood throughout #NoSitSunday for the Wisconsin win. After that game he told his nephew, "I want to tell you something. This is probably my last year on the planet. And that team is going to win a game in the NCAA. That's going to be the first [Nebraska] team to win a game in the NCAA."

Miles tells his coaches and players he talked to David on the phone for fifteen minutes that morning. Then he tells them about how scared he was last season during his own father's heart surgery and having to wait a week to find out if he'd survive. He tells them about standing in a hospital hallway, outside his dad's room, where Tip asked the doctor to just give him two more years of life.

"My boy's going to get them in the NCAA Tournament, and they're gonna win within two years," Tip said without knowing his son was listening.

Tip is in great health now, and he may realize his dream tomorrow.

"There are so many people who want you to be successful and really, truly believe in you," Miles says. "Let me tell you about one I just met."

The team hears the story of Ryan Hanigan and his family and what Nebraska basketball means to them. How connections and memories with John are intertwined with Husker basketball and its history, past, and especially present.

"Understand the impact you're having on people all across the country," he finishes. "You're really on to something special because you're people with talent. You're together. You're not perfect. . . . This is a thing bigger than yourself. A thing bigger than us as a team. I expect championship conduct tomorrow night. Determined, tough-minded junkyard dogs."

Everyone stays to eat a buffet dinner. But Miles goes back down to the Marriott bar and watches Saul Phillips and the Bison beat Oklahoma, 80–75, while sitting with Tip and Alyce and other family. Saul has done what Miles wants to do.

"Good for him," Miles says. "You know, he didn't get enough credit five years ago when he got to the tournament. Everyone gave me the credit."

Tomorrow would be Miles's turn.

46

Nothing goes right from the moment the Huskers show up to try to make history.

When the bus drops them at AT&T Center the next morning, players and coaches show their IDs and crowd into a service elevator, which takes them to the wrong floor, back to where they started, and gets stuck.

Miles complains from the back wall.

The elevator operator barks back, "Got it, Coach."

The coaches' locker room, about four by ten feet, has only two chairs and four lockers for the seven coaches.

Walt Pitchford misses his first three, and Baylor's Cory Jefferson dunks on him at the other end. The Bears build a 17–7 lead, and Nebraska can't stop fouling. Terran Petteway and Tai Webster and then Shavon Shields and Leslee Smith get their second fouls midway through the first half. The Huskers are also turning the ball over against Baylor's press and half-court zone.

They can't make shots, as Miles had worried the night before while eating a peppercorn steak away from his team. By halftime Baylor holds a 29–16 lead.

The Huskers are 0-11 from the three-point line and have almost as many fouls (thirteen) as points (sixteen). Miles is livid about the offensive ineptitude, and before he gets to all the guilty parties, he starts on scoreless Walter Pitchford in the halftime locker room before he even meets with coaches to figure things out. Pitchford starts arguing back.

Shields stands to intervene with his we-can't-get-frustrated mantra. He says they're doing the same thing they did in the Ohio State collapse.

"Let's go," he shouts.

Miles retreats to the coaches' closet, and the players are silent for six minutes. The good news is the Huskers held Baylor to 33 percent shooting, which kept them in the game. When he returns to the team Miles says the Iowa State Cyclones bucked up and manned up when Baylor hit them early, and they came back to win. The Huskers can do it, too.

"You gotta have a tough mentality," he says. "I'm on your ass. I'm pressing buttons. I'm getting good responses out of some, not so good out of others. Guys, listen, if I don't believe in you, Walt, I'm not gonna play you. I believe in you. You can do it."

What happens in the second half would take time and distance for Miles to ever understand, much less explain to his mother.

The Huskers cut the lead to nine when Pitchford blocks Jefferson at the rim and Ray Gallegos hits a three at the other end. But Baylor extends the lead back to fourteen when Smith gets called for a blocking foul against Rico Gathers. Miles runs out to the scorer's table to complain that the shot clock wasn't working. Atlantic Coast Conference referee Karl Hess, infamous on Internet message boards and social media, calls his second technical on Miles in the last 2:36 of play.

Miles is in shock. He's never been ejected from a game. Ever. He's had four technicals in his last six years in coaching. He tries to explain to the officials and the official scorers he just wanted to notify them the shot clock had stopped. But Hess boots him.

Baylor hits four straight free throws, just like it did on the first technical, to stretch the lead to eighteen points.

Miles is exiled from the biggest game of his career with 11:17 to play. Even more bizarre, Miles can't find a way to watch Craig Smith coach the rest of the game. The tiny television in the locker room can't find the feed. He goes to the Turner Sports–CBS green room but gets kicked out by NCAA officials, who direct him back to his locker room.

On his way back he wishes Creighton luck at the Bluejay locker room. The Jays had been watching, and Greg McDermott pats Miles on the back and invites him in to watch for a few minutes.

For about 4 minutes of play, Miles is stuck in the Huskers'

locker room with his boss, Marc Boehm, NCAA site administrator Doug Fullerton—explaining why he'd been kicked out, even though Miles was right about the clock—and an arena technician, banging on the tiny television.

"Karl saw you out of the box and thought you were charging him over the call," says Fullerton, who is also the commissioner of the Big Sky Conference.

Miles is calm. He sits with his hand over his mouth.

He tells the technician to "be careful" while she stands on a chair to figure out the TV.

"Good to see you," Miles says without any sarcasm as Fullerton starts to leave.

Fullerton is apologetic and blames "Murphy's Law."

Miles finally gets to see the final minutes of the Husker season on the small screen in his locker room. With 3:50 left, and the Huskers down by eighteen, he sees a replay of the technical. He stands and starts picking up empty Gatorade bottles and nutrition-bar wrappers throughout the locker room, a practice he picked up in part from his old athletic director Jim Kretchman at Northern State.

Twenty years earlier, then an assistant at Northern in Aberdeen, Miles found out he got his first head-coaching job at Mayville State. He immediately went into Kretchman's office for advice.

"Coach, what happens if I'm not successful?" he asked Kretchman, who had been a mentor throughout Miles's six years of running the JV team and driving back roads while recruiting across the upper Midwest, from one Hardee's special meal to the next. Miles viewed Kretchman as a philosopher of athletics.

"Recruit the right kind of guys," the AD said. "Coach them the right way. Leave the locker room cleaner than it was when you got there. The right people will notice. If they don't, the janitor will appreciate that, and there's something to be said about making the janitor happy, too."

...

In the locker room Tim Miles sits with Marc Boehm to watch the final minutes of the game.

"Let's say we come back and win," he says. "Am I suspended for the next game?"

The question wouldn't matter. Petteway, Shields, and Gallegos play well down the stretch, cutting a 60–40 Baylor lead to 67–56 with 1:47 left, but they run out of time. Miles shuts the TV off before the final buzzer.

"Tim," Boehm says, "absolutely fantastic year."

"Thanks."

After the game Karl Hess releases a statement that doesn't include an apology.

Baylor would shoot forty-eight free throws to Nebraska's sixteen.

But Miles knows his team didn't deserve to win. He didn't deserve to win. No excuses.

"We're so fragile," he says to Boehm.

Smith brings a defeated team to the locker room with a 74–60 loss. Hand slaps and hugs from Shavon Shields and Kenya Hunter.

"Guys, listen, I apologize for getting run out," Miles says. "It's a bad example on my part. I want you guys to know that. . . . Second of all, we didn't play our best today. We weren't together today, and we have to figure that out."

He tells them they played hard and never quit, but they can't get consumed with themselves like they did in the last two games. He talks up the seniors.

"At the end of today, when I look at today's game, we know why we lost," he says. "How we cure that and how we fight that is going to take time and maturity."

He blames himself for some of that. He tells them to ignore the officiating when they talk to media.

"Hopefully, we can earn our way back into this tournament next year," he says. "Are we good?"

He doesn't wait for an answer.

"Let's take a knee."
A few seconds later, "Team on three."
Petteway: "One. Two. Three."
Team: "Team."

Back at the hotel, the team has an hour to pack up before the bus leaves for the airport. In the lobby Tip and Alyce Miles sit at a table, surrounded by family complaining about officiating and waiting for the baby boy. Kari Miles has a Stetson for her husband, one of many unexpected things, most of them inside his head, he'll take home from San Antonio.

The team enters the lobby to big cheers, and Miles hugs his wife, his kids, and his parents. He thanks everyone for driving down.

He sneaks off to the side of the group to explain his technical fouls in whispers to Gabe, but Alyce loudly asks him why he got that second one. What was all the fuss about?

So Tim Miles has to explain his behavior to his mother.

"Ooooooooooh," she says. "Well."

Tip tells him they'll win in the tournament next year.

"Well, we've got work to do," Tim says.

Alyce secretly has a bigger worry than the technicals her son got whistled for today. What she worries about is whether all this basketball business will make the family forget it's Friday.

"Boy," she says, "I hope they remember it's still Lent."

EPILOGUE

Kevin Miles says his little brother will always be the littlest dog in the fight no matter how big he gets.

When they were kids in Doland, he would beat on Tim when he was too annoying, too loud, too cocky. Nonstop with that Nerf hoop on the door. Kevin would hold Tim down until he said "Uncle." Then the boy would come right back for more with everything he had, claiming he'd had his fingers crossed when he admitted defeat.

Alyce would finally call her own time-out before heading back to the table to get the newspaper out. Tim would be sentenced to the blue chair in the living room, seething, and Kevin, facing him from the hallway bench fifteen feet away, would mouth these words: "I'm going to kill you."

And Tim Miles would grin back.

Craig Smith says Coach will always have the mentality of an undersize fighter with a chip on his shoulder. The kid from a town nobody knows. The player who couldn't make an NAIA roster at a school named after the Virgin Mary. The graduate assistant who got turned down by a half-dozen schools before taking on a 2-22 program. The guy who knows he wasn't the fans' first choice to replace Doc Sadler at Nebraska. The Big Ten team picked to finish last.

Miles has a card taped to his computer in his office from a coach who jokingly told him he'd never beat Tom Izzo. When the Huskers beat Izzo, Miles didn't throw away the card.

"That challenge will always be there," Smith says, "no matter how far he goes in this business."

Smith has been with Miles most of his career and considers the 2013–14 Husker season Miles's best coaching job during his 20 years in the business. Coach recognized the system wasn't working, and he had the humility to own up to it and mess with the recipe. The Huskers finished fourth in the Big Ten, even though they were in the bottom three in seven of ten crucial statistical categories. They made a run that almost turned into the greatest season in Nebraska's 119-year history.

In the first week of April, Oregon coach Dana Altman presented Miles with the Jim Phelan National Coach of the Year Award. Creighton's Greg McDermott, Michigan's John Beilein, and UCLA's Steve Alford had been finalists. Another trophy and Tombstone frozen pizza.

Six weeks after returning from San Antonio, Miles pulls everyone into the Hendricks film room for a team meeting.

Mike Peltz and Ray Gallegos are gone, out of eligibility. Three scout teamers have transferred to smaller schools to get more playing time. Smith, his longest-tenured assistant and one of his best friends, has taken the head-coaching job at the University of South Dakota. Miles called everyone he knew to get him on the Coyotes' radar and then coached him through the interviews. Operations guy Jayden Olson has joined North Dakota State's staff as an assistant.

Veteran head coach Jim Molinari, whose Western Illinois team lost at Pinnacle Bank Arena in November, has replaced Smith and sits in the back with Chris Harriman and Kenya Hunter.

"He was my three hundredth win," Miles says to the team

when introducing him. "So thanks for that. He truly cares about players. We're lucky to have him."

Miles gives his difference makers, winners, and losers speech. He asks the team to figure out where they land on that scale. Then he tells them exactly where they are and where they need to be before next season. Together, they conclude they have two difference makers in Terran Petteway and Shavon Shields, if that's what they want to be. The rest of them could be winners, at the very least.

With nearly all of its rotation coming back, the Huskers would enter the 2014–15 season ranked in the Top 25. They beat Michigan State, which made the Elite Eight. They beat Wisconsin, which went to the Final Four. Miles figures they need to change their identity from "Us Always" to "Why Not Us?"

Privately, with the players out on the Hendricks court in their sandbox, he wonders if they'll have the togetherness and toughness to win the whole damn NCAA Tournament. The Tougherness. Or will they lose out to the frustration and fragility?

Then he flashes a Doland grin and heads to the court.